GAFFER

Tom Jones

GAFFER

i
Life as I have loved it

Tom Jones

T. W. Jones

A Square One Publication

First published in 1993 by
Square One Publications
Saga House, Sansome Place, Worcester, WR1 1UA

© Tom Jones 1993

British Library Cataloguing in Publication Data
is available for this book

ISBN 1: 1 872017 68 1

Typeset in Times 11 on 14 by Avon Dataset, Bidford-on-Avon,
Warwickshire B50 4JH
Printed in England by Biddles Ltd, Guildford

To Rosie

My love, my life
my friend, my wife

CONTENTS

CHAPTER I

Land Of My Fathers

I was sixty years old when I fell truly in love for the first and only time in a long life of dalliance. The old song ends '....but it's when he thinks he's past love, that is when he meets his last love, and he loves her as he's never loved before.'

On 17th March when I was in my sixtieth year I finally met my destiny at the "Hunt Supporters'" dance. The previous evening I had forecast a fine day after the late rains and next morning when I looked out the earth seemed to have been created anew. Spring had sprung four days early and the sunshine, breaking the bonds of winter, declared that this was a very special St. Patrick's Day.

I had felt when I awoke, before the reason of day re-entered my mind, that some great happiness was awaiting me and had imagined for the moment that the source of this exhilaration was the final freedom from the worries of my business. But, as I dreamily cast about for further explanations, I remembered that I was about to fulfil one of my life's ambitions by accepting the Mastership of the South Shropshire Hunt and that, as Master-Elect, I was invited that very evening to attend the Supporters' dinner and dance at the Shropshire Lad. Good, very good. But, when I got out of bed and gazed through my window I felt that I had been renewed with the world and was now beginning a fresh and more abundant life, I just knew in my bones that there was something more. Something truly exciting waiting round the corner that would change my life dramatically. Looking back I have never experienced that same feeling before or since.

The evening was always going to be a success. I was among good friends. After an excellent dinner Brian Roberts and I were introduced as next season's Joint Masters. Then came the speeches, including one from our guest, the former champion jump jockey Dick Francis, now starting on his way to further fame as a novelist.

When we all went into dance I was still imbued with that same strange feeling of suppressed excitement that had been my constant companion throughout that momentous day. I have never fancied myself on the floor and indeed many girls have accused me of having two left feet, but I enjoyed my usual dances with Marion Griffiths and Peggy Gibbs, the delightful wives of the Chairman and Vice-Chairman respectively. Sitting next to them with a man whom I presumed was her husband was a beautiful blond girl. I summoned up the courage and asked her to dance with me. Her husband nodded his consent and we took the floor. From the moment our eyes met and our arms went round each other I knew suddenly that this was the greatest moment of my life. It was the most extraordinary sensation. I was lost to the world and, although for very different reasons, I had some idea of what St. Paul must have experienced on the road to Damascus. I can honestly say that my feet did not touch the ground and I felt as though I was dancing on air. Long after the band had finished we were still dancing together in the middle of the room. In those few minutes we knew that we two, surmounting all obstacles and forsaking all others, were fated to live together. We were both still shaking all over when I returned her to her husband. Before leaving the dance I discovered that this lovely young lady was Mrs. Rosemarie Jones, now 29 years old, whom I had known when she was a little girl called Rosemarie Lock, the daughter of one of my great friends, Jim Lock of Bomer. I used to make a point of calling in at Bomer Farm on my way back from hunting. There was always a cup of tea well laced with Scotch waiting for me and I used to see this dear little blond girl running around the farm. Jim died in 1946. A very good horseman, he was riding with me in a point-to-point at Eyton and was pushed out through the wing. The woodwork went into his kidney and he died about six months later. I hadn't seen Rosie again since those far-off days but we both knew now that we would soon be together, although it was some months later before our paths crossed again.

I went straight home to bed knowing that the expectations of that great day had been fulfilled. I had many good friends in Ireland and I shall always be eternally grateful to St. Patrick! As I lay in bed with the curtains open looking at the moon I refected that this was in truth a turning point in my life. I had found a wonderful lady. Fifty one years earlier I had lost one. I cast back to that day in 1919 just after the First World War. Life was fun for a small boy on the farm. I had just finished cleaning out my ferrets and had slipped one of them under the lining of my coat when my mother walked past carrying two buckets of eggs. Tall, dark and handsome, at 44 she was seven months pregnant with her seventh child. I still remember the silver V in her black hair as she leant down to kiss me.

"Which one have you got in there?" she said. "Tom, Dick or Harry? What a naughty little boy you are!" She laughed as she went on her way. That was the last time I saw her. Within an hour she had died of a prolapse. There was I, her third child, still in short trousers and we had known each other for just nine years. The first lady in my life was gone for ever. How she would have loved Rosie if they had ever been able to meet. Inevitably her death was to lead to great changes in all our lives.

Those lovely grey-green mountains of Wales, famed in song and story are not just romantic ornaments. From time immemorial they have been the bastions of England protecting the western approaches of our little island from the ravages of the Atlantic ocean. In particular, they shelter from the stormy blasts the ancient county which lies in their lea, Salop or Shropshire as it is now called.

As the foul weather blusters in ferociously, firing barrages of rain, hail, sleet or snow, it strikes those noble hills and is forced to rise, not descending again until Wyre Forest near Kidderminster 50 miles to the east in Worcestershire. Small wonder that the fertile area of Shropshire which has thus always escaped the worst is known as the Wheatland, a name borne proudly by its pack of foxhounds.

Shrewsbury, the county town on the river Severn so

picturesque and quaint with its hilly crooked streets and the many black-and-white timbered houses, its famous public school which was founded by Edward VI in 1551 and its lovely churches, including the imposing redstone abbey church of the Holy Cross which dates back to the 11th. century. At Shrewsbury was fought the battle between Henry IV and the Percys (1403) when Hotspur lost his life and the place is now marked by the church of Battlefield. The county of Shropshire contains many beautiful ruins such as Shrewsbury Abbey and there were no fewer than thirty two castles, of which Ludlow and Stokesay were perhaps the finest. Shropshire was closely settled by the Romans and was added to the kingdom of Mercia by Offa who constructed Watt's Dyke and Offa's Dyke to defend it from the raids of the Welsh. Our large tourist population has been greatly increased by the cult of Brother Cadfael in the mediaeval whodunnit books of Edith Pargeter writing under her pen name of Ellis Peters.

It is essentially a farming county and my family have lived and farmed at Babbins Wood Farm, Whittington near Oswestry for three hundred years. Another old town, Oswestry's famous church originally belonged to a monastery founded in memory of Oswald who was killed here in 642.

My great-grandfather Thomas Jones started farming at Babbins Wood in 1812, three years before the Battle of Waterloo. He was renowned throughout the county as a good, sober, Christian, clean-living, non-smoking monogamous man. I won't pretend to have inherited all those qualities! But above all he was famed throughout the Midlands as a supreme farmer, stockman and cattle dealer and I believe that these skills and knowledge have travelled down the tail-male line to me.

In the early part of the 19th. century farming was difficult and my great-grandfather inevitably had some lean years. It is worth recording for posterity his modus operandi. Each month of February, March, April and May he would buy 400 cattle at 12 to 18 months old which had been reared by the Welsh hill farmers. Each month these cattle would be brought back to Babbins Wood and each month he would send four men and two dogs to walk 400 cattle all the way to Northampton. This took fourteen days. Great-grandfather followed on in the horse and trap with two spare horses tied behind. He would catch up the cattle at Gailey which was 46 miles from Babbins Wood. There Grandad would sort out the fat cattle which he and two men would take on to sell to the butchers in Birmingham. They then travelled 40 miles to Northampton where they met up with the remainder of the cattle. In those days Northampton had the best feeding grass in the whole of England, the famous Pytchley country, and those good farmers, who talked like Australians, loved the Welsh Blacks which fattened up very quickly on their good grass. So Grandfather himself would auction them in bunches to the local farmers who would sell them on into London and Birmingham in the autumn when they were fat. Not only did he buy cattle in the Spring but he would also buy a similar amount in the autumn months of September, October and November which he would then sell to the Shropshire farmers who fattened them indoors. Great-grandfather and his entourage became a regular sight on the route to Gailey and Northampton, establishing many valuable regular contacts.

It was a time of far-reaching developments. In 1825 the first railway was opened — from Stockton to Darlington — and the following year saw the first crossing of the Atlantic under steam by a Dutch ship called the Curacao. But the difficulties of transport and therefore of marketing, coupled with the vagaries of the English weather made farming a very precarious living even for a good big farmer. Great-grandfather was good and, by the standards of those days, big. At Babbins Wood he was farming 400 acres at the considerable rent of £300 a year. Babbins Wood was part of the Halstone Estate owned by an eccentric sportsman called "Mad Mytton", whose nickname was well-earned. Those golden days were not as golden as they are frequently painted. At a time when everything depended on man and horse, even the very best, most skilful farmers were constantly at the mercy of nature and could be devastated in a year of sickness and atrocious weather.

Towards the end of such a year, Great-grandfather, finding himself unable to pay his rent, decided to confront the landlord. On arrival at the Hall one winter evening, he was received by a very pompous butler who showed him into the dining-room where Mytton, clad in his customary scarlet evening coat, was enjoying his evening meal. When he explained his predicament Mytton grinned and turned to the butler, "Jenkins, bring me a large jug of beer."

To Great-grandfather he said, "Jones, you're a gambling man, aren't you?" Now nothing could have been further from the truth but Great-grandfather realised that this was not the time to argue the point! His host picked up a large pot of mustard.

"Sit down, man," he said. "Now, if you can eat all that mustard and wash it down with a jug of beer, I'll let you off the rent!" Without hesitation Great-grandfather downed the lot and, much to Mad Mytton's amusement, succeeded in keeping it down until, making a hasty exit he threw up all over the hall flags. He'd delighted his landlord and saved his rent but the butler was not best pleased! Now this was typical of Mad Mytton who got a bit of his own back later that same year when they met while walking near the river Perry. After the usual pleasantries Mytton asked "Can you swim, Jones?"

"No, sir."

"Well, here's your chance to learn." Quick as a flash, he pushed him into the river and went on his way laughing heartily.

Nothing daunted Great-grandfather struggled to the bank bearing no malice. A vomit and a soaking were nothing compared with saving a whole year's rent.

My great-grandfather set a fine example to his animals in the fertility stakes, siring eight daughters and three sons of whom the youngest, my grandfather, was born in 1844, seven years after Queen Victoria had succeeded to the throne and two years before the repeal of the Corn Laws. Since farming was so precarious Great-grandfather did not want his youngestson to go into the family business and so, when the time came, he was apprenticed to a draper in Ellesmere. Although he was well-fed he got very little money, but, being a typical Jones, he managed to think up ways to get round this short-fall. He and the other apprentice enjoyed going to the theatre and so, by clubbing together to buy a ticket, one would use it to see the first half and the other would then change over in the interval and see the second half. The rest of the evening would be spent in catching up with what each other had seen!

Nevertheless after six months the call of the land overcame the doubtful joys of counting buttons and selling cotton and Grandad went home to the farm at Babbins Wood.

1871, which saw the end of the Franco-Prussian War and the legalising of the Trade Unions in Britain, was the year when he met and married my grandmother, left home and took a farm at Clynmaddock between Abermule and Kerry. They remained on this good arable farm until 1880 when he rented Crossgreen Farm at Berwick near Shrewsbury. As I said earlier the old town on the Severn is situated on a peninsular and communicates with the opposite banks by the English and Welsh Bridges which were re-constructed in 1774 and 1795 respectively. Since then the English Bridge has been re-constructed again and widened in 1927. Since my grandfather's day the Kingsland and Geyfriars Bridges were added. Crossgreen Farm was not far from Shrewsbury Prison, the Infirmary and the major schools. Grandfather was astute enough to realise that if he started a milk round in that area he should make plenty of money and so he bought 25 cows and some Hereford cows with suckling calves and went into milk. His new venture was an instant success. Demand for his milk grew so much that he was buying from neighbouring farmers to keep up with the demand. Business was thriving and Grandfather was well on the way to prosperity when nature intervened once again with five really wet years which caused the river to flood three years running, ruining all his hay and corn. Like many others in his despair he found comfort in the bottle and gradually his drinking became a problem. Continuing his flourishing milk round he would rise at the crack of dawn, load the churns onto the cart and make his way round the Prison, Infirmary and the schools, leaving their daily orders and, with his cart empty, ending his journey very conveniently in the late morning at the Lion and Pheasant which is situated near the English Bridge in Shrewsbury. There he would drown his sorrows as thoroughly as nature had drowned his hay and corn and, at closing time, the landlord would load him bodily into the cart, give a good slap to the horse which could then be relied upon to get him home. A definite advantage over the motor car and no Breathalysers to worry about!

At this stage my splendid grandfather, like many another man before or since, was saved by his wife, an equally strong character who, in 1886, decided that she had had enough of pouring him out of the trap every night and sobering him up ready for the next milk round in the morning. So, taking matters into her own hands, she persuaded him to move and to rent a farm on the estate of Lord Barnard who owned a vast area from the Clee Hills to Wem. A good stock farm, it was situated at Norton near Stottesden, Cleobury Mortimer.

The move was complicated by Grandfather's flock of Shropshire sheep which had to be walked from Crossgreen Farm to the new farm at Norton. This journey took three days because it became a sort of maternity procession for my father, who was thirteen years old at the time, four men and two dogs. It was springtime and the ewes were dropping their lambs all along the way. Father had the job loading the ewes and new-born lambs into two waggons which travelled alongside. When those waggons got full they would leave surplus ewes and lambs at the farms they passed on the way to be collected later. Much to the relief of Father, who, doing the work of a man, took his responsibilities seriously, all arrived safely at the other end. The moves meant that Father had to change schools. First from Clyn Maddock and then from Crossgreen near Shrewsbury. Like most of his family, he was a clever lad but, although he enjoyed school, he was much happier on the farm.

One of the best features about going to school was his pony which was the only means of transport in those days. He would ride that pony everywhere and it was normally very reliable. It only let him down once when he went with his friends to a local dance to celebrate Queen Victoria's Silver Jubilee in June 1887. Several naughty harmless schoolboy tricks have been lost over the years; for example, if you can place the hand of a soundly sleeping friend in a bowl of water, he or she will wet the bed. Similarly if you hold a hen, tuck its head under its wing and rock it, it will fall asleep. At this particular dance my father left his faithful pony in the stable and went off to enjoy himself. While he was drinking rather more cider than was good for a boy of his age, his friends placed a soundly-sleeping hen on Father's saddle. Leaving the dance eventually slightly the worse for wear he led his pony from the stable and the hen woke up, flapped its wings, squawked and startled the pony which broke free and galloped all the way back to the farm leaving my father a four-mile walk in which to sober up!

Back at Norton all went well. It was a good mixed farm and Grandfather grew oats, wheat, beans, swedes and mangolds of which he fed a great deal to the cattle. He had a suckler herd of Hereford cows and a big flock of ewes. He was drinking normally again but inevitably the financial side was up and down. In 1888 he had to sell his ewes to pay the rent. Nevertheless by now he was a popular, respected man, admired for being lucky and in Shropshire we reckon that you make your own luck. Invited to judge at Welshpool Show, he was staying at the Oak and one night, drinking with his friends, he was persuaded to buy a hundred Welsh ewes, assured that he need not pay the £50 for them until the Welshpool Show in twelve months time. This gentlemen's agreement was far better than any of our modern hire-purchase schemes!

Grandfather went to Welshpool station and arranged for the ewes to go to Cresage station, the nearest staion to Norton where he had left his horse and trap. He caught the next train and the sheep would arive at Cressage at 8am the following morning. He got back to Norton at midnight and got Father out of bed to fetch the sheep from Cressage. Luckily it was a moonlit night and Father went across country, jumping hedges and ditches on the way which was not too easy in the dark. Unluckily for him he misjudged one hedge bank and landed in a ditch full of water, eventually arriving at the station wet and cold but on time to meet the train. Many's the time he has shown me the spot and laughed about his predicament. You had to be tough in those days.

Grandfather had kept his Shropshire rams which he now put onto the Welsh ewes. In those days the heads of Shropshire sheep were completely covered in wool and, if you did not clip back the wool that hung down in front of their eyes, they would go completely blind. Grandfather reasoned that by crossing the Shropshire rams with the Welsh ewes he could breed this out and he was proved right. This put the Jones family on the map because these sheep became the forerunner of the Clun sheep that are so popular today. He was rightly very proud of his sheep, took them to all the local shows and won many prizes with them. He became very well known and much loved, judging at Welshpool Show from 1875 to 1914, followed by my father from the end of the First World War in 1919 to 1939 when the Second World War started and I took over from 1945 until 1983.

Grandfather was a great character and an inspiration to me. From my earliest boyhood I recall some of his words of advice which I have tried manfully to follow all my life.

One day when I was only seven he said to me: "Tom, if you want your farm to be full, you want a young cock on an old bull". At that age I didn't really understand what he meant but he told me years later: "It's like this — a young bull and an old bull were walking down a grassy lane and saw twenty lovely heifers over the hedge. The young bull said: 'Oh Dad, let's run and jump over the hedge and have one of those!' His Dad replied: 'No, son. Let's walk down slowly, find a gap in the hedge and have the lot!'" That was the first time I had heard what today is a very old well-worn joke, but at the tender age of twelve I took his advice seriously to heart and have always tried to the best of my ability to follow it ever since. Happily I feel I've succeeded!

Another day when I visited him I was wearing a new pair of boots of which I was very proud. Grandfather admired them and then put his hand on my shoulder, saying very solemnly: "The longer the steps thee take, lad, the longer the boots will last." Which, when I thought it over, was good advice. I just wished I was taller with longer legs which would have made them last twice as long.

Grandad had a wheelbarrow which he insisted had lasted him for fifty years. The fact that it had had four new bodies and three new wheels in its life did not count. To him it was the same old wheelbarrow!

When it came to picking the best farm, his advice was quite simple. "Never take a farm, lad, unless there's plenty of water and thistles big enough to tie a horse to." I have found this good advice. If you have ground that grows good thistles, you can grow anything. With Grandad as my mentor, life augured well.

He retired in 1921 to The Elms, High Ercall, where he lived until his death in 1937 at the great age of 93. Typically he kept busy to the end of his days. In addition to the house he owned some buildings in the village where he kept 200 hens and he also had a large garden where he grew all his own vegetables. About a mile from his home near Roden he had about 10 acres of pasture where he kept the best ten Hereford bullocks that he could buy at Shrewsbury Market each spring. Back in 1884 he had bought a bucket, ten round cast iron bowls and a tin hut from William Howe in Shrewsbury. In his old age he would have half a ton of Bibby's feed nuts delivered regularly and every morning he would go down to his hut and feed the cattle. If it was a sunny day he would sit in his old wicker chair watching them feed. He knew exactly how much his bucket held and would give the cattle 4lbs. of nuts a day. On rainy days he sat in his hut, smoking his pipe. When the cattle had finished feeding he would tidy up, lock up and then go to the Cleveland Arms in the village where he would enjoy two bottles of Whitbread before returning home at one o'clock. I loved that old man. He was a fine farmer, a good hearty, tidy fellow with a wicked twinkle in his eye and he always had a tale to tell. He died as he would have wished. He had always tended his big garden and in April when he was 93 he went back to the house saying: "Maggie, I've finished planting the garden. I think I'll go to bed." Next morning he was dead. That is the way to live and that is the way to die.

When he died I bought his tin hut, his bucket and his bowls and determined that I would do as he had done in life and in retirement. I certainly had a pretty full life, living up to his standards as best as I could and I've done most of the things he would have wanted me to, most of what I want, including most of the heifers and, now I'm retired I've set up the hut but instead of cattle I've got sheep. I've kept back the best of the heifers, though, and she's making sure I don't stray! At 82 I don't feel quite the same urge to roam!

Grandfather was very good to my father and in 1903 set him up at Weston Farm, Monkhampton. This was a big farm which had been very badly farmed and was therefore rent-free for the first twelve months. Father had not much capital but Grandfather let him have some of his old ewes and a few cattle to get started.

Two of Father's sisters kept house for him, looking after the hens, and every week taking the eggs, dressed poultry, butter and the cheese produced from the twenty-cow herd to sell at the market in Bridgenorth. But then Father met and fell in love with my mother Alice Beaman, who was a nurse at Wolverhampton Hospital. A fine woman who came from a very old Herefordshire farming family, she was a good housekeeper and an excellent judge of stock. She must have been a good judge to pick out my father! People said that if anything she was a better farmer than he. Her family also had close connections with France. One of her ancestors was said to have fled the French Revolution to save his neck from the guillotine. Maybe we have some aristocratic French blood in our veins which probably accounts for Mother's enterprise and for her excellent cooking.

She had four sisters and two brothers of whom one broke his neck riding horses and the other went broke from backing them! As I grew up with a lifelong passion for horses my father used to remind me that I was the only one of his children who took after those two uncles. I like to think I also inherited some of their better qualities — although I can't speak French. Mother's sisters all married well, three to farmers and the fourth to a man with a haulage business which, in those days, was always done by horse and cart, of course. They were all very well respected and none of them either broke their necks or went broke!

Like his father before him my father farmed well and was also a very tidy farmer. There was never a weed on the whole farm. He was good with his men and always taught us boys that you must treat your employees well because whatever they earned they were earning for you. He practised what he preached. Tom Davies and Ernie Jones, whom he took on in 1903 and 1904 both worked for him for the rest of their lives, happy and contented.

Tom Davies became a champion hedge-layer, unbeatable in all the local competitions. Even a rabbit would have had a job getting through any of the hedges he laid. He told me: "If you want a good, level hedge, Tom, keep your tools sharp." That's what I have always endeavoured to do. His son is 75 but still goes to Uppington Farm every year to tidy up.

Not only was my father a good farmer, winning the second prize for the best-kept farm in Shropshire at the 1914 Royal Show when the first prize was won by Mr. William Everall of Shawarding Castle, but he was also a good husband, keeping my mother happy, busy and productive! My eldest brother John was born in 1907, my sister Mary in 1908. I first saw the light of day two years later, Arthur in 1912, George in 1914 and, finally, Margaret in 1916 — six of us in all. It is hard to imagine how Mother coped with so many babies and small children. Somehow we seem to have lost the art today. Either we men are not keeping our tools sharp enough or we are being outmanoeuvred by modern practices. The noble profession of housewife and mother and the family is the foundation of civilisation.I remember my early childhood years as an idyllic mix of family and farm with all the chickens, ducks, geese, turkeys, animals and, most of all, the horses. Horses have been the constant love in my life. There was never a dull moment. So many exciting things happened on the farm — the thrills and spills that only a large family can bring. There was a security and continuity to life at this time and although, compared with today, the pace of life was much slower, I feel it was undoubtedly sounder and more enjoyable.

"Old men forget", said Shakespeare's Henry V. Maybe, but I have found that those who have spent their lives with animals, particularly with horses, remember much more than others. There has always been a horse. I am told that Atty Persse, one of the greatest of all racehorse trainers, at the age of 90, could remember his entire life — not just childhood and the early days, but yesterday, the day before and the middle years because there were always horses at every stage, in Ireland, England, France and America to jog his memory.

I still remember the day I fell out of the pram onto my head. I was a toddler of about three and a half at the time. Mother had several maids to help her in the large farmhouse because with six children and all the butter, cheese and poultry to dress for the market, she needed quite a bit of help. Every afternoon one of the maids was detailed to take my brother Arthur and me for a walk. Arthur, two years younger, rode in the pram while I sat on the edge of it. When Alice met a friend pushing another pram and they stopped for a long chat she was too engrossed to notice that I had fallen asleep. I toppled forward upsetting the pram on top of Arthur. Even today I clearly remember my head hitting the ground very hard and thought that by the amount of stars it must be night. Poor Arthur screamed, I screamed and both maids screamed! The moral of this story is keep well away when women get together for a gossip. You'll never come out of it well. In fact you'll be lucky if you only come out with a sore head.

My next most vivid memory was of my eldest brother John, my best friend, ally and hero. Of course long before the days of television we were able to be proper little boys making our own enjoyment and on a big farm there was plenty of room for mischief. Our escapades were many, varied and mostly naughty. One day we had been playing in the yard and I dared John to climb the gate into the foldyard, where the suckling cows were. John, aged seven, climbed the high gate, stood at the top, shouted 'I'm the king of the castle' and promptly fell over into the yard full of cows who did not appreciate this noisy intrusion. As John got up one old lady with very large curving pointed horns lunged at him and he ran screaming towards the far wall with the cow bellowing in hot pursuit. She rammed him up against the wall but God must have been watching over us that day because her horns fitted neatly round his body and became embedded in the sandstone wall. The marks are there to this day. Hearing our screams Father raced out of the cowhouse shouting and everyone else stopped what they were doing. The whole farmyard held its breath while Father managed to rescue John. We were both soundly beaten and richly deserved it. Father roared 'Now you know why rules are made — to be obeyed.' It was one of the many lessons we had to learn, but life on the farm was never dull. We learnt a different kind of lesson at school.

I started school when I was four years old in 1914, the year that war broke out. John and Mary were already there and together we walked 2 miles to Brockton school. Even though I was scarcely more than a toddler we thought nothing of that sort of walk and thoroughly enjoyed it. Our neighbouring farmer Mr. Barker had three daughters who usually joined up with us. On the way to school we passed a brook and usually found time to poke sticks into the water. It was very clear and if you poked hard and moved the stones around you could see the fish swimming out from underneath. When you poked your stick into the bank trout would come out. Sometimes we would take jam jars and on the way home would collect frog's spawn which we would watch hatching out into tadpoles at home. We had a lot of fun and usually arrived at school happy but rather bedraggled. About a hundred yards before the school there was a humpback bridge on which we could play the game that some years later A.A. Milne's Christopher Robin was to call Pooh sticks. We would drop our chosen sticks on one side of the bridge then race across to the other to see who was the winner. One of our farm hands watching us doing this on his way to work laughed at me being the youngest and the smallest saying that I was so short in the leg that I wore the backside out of my trousers going down the other side of the bridge! I always wished I had longer legs. I've just had two new steel knees fitted and since then I find I am one and a half inches taller but it's taken me 82 years and modern medicine to achieve this.

One very wet day we left home wrapped up in sou'westers,

leggings and galoshes. We had nearly arrived at school when, as we trudged along with our heads down battling against the wind and rain, we found we were walking through fish. A big lake and dam near the school had been burst by the heavy rain. We thought it was wonderful wading through all this fish until sister Mary started to scream. A huge pike had coiled itself round her feet, wet and shiny skin and a huge mouth full of sharp teeth. It was a monster fish, one of the ugliest I have ever seen. That was one of the few occasions when we were all relieved to get safely into school.

School consisted of two downstairs rooms and one room upstairs. One day when we arrived at school there was great excitement because a very large pig had come through the door, rushed up the stairs and refused to leave. We were delighted but the teacher was hysterical. Eventually with extra help from the farm next door we all pushed and shoved and managed to persuade this pig that it would be better to go back to its stye to remain well-fed if illiterate.

It was at Brockton school that I learnt the wonderful flavour of new boiled potatoes dug fresh from the garden. One of our school friends who lived in the village only a few doors away went home for lunch. One day he arrived back bringing a new potato each for all of us. I think it was the best potato I have ever tasted. I still grow my own potatoes to try to recapture that early memory. There was the time when he came back late from lunch and was asked by the teacher 'Why are you late, Johnny?' Johnny replied 'Well, miss, we had tatoes for lunch.' 'What happened to the 'po', Johnny?' she asked. 'Oh we ain't got one, miss. We use a jam jar. Me and me Dad manage fine but me Mam makes a terrible mess.' So much for grammar!

One of the most notable features of farm life over the years, particularly in Devon, Somerset, Shropshire and Herefordshire, has been cider. In many parts there was a seemingly endless supply and I have known many good strong hard-working farm-hands who, throughout their lives, never drew a truly sober breath. Some would start before breakfast and keep going on and off throughout the day.

When we moved to Weston in 1903 Father planted an orchard of cider apples. He made some of the finest strong cider in the world but, in giving you his recipe, I am sure that today some interfering busybody official would put a stop to it in the interests of 'hygiene'. When the apples were ripe, those that had fallen on the ground were kept separate and the others were harvested and put into a large clamp with hurdles around it. Then the fallen bruised apples were placed on top. Now we made sure that all the hens, ducks, geese and anything else that could walk, went backwards and forwards constantly over the top of the clamp answering the call of nature and adding their muck to the apples to be washed down by the rain. At the beginning of November the cider mill would arrive to make the apples into cider. Now, below the farmhouse was a very large cellar where there were thirteen hogsheads. I believe that each held about 50 gallons — a lot of cider! Troughings were placed from the cider mill down the slopes in the cellar to the hogsheads so that as the apples from the clamp were shovelled into the mill, the juice ran down the troughs into the hogsheads. Of course water was needed too, so there was one man who would carry two four-gallon buckets of water from the pool where the same ducks and geese were swimming that had nested on top of the apple clamp. The local saying was that the thicker the water, the better the cider. So they shovelled the apples and added the water to achieve the right mix.

There was one special barrel that was made for the house which was better and stronger than the rest and had all sorts of special things added to it to achieve its strength — beef and sugar, for example, producing the most extraordinary cider. The rest was made for the men. In those days farm workers received comparatively low wages but they had a cottage or lodgings and free milk while every morning they took a half gallon wooden barrel of cider out with them which kept them happy for the rest of the day.

It was horses that kept me happy. Father and Mother used to sit me on their backs but I must have been about five when I had my first ride. John, Mary and I all climbed onto the back of one of Father's old driving cobs. John, who was the biggest, got on first and pulled Mary up behind. I climbed onto a trough and was yanked on behind her by the other two. Now holding on tight to Mary, who in turn was holding on like grim death to John, we cantered up the field. It was very exciting but my triumph was very short-lived because the cob climbed a bank and I rolled off hard onto my backside. The seeds of a lifelong passion had been sown.

During those years horses played a major role in the life of the farm and also in our social life. They were the main form of transport and power. I'm afraid that I find it somewhat annoying and rather pathetic when I hear the so-called 'experts' of today talking as though they had invented the horse. Our grandfathers, born in the happy years before motor cars, had to rely on the horse for everything, to do their shopping, to travel around, to work on the farm, to get the doctor for a sick child. Inevitably, they had to know more about the animal than we can today in an age of universal mechanisation. So often their ideas were plain common sense and considerably kinder than methods employed today. People complain about blinkers, for example. But after all every cart and carriage horse had by law to be equipped with blinkers or 'winkers' to stop him shying at things in the hedge, to keep his mind on the job, to make him a safe conveyance. They were as normal and necessary as side-lights on a motor car.

Take another example. A chronic rearer — always a nuisance and frequently dangerous. So many people think they know the answer and it's usually rough, cruel and so seldom a hundred per cent effective that such horses are often condemned as unrideable. The whip between the ears, a bottle of oil smashed over the head to give the feel of blood, the savagely-placed Chifney bit and so on. Our grandfathers had no need for such treatment. They would simply remove the horse's hind shoes and run him out on sharp gravel. An excellent method. Fuss-proof and most effective. The last thing he wants is to rear and place all his considerable weight on his soft frogs. Above all, it's practical common sense. Any young man who thinks he knows better than his forebears about horses is in for a rude awakening.

That 1914 – 18 war was a strange and terrible affair about which even the grown-ups knew very little. Young men would go off to war and, when they failed to return, we became used to tears being shed by their relations but, with no wireless and in the country a scarcity of newspapers very few people ever appreciated the ghastly extent of those appalling casualty lists and the fact that the life-expectancy of an officer in that 'war to end all wars' was somewhat lower than that of a condemned man on 'death row'. It was not that people were callous. They just didn't know the horror of the trenches. If Robert Graves had published his 'Goodbye to all That' in those days he would probably have been condemned as a traitor. When they did come home on leave they never talked about it and if they had I doubt if anyone would have believed them.

By 1916 horses were much in demand by the Army. Father set off for Bridgenorth auction on a Monday as usual but, when he got there, the Army commandeered his horse. He received £50 for the animal and, as he needed to get back home to the farm, he decided to buy a Model T Ford. It was rare to own a car in those days and Father had hardly ever seen one let alone driven one. Nevertheless he was a capable competent man and after a little elementary instruction succeeded in driving it home scattering ducks, geese and hens as he entered the yard. We were all amazed at this new wonder and I remember climbing all over it pushing knobs and levers, stroking it and jumping up and down on the seats. Father was very proud and pleased with his purchase and the car remained the talking point for days, not only on the farm but at school and in the village. We never let on that our pride and joy was almost impossible to start in the mornings. Father soon learnt to back it into the shed at night so that it was easy to tie a horse onto it in the morning to give it the extra horse-power to get it going. Unfortunately not even this method was always without its problems. One day, after hooking a large carthorse onto the car, the horse had sucessfully pulled the car for a full fifteen yards when the engine sputtered into life and backfired loudly with an enormous bang. The terrified horse bolted at full speed taking

Father and car along with it. It was some time before he managed to stop it after vigorously applying the brake and the hand-brake!

CHAPTER II

Lucton

1917 was a momentous year. While the ghastly trench warfare continued in France and the Low Countries, the Americans entered the war, unrestricted submarine warfare began, Russia was completely overturned by the communist revolution and the seed of bitter future conflict was sown when the Balfour Declaration recognised Palestine as a 'national home' for the Jews.

Although understandably ignorant of all these happenings, life was exciting enough for a small Shropshire lad. In March we moved our home. They say that moving house is one of the most traumatic events in our lives but I found it really exciting. Our new home was Avenue Farm at Uppington which Father had first heard about in Wellington market the previous autumn. It was reputed to be one of the worst farms in Shropshire having been occupied by a man whose hobbies centred chiefly on a certain lady in Birmingham which left him little energy or interest for farming. Rumour had it that he only had time to look over the hedges before rushing back to Birmingham where his energies were channelled into more satisfying pursuits!

My father decided that there was a great deal of potential in the farm. He believed that although the fields had not been grazed for three years and were covered in tussocks of old grass which were sour to any but the most hungry stock, with hard work and proper farming practices it could turn out well. So he went to see Colonel Sowerby who managed Lord Barnard's estate and arranged to rent the farm, which lies in a beautiful situation just at the foot of the Wrekin. One expert said: "That is the worst farm in Shropshire" but Father knew different.

During the winter he sent a man to plough the arable land and in the spring we moved from Weston Farm, Monkhopton.

Uppington was fifteen miles away from Weston so that all the stock had to be herded there while the horses pulled the carts with all our furniture and worldly possessions. To me the highlight of the move was packing the hens into hay cratches half filled with hay. The old Welsh cob pulled out of the cobbled yard at Weston with the stunted steel wheels behind making enough noise to frighten the poor silly hens out of ever laying another egg! However, this was nothing to what they have to put up with nowadays and production resumed within a matter of days.

Avenue Farm was well laid out. Every field had a road and about a hundred acres were adjacent to the A5. Realising that he must get some stock to graze the poor grassland, Father had a brilliant idea. Now just down at Leighton there was big remount depot where they were receiving 200 horses a month from Canada to be broken in and trained before being sent to the Front. Since initially these horses were starving after a long boat journey and would eat anything Father reasoned that they would eat his poor grass. So he arranged with the Army to bring him 200 a month straight from Shrewsbury Station and onto the farm. They were so hungry that they ate everything in sight, even the boughs and twigs in the hedges but they did the ground a lot of good. At the end of the month they were collected up by about a dozen soldiers and taken onto Leighton to be replaced immediately by another batch of 200. So Father managed to get his grass improved free of charge. One day when Father had decided to plough up some of the fields which were full of scutch (flax) he sent two of our Land Army girls down to cock up the scutch. I remember them well, happy, buxom, lusty lasses. It was a day when the soldiers from Leighton had delivered a batch of remounts. Seeing no activity in the fields Father went down to investigate. He heard squeals and giggles and there behind one of the cocks were both girls being well covered by the soldiers. He sacked them on the spot and the local papers headlined 'Local farmer sacks Land Girls for making love to soldiers'. We had a minor scandal on the farm.

Moving to Uppington meant that John, Mary and I had to change schools. We went to Wellington Grammar School which was four miles from the farm and set off each day from home in the horse and trap. Before we started Father gave John some lessons on driving the pony and trap because, after all, he was only nine years old. However he learnt quickly and were soon on our own. We would leave the trap at Ercall Garage and then walk three hundred yards up to the school which was at the top of New Street, Wellington. At the end of the day we'd pick up the trap and jog on home. All went well until our quiet old pony went lame and Father bought another with an excellent reputation from a man called Groves from Burcot, a farm off the A5 road on the way to Wellington.

Quite excited with the new pony we three set off for school the next morning and were trotting along well until we got to the Umbrella House cross-roads, which used to be the old toll house. Suddenly the pony turned left and took off, defying all our frantic efforts and galloped on home to the Groves' yard at Burcot. His former owner helped us to turn him round and sent us on our way again but as soon as we got to the Umbrella cross-roads the pony whipped round and galloped back home. Despite all Groves' efforts that pony got the better of us and Father made him take him back. We had a lot of fun and missed school for the day. Father found another pony who served us well for the next few years.

I remember my time at Wellington School as very happy although the Headmaster Mr. Webb was extremely strict and made frequent use of the cane, most of the time on me! He hated dirty hands and finger nails and, as we found it very difficult to keep clean during our journey by pony trap, we were constantly in the dog-house. Perhaps because she was a girl Mary didn't attract the dirt so much and it was John and I who seemed to be bending over for him on most occasions.

It was a good school with a good mix of people and most of my Wellington school friends have remained good friends ever after. There were local farmers sons and the children of local business people such as Murphies from Wrekin Brewery. The Gwynnes, solicitors, Epsley, also solicitors; Roy Adams, whose family owned Bomley's; Pearces, Builders' Suppliers, who also owned Ercall Quarry; Boffeys, who had a big shop in New Street; my uncles Ernest and Bob who owned Morgans, the grocers in the Square. I often stayed with them as they had a son called Russell at school. I shall always remember going to Morgans shop and watching their apprentice Bernard Farmer blending teas to sell. He sat on a stool with several tea chests round him taking small scoops of tea out of each in turn and filling square pieces of paper which he had made into cones. In 1930 my cousin Russell went to Welshpool and joined a Mr. Edwards to form a wholesale grocers business called Morgan Edwards, which later started Spar Supermarkets. Russell took with him Farmer the apprentice who stayed with Morgan Edwards and Spar until he was 70. Russell didn't stay many years but Mr. Farmer stayed on and I think he was the brains behind Morgan Edwards and Spar.Halcyon days which were shattered temporarily by Mother's death in 1919. However none of us young as we were at the time, has ever forgotten that dramatic shock when she just dropped down dead.

Colonel Sowerby, the land agent, had a family of almost exactly the same age as ours. Tom, Florence, Michael, Sandy, Simon and baby Susan. It seems extraordinary, looking back now, that we should be so close in ages and as neighbours, of course, we all played together. The day Mother died Mrs. Sowerby collected all six of us and took us home with her where we stayed until my aunts came over to look after the house and care for Father and the family. Aunt Mary stayed to take charge and soon the five school-age members of the family were booked into boarding school.

John and I being the two oldest sons were sent to Lucton in Herefordshire. John and I had always been good pals and I really looked up to him so that I was relieved that he and I were together on this first trip away from home as his companionship and guidance were now more important to me than ever. Mary was sent to Bridgnorth; Arthur and George were sent to a little infant school in Preese leaving baby Margaret at home.

John and I shared one large suitcase packed by Aunt Mary

and after saying our goodbyes to the farm, the men and the horses, Father drove us to Lucton School.

It was a small public school with about a hundred and twenty boarders and thirty day boys, mostly the sons of farmers and business people from the surrounding area. Although it was strange at first, we made friends easily and it took us surprisingly little time to settle in. But the food was a terrible shock for growing boys bred and reared on a farm. It was 1919 and after five years of war the standard of school food had dropped to an all-time low. Missing the plentiful supply of fresh milk, eggs, bacon and poultry at home, we were absolutely starving by the end of the first term. We had started in September and so, after Christmas, we took back rabbit wires. A gang of us used to go out, lay the wires and catch rabbits which we'd cook in a tin can. We made a fire in the woods to cook them with potatoes which we picked from the fields. We supplemented our diet with duck and moorhen eggs which we could find round the local countryside. As the school was in the middle of Herefordshire there were many orchards around and we were always scrumping for apples and pears. John and I soon started a thriving little business. We had to wear long blue mackintoshes for school which had loose linings at the bottom. At night we would slip out of school through a window and fill the linings of our coats with apples and pears which we would sell the following day at three for a penny. That second Autumn Term we had managed to make 7/6d by November 1. We persuaded the man who looked after the playing fields to buy us some fireworks because he used to go into town once a week. Of course we couldn't resist letting one off the day before Guy Fawkes' Day. We were caught and the Headmaster confiscated the lot! Later we decided to collect mistletoe which grew in abundance in the withy and apple trees near the school. We soon collected a huge pile and hid it in a tree covered with ivy near the school ready to sell for Christmas. On the day we were due to go home we went to collect the mistletoe and discovered that the birds had taken all the berries! The following year we were wiser. We hid the mistletoe in a loft where the birds could not get it and we made quite a bit of money selling it in Shrewsbury before Christmas.

I found school work difficult and had great trouble concentrating. There were so many other distractions and my reports at the end of term were always appalling. I was constantly in trouble. We had a marks system. When you were caught doing something wrong you got so many marks — for six marks you got half an hour's detention; twelve marks one hour detention; and if you had more than twelve marks you got a stroke of the cane for every mark over twelve. Thank goodness they weren't allowed to go over twelve strokes! The first term was disastrous for not only did I have an hour's detention every Wednesday and Saturday but I also had twelve strokes both days. It was the Headmaster who usually caned me and he beat me so often that he said once: "Jones, you must think I like beating you!" Mr. Pitt was a wonderful Headmaster, a very good man, even though I had the cane so regularly. In fact he gave it to me at the end of my last term!

All this punishment certainly toughened me up. Not only was I constantly caned but my brother John used me as his punchbag. He was a very good boxer and after practising on me all the holidays would go back to school and win prizes. I got a bit fed up with getting hammered like this and so one term I got our school PT instructor to teach me to wrestle and next time John wanted me to box I told him I'd rather have a go with bare fists. I soon beat him.

During the next holidays Dad let us dig up a patch in the orchard and we planted potatoes. We had a really good crop and took them in a pony and trap to Wellington where we managed to sell them and make enough money to buy two pairs of boxing gloves.

I couldn't resist a dare whether it was climbing to the top of the highest ash tree to fetch down a crow's nest or collecting cricket balls from three storeys up. Unfortunately I often got caught in the act and ended up being caned yet again.

Every Saturday we would collect our pocket money, sixpence, and I would spend it all in the tuck shop, usually making myself sick. We had a marvellous Matron who was really kind when you were ill but her cure for everything was

'Gregory Powders'. So vile was this cure that you recovered instantly whatever was wrong with you.

I was easily distracted at school and, having had my first day's hunting one Christmas holiday in 1919, I became horse-mad to the exclusion of everything else. An uncle, Arthur Adams, who was then living in Wellington had an old pony which we kept at Uppington for him. I rode this pony when hounds met at Uppington for that first day's hunting. A fox was found in Uppington coverts at the big house where Colonel Sowerby lived and away they went to Charton's Hill. Just before we got there I came to a hunting wicket. The pony was fat and my legs were sticking out on both sides. I caught one leg on the gate post and came down into the mud. Three horses jumped over me but luckily I wasn't hurt and I still came back having enjoyed my very first experience of fox-hunting. As every true farmer and countryman knows it will always remain the greatest sport in the world. At the age of nine I had started a lifetime's enjoyment.

Mr. Evans had the farm in Lucton village near our playing fields. He had fifty mares running on Bircher Common, about two miles away. In the autumn he would wean the foals and bring them back to the farm to be wormed and castrated. If posible I was there to help. They would sell some as foals and those they kept would be broken in as two-year-olds. One year they put me on a two-year-old and away we went full gallop all round the playing fields and back over a wicket between two buildings into the yard. Even in those days I took a lot of dislodging from a horse's back. I learnt a lot about horses but my school work remained abysmal although, fortunately, I was good at exams and even won two scholarships.

The Evans made some very good cider which this schoolboy spent a lot of time sampling, sitting on the benches in the cider house and drinking it from a sawn-off cow's horn which had the end plugged up. I used to get paralytic and even more susceptible to dares. One day they persuaded me to shear one of the farm lads who had refused to cut his hair. The biggest Evans boy held him down and I turned the shearing machine on and took a 4" swathe out of the middle of his head. He looked a fair old sight for quite a long while!

School became even more bearable when I managed to get into the junior football team through realising that most boys couldn't kick with their left foot. So the school was always short of outside lefts. I begged an old football from a friend and spent the whole of the summer holidays kicking it between two goal posts I had chalked on one of the walls at home until I could kick as well with my left foot as my right. So, when I returned to school I had a trial and got into the junior team which certainly improved life. We had a lot of away matches and we would travel in a four-wheel waggon with a pair of horses which was called a brake. We went all over the place and always were given super food. Looking back I find that we judged the quality of a school by the standard of its food. My favourite was St. Michael's at Tenbury. The food there was superb following a good, hot bathe in the huge communal bath. Then clean and full we would be allowed to go forth into the town to see what other mischief we could find.

Sometimes we really overdid it with ham and eggs and sweets and bottles of lemonade — those lovely old ones with a marble in the top which you had to knock down before you could drink. What days we had and we were nearly all sick in the brake on the way home! So my winter terms became really full and happy and when the Easter term came round, much to my surprise and pleasure I was picked for the junior hockey team. My good fortune continued until the summer term which was not so good as I didn't like cricket or swimming which were the two main activities, but I proved to be quite good at athletics. My best distance was the quarter mile. Brother John wasn't too bad either and we finished first and second in the cross-country.

My hero at school was Tom Milner, four years older, Head Prefect and Captain at cricket and football, a really good fellow for whom I had the greatest admiration. I felt he was a kindred spirit. One day Tom and his friend Bradbury Green were tickling trout in the river when they were caught by a particularly odious keeper who was about to march them off to the police station. With no hesitation the two boys picked him up and threw him into the river. They had no more trouble from him. Bradbury was killed on his motor bicycle soon after leaving school but Tom still farms quite near to me and I've had no reason to change my opinion of him.

At the end of our second term at Lucton we arrived home to find a new mother. Father had married his housekeeper Maud Albutt, a good-looking woman of whom he remained very fond for the rest of his life. Although we felt no love for each other I accepted her. There's no doubt that she was extremely good for us. She was strict but she taught us manners — to walk on the outside of the pavement, to escort women across the street, the things that mattered. When my sister slouched at table she would put a board up her back. Above all, she looked after my father, with his large family, maintained his household to a high standard and was an excellent all-round farmer's wife.

My cousins Jack and Ben Gittings, who lived near Lucton at Shobden, didn't need to board. They were a source of constant envy for me, because living so close, they rode to school every day on their ponies. Jack had a wonderful show pony on whom he won many prizes at the top shows. Ben was an equally brilliant horseman. Each term he would have a new pony to break and he would often be late for school because it had thrown him on the way but, by the end of the term, he would have produced an animal with perfect manners. Later on they both rode some excellent point-to-pointers. Little did I know at the time that before many years were out I would be joining them 'between the flags'.

Jack and I often saw each other in later life. He became an outstanding international professional horseman and one of the best hunter judges in the world.

I knew now that horses were to play a major part in my life. In addition to hunting I have learnt from the age of nine about the other wonderful sport which stems from it — racing. The war had ended with the Armistice signed on 11 November 1918 and great had been the local celebrations. In the spring of 1919 we were thrilled to be taken to the local point-to-points by our father and mother as soon as these splendid events started up again. The real inspiration came in April when our own great local horse Poethlyn won the Grand National. Bred by Major

Hugh Peel near Whitchurch in 1910,he was such a weak, sickly yearling he was sold to a hotelier in Shrewsbury for just £7. However the following year his breeders bought him back again for £50 and Hugh Peel gave him to his wife. At the end of 1915 the Aintree course near Liverpool was taken over by the War Office and closed to racing with the result that the Grand National was transferred to Gatwick and there in 1918, ridden by Lester Piggott's grandfather Ernie, Poethlyn won the third and last substitute National.

In April 1919 five months after the end of the war the country was still celebrating the Armistice and huge crowds flocked to Aintree particularly from our part of the world. They all wanted to cheer their favourite to a second National victory. The field included past winners Sunloch, Vermouth and Ally Sloper and future winners Sergeant Murphy and Shaun Spadah.

That year Mrs.Peel's big brave nine-year-old was carrying 12st. 7lb. Only Cloister and Jerry M had carried that weight to victory in the National. But his supporters feared nothing. Men celebrating their release from trenches, destroyers and merchant ships rushed to Aintree for a race which seemed to stand for England in a shattered world. Crowds were larger than ever before; the mood was a desperate gaiety. It was a day when the favourite had to win and they backed him down to favourite at 11 to 4. Although he was sometimes an erratic jumper and needed all his strength to cover those four and a half miles he had become the nation's hero. He didn't let his supporters down. Ernie Piggott who had won on him at Gatwick rode a wonderful race and won confidently from the Irish horse Ballyboggan ridden by Willie Head, who became a top-class international trainer at Chantilly and was the father of Alec who was to be France's finest trainer. Incidentally Mrs. Hugh Peel was the first woman to own a successive Grand National winner. All I know is that for some time there wasn't a sober breath drawn in Shrewsbury or Wellington. Our own horse had won the world's greatest steeplechase.

The impact on a nine-year-old boy was immense. On my rides I would imagine myself as Ernie Piggott and my pony as Poethlyn. I'd got the racing bug!

30

So at school at the age of nearly thirteen I certainly envied Jack and Ben Gittings but I also had other things to occupy my mind. There I was frittering away my school time, enjoying my sport and beginning to be aware of sex. We all spent much of our spare time talking about it. I have a picture postcard of two small boys talking and the larger one asks 'How old are you? Five or six?' The little one answers 'I don't know.' 'Well' says the big one, 'Are you worried about girls?' 'No.' 'Then you're five!'

Well, I can tell you that by the time we were thirteen sex was our major topic of conversation. Of course there was no television or tabloid newspapers to fill in the gory details and to degrade this wonderful sexual act. But as country boys we had been reared with animals and as little animals ourselves we knew enough about nature that we needed no instruction in the ways of 'the birds and the bees'.

From the very beginning we decided that the whole thing was fun. We had no hang-ups. As little male animals we compared each other's equipment in the communal baths. We had our wet dreams and we discussed the physical attributes or otherwise of girls, matrons and mistresses. I think this attitude influenced our whole lives. Sex was a lovely, wonderful, natural, happy experience between men and women and we just couldn't wait to get involved. That is why there was never any sodomy at Lucton but we spent our time, as I say, discussing sex and picked up as many naughty schoolboy stories about it as we could.

I remember laughing all the way back from a football match at Cleobury at the story of the randy vicar and curate who were always arguing about who had made love to the most women in the parish.

Determined to settle the matter once and for all, one Sunday they stood together in the organ loft watching the congregation come into church for Matins and arranged that they would say 'Pip' for each of their own respective conquests. So 'Pip' said the vicar as a middle-aged lady entered and, when an eighteen-year-old girl came in his curate said 'Pip' and so on until finally the padre's own wife and daughter came in. He smiled smugly

sure that now he had won the argument. 'Pip', he said
. . . . 'Pip, pip' said his curate! My respect for the church grew
when I heard this. I longed for the day when I would be able to
say 'Pip, pip, pip,...' myself. Little did I realise that I would not
have all that long to wait.

At the time when I was becoming aware of my sexuality my
Father decided that he could not afford to keep Arthur and me
at school any longer. We both sat for scholarships to
Bridgenorth Grammar School and, much to my amazement, I
won two scholarships. It turned out that I was very good at
exams. We both boarded there as, with the awards, it was very
cheap and we soon made many friends. I got to know my
Housemaster 'Slasher' Smith particularly well because, like my
previous Headmaster, he spent a fair bit of time thrashing me
and lecturing me. As the youngest member of the 1st. XI's at
football and hockey I spent even more time on sport. I became
captain of the Junior Athletics and so had a say in choosing the
teams. My running improved immensely and I won the quarter
mile in 1924 in a record-breaking 53 seconds. I blotted my
copybook, however, in the cross-country. Ralph Smith, whose
father kept a shoe shop in Bridgenorth and who had a pretty
sister, and I were stretching out the last half mile of the seven
mile run together and we decided just for a laugh not to
challenge each other but to cross the finishing line with arms
linked. Slasher, looking grim, strode away leaving the gym
master to give us a hell of a rocket in front of all the
parents,guests and younger boys. In real disgrace we were
excluded from the prize-giving.

Shortly after this Father announced that I would be leaving
school at the end of term. It came as a shock and I suddenly
realized what a fool I had been wasting my time. The imminent
threat of leaving did what the cane, detention and loss of
privileges had failed to do and I learnt more in that last term
than I had ever done. I found that I really enjoyed the
experience. At the end of term prize-giving I actually envied the
boys who had won prizes and it was with a heavy heart that I
packed my case into the Ford and travelled home to Uppington.
Although John had already left school Father just could not

afford the fees of five of us away boarding. So Arthur, who had joined me at Lucton, had to leave at the same time and cycle to a school in Shrewsbury. Nevertheless, like all good farmers, my father, who was a fine horseman, still managed to hunt. Uncle Charley Dorrell who farmed at Ellerdine, had gone bust when the slump really started in 1921 and emigrated to Rhodesia. He always kept a few thoroughbred horses and he had a very small undergrown three-year-old mare called Miss Cleveland. Father bought her and one of our men, Joby Watkins, rode her home. I almost despaired when he came into the yard riding bareback. The little horse was covered in lice, as thin as a herring, looking like 'the high mettled racer shortly before its demise'. Father wormed her, turned her out and let her summer well on our good keep so that she built up plenty of condition by the time she was four and he started hunting her in the autumn. He always started them at four because he said that they went straight and had no bad habits. He hunted Miss Cleveland at four, five and six before he sold her to Jack Smith of Dryton, where the point-to-point course is now, and he went on to win the Members' Race with her. In fact he won the Members' at the North Shropshire point-to-point two years in succession.

My best memory of Miss Cleveland was the day when I was out with the men spreading muck in a field behind the blacksmith's shop. Now the fields at Uppington had very big hedges, good tough fences of at least four foot, well brushed and very thick. Suddenly hounds were in the field where we were working. They had found a fox at Ravenshawe Gorse, which is now Atcham aerodrome, and run right through Charlton across the A5, across a fifty-three-acre field heading straight for the Wrekin. Hounds came in full cry past us and then, not five hundred yards behind the tail hound, over the fence came Father on this little Miss Cleveland. We all shouted to him and I knew that this was the life for me. One day I resolved to be Master of Foxhounds.

33

CHAPTER III

The Farmer's Boy

Uppington is a beautiful farmhouse nestling at the foot of the Wrekin with its bay windows giving a glorious view of gentle slopes and hedgerows. I always loved that moment when we pulled up in front of the stone walls and walked through the arch of the massive yew hedge into the warmth of the kitchen with its big black old-fashioned range, the fire glowing and the huge stew-pot simmering on the hob. This particular moment was always tinged with sadness because I still missed my mother. Our step-mother tried hard to look after us all and, as I said, set standards of cleanliness and dress which have stood me in good stead throughout my life, but she was in a difficult position. John, in particular, could never forget Mother and, being a stubborn character, determined never to like or accept Maud. As far as I was concerned she had very little warmth and this I missed. So I grew up with a subconscious need for love and affection which perhaps accounts for the many and varied amorous interludes in my life. At least that's my story and I'm sticking to it!

The day after I left school was the first day in my working life. Father drove me into Shrewsbury and kitted me out with two flannel shirts, two pairs of cord breeches, a pair of hob-nailed boots, leggings, an oilskin coat and a cap. That was my last day of leisure.

The next morning I was woken at 5.30 am to start work. I had five cows to milk the first morning and gradually worked up to nine. There were six men, John and myself for the seventy-four milkers. We usually finished at 7.45 am. We had an order for 102 gallons a day from Chetwynds of West Bromwich which had to be taken to the railway station at

Walcott where the train arrived at 8.15. So it was quite a job getting there on time, especially on a Sunday when the train actually started at 7.45. I must admit to feeling nervous. I had done a little milking but was never in the same league as the regular milkers and so, as the early morning mist cleared, I helped John bring the cows up from the meadow with Bess the sheepdog running backwards and forwards to make sure that the beasts didn't stray as they filed in an orderly fashion into the cowshed.

As I took a milking stool down from the rack I hoped the cows didn't realise how nervous I was. They obviously tried to make me feel at home by promptly emptying themselves with fresh muck all over my new boots and leggings. I had given Hannah, my first cow, two scoops of corn in the manger and she was content to munch this as I patted her rump and pushed my shoulder into her, preparing to milk. Father always said that you should never be frightened of animals because they immediately sense it and then the cows tend to kick out knocking you and/or the milk for six. Things went well and soon the milk was flowing into the bucket gradually rising up the sides. So, stool in hand, I passed onto the second and third, giving each two scoops of corn and gradually gaining confidence; the milk flowed and the bucket filled. So I came to Milly, the fourth cow, who had teats as thick as lambs' legs. They stuck out one at each corner and there was a fifth smaller one half way up the rear of her udder. I was rapidly getting covered in green muck and my fingers were beginning to ache with the continual squeezing which begins with the thumb and forefinger and works slowly down closing each finger in succession to the little finger. Milly was hard work. The tension had to be just right or the whole movement was wasted. The near fore teat stuck out at an odd angle — it had obviously been trodden on by another cow as she lay in her stall — and, as I milked it, a fine stream of warm milk shot across my face and clean smock, completely missing the bucket. I struggled to keep the teat at the right angle so that it ended up filling the bucket and not me!

I was feeling quite pleased with myself when I reached

Megan, the last of my five cows. Giving her the usual two scoops of corn and settling down on my stool, I reached for her teats. The milk hissed down in an even flow into the bucket which was nearly full now, forming ripples as it hit the surface, and my mind wandered temporarily, mesmerised by the warmth of the cow's flank and the swirling milk. Bang! I was brought back to earth with a start as her foot knocked the bucket flying and, much to my horror, the milk ran away over the cobbles, turning from white to green as it flowed along. I grabbed the bucket and looked with dismay at what little remained. Looking furtively along the line of milkers to see if anyone else had noticed, I frantically squeezed Megan's teats harder but of course I couldn't make up for the lost milk and just made my fingers ache worse than ever. It was not a good start, but at least I had learnt that you never had to lose concentration whatever you were doing.

So we had all finished by 7.45 am. You had to push really hard every day to get the milking done in time before the float arrived to take the full churns to Walcott Station. It was always a relief to hear the grey cob stretching out at a brisk trot with the milk churns rattling over the cobbles.

There's no doubt, picturesque though it may seem, that milking was very primitive in those days. As I said, all the cowshed floors were cobbled. There was only a slight depression behind the animals which was totally inadequate to cope with all the muck and before you had milked two cows you would be plastered with it. The smocks we wore were supposed to last a week and it is a mystery to me that people didn't get all sorts of diseases from milk. TB was often attributed to it and I think that could well have been the case.

The next job was to feed the calves. We had thirty to forty calves and they each had to have half a gallon of milk a day. Any milk that was left over from the day's milking was then taken into the dairy for cream and butter.

That left the buckets to be washed and the cattle to feed. The cattle that were nearly ready for market would have a wisket of mangolds between three, while the smaller store cattle would have a wisket between four or five. A wisket was made of wicker and would hold nearly 60 lbs. of mixed mangolds and chaff which had to be carried across the covered yards to the cattle.

Then the corn was weighed up every morning for the horses — oats, bran and a certain amount of maize flakes. We averaged about sixteen horses all that time. They were looked after by three waggoners and one apprentice lad — four horses each. By 9 am we were ready for breakfast, and when I say 'Ready' I mean ready! I was always ravenous, particularly as I was still a growing boy.

My first two months were spent milking in the morning and the rest of the time I helped the shepherd with the sheep. We lambed 300 big Oxford ewes, monsters whom I had trouble turning over because of their size. I devised a method putting my right arm underneath them and catching hold of the far leg and pulling it so as to put them on their backsides. When I reared them up it was as much as I could do to hold them as they stood as high as I did and I had a struggle to stay on my feet. The week before we started lambing in March the shepherd left us — he wasn't much good anyway but it meant that I had a tremendous burden on my shoulders. I weighed only about seven stone but I suppose I must have been strong and healthy. We had all the ewes lambing outside in a four-acre patch at the back of the house and we had iron hurdles to funnel off seven pens and a shelter which could be lined with straw. When the ewe was lambing you could run her into the funnel and catch her up against the hedge in the shelter and the straw would protect her from the wind. The weather was usually wet and cold and we put timber across the top of some of the hurdles and covered them with straw creating a kind of pen. We had seven of these contraptions in each field. The job meant going out at all hours with a hurricane lamp and it was quite scary. I was afraid of the dark at that age and, looking back, I think it was one of the worst times of my life. Sometimes a bad case would need attention all night. Father usually helped or got one of the men to give me a hand if necessary so that I did get a little time in bed. But that season almost killed me.

Nevertheless, as I got even fitter, I still had time for a bit of mischief. Our neighbour Jack Reynolds was a bachelor living with his sister. They kept a goat and one morning when I was taking some ewes and lambs past their house I saw a little goat on their front lawn. After moving the ewes down the avenue I walked back round past the blacksmith's shop which was a favourite stopping place for me to have a natter and to get warm. I suppose it was rather naughty of me but I said to Tom Gamble the blacksmith: 'Miss Reynolds has got a kid'. He said: 'Don't be so silly, she's never been married.'

Next morning I was taking the ewes down by their house again when Miss Reynolds came running out shouting at me: 'You nasty little boy ....telling everyone I've got a baby!' I argued that I'd only said she had a kid on the lawn. The story had got quickly back to her as her brother was taking out the blacksmith's sister at the time. I always seemed to be in this kind of mischievous trouble.

Moreover it was about this time when I had my first sexual experience. Father and my step-mother always went to Shrewsbury on a Saturday afternoon, usually staying to have a meal and go to the 'pictures', arriving home about 9 pm. I was left to see to the milking, wash out and feed forty calves. It was usually about 6.30 pm when I'd finished. On this particular evening I was washing the buckets up and swilling the floor down, and as I bent over I felt a hand between my legs. I whipped round and saw the younger of our two maids who must have been nearly seventeen years old. I grabbed hold of her in fun and I discovered she was wearing no knickers. Gulping and trembling with excitement I let her take me to the place where we cooled the milk off, a little building which housed potatoes and vegetables for the house. It was too much, and it was soon all over but it wasn't long before she had me well trained. Every Saturday night from then on we had a marvellous time together. I shall always be grateful to that lass for teaching me so much. Inevitably, however, as time went by, we grew too bold about our love nests. One night I was well in the saddle in front of the kitchen fire when the door opened and in walked Father. I jumped up and ran out to the yard as fast as

I could, pulling up my trousers. I hid on top of the hay bay and stayed there all night. Eventually, of course, I was hungry and had to come down whereupon Father gave me a monumental rocket and told me what would happen if I ever saw that girl again. I never did see her again because she was promptly dismissed but the experience stood me in very good stead.

A little later I was telling the story to a friend, Maurice Edwards, who told me that he had much the same experience but he had been in bed with the maid in her room and was hard at it when the door opened and his father came in. The irate parent said: 'What the hell are you doing? I suppose you'll start smoking next!' Maurice ran downstairs out of the way. Thinking about it afterwards he began to wonder what his father had been doing up there in any case and wondered why he hadn't come down straight away!

My father was a brilliant farmer — too good. At this time he was farming 470 acres. Every hedge was beautifully laid, every gate opened smoothly. He had sixteen men working for him all the time. Everything was swept up and you couldn't see a weed on any part of the farm. That was why he never made a lot of money and why I had to work for him for nothing. If I wanted to go out I would get, perhaps, half a crown, but we had the rabbits. My brother and I used to catch as many rabbits as possible. We worked with the men sixty hours a week and if they finished at six, we finished at half past. Moreover we worked until twelve o'clock on a Saturday and, of course, we had to milk again in the afternoon. So the only way we could catch rabbits — I always had ferrets — was on a Saturday, when we would take a bit of bread and cheese and set off with our nets, wires and every possible aid. We could sell them for about 6d. a brace.

Of course the corn harvest afforded an opportunity to kill off a lot of rabbits and people came from all around. There would be many guns and every care was needed so that no-one was accidentally shot. I remember one man shooting the binder which scared the horses badly. Organisation of these events was crucial. The binder would go round and round and then stop, leaving the rabbits caught in the middle. Then they would start coming out, one, two, three at a time. The excitement was tremendous. I've seen a hundred rabbits killed in one day.

During that first year at home I realised that farm workers were the salt of the earth. I'd known most of our men intimately for many years, especially old Thomas and Ernie. Every job which our sixteen men undertook was a source of pride for them. Father chose his men well and any mistakes he made in that respect were soon rectified. Bad ones got their marching orders quickly. Although he was very strict, he was a good boss and was much respected by his workers. There wasn't a single job on the farm which he couldn't do as well as, if not better, than the men. Following his example, I soon realised that, if I couldn't do a job properly, I would never be a good farmer, so I owe much to old Tom Davies and his supervision. The first job I did with him was putting posts in and to fill in I shovelled in some turf. He made me get on my hands and knees and pull it out because he said that would rot the post.

Every job on the farm was an art, even muck lugging and muck filling. To spread muck properly you had to twist each forkful and open it out by throwing it and then go back to dress it. Tom Davies was the best I've ever seen in my life. He would just twist the fork and there would be no need to dress it because every inch of the ground would be covered.

Ploughing and sowing the spring crops was a big job and the ploughmen would take a pride in their straight lines. There was a saying that if a countryman got crooked furrows, he could go down next morning and pick up the rabbits that had broken their necks hitting the curves in the furrows!

Sowing had to be quite straight so that you didn't overlap. It was all a matter of acquired skill. Sowing clover seeds was another skill which Tom Davies had off to a fine art. They were sown out of a bucket using thumb and two fingers and you would sow five-yard butts. Sticks up the field would ensure straight courses. These sticks had to be placed up and down the field after each sowing. The wind direction had to be considered in sowing too. When harvesting after Tom had sown you couldn't find a place which he had missed. And, after all, he would be sowing some 80 acres each year.

Fertilizer was spread by hand in those days, too, and it had to be mixed, six hundredweights to the acre for root crops or sugar beet (3cwt. phosphate, 1½ cwt. of potash and 1½ cwt. sulphate of ammonia). When this mixture was prepared it had to be spread almost immediately and, if it rained the day after mixing, it would set and have to be broken up again which meant that the whole procedure had to be repeated before spreading. In bags it became lumpy and before tipping it out you had to bang the bags with shovels. The whole system was, however, quite methodical and calculated.

In summer the hedges had to be brushed and, to do a good job here, it was essential to keep the brushing hook sharp. This was another of Tom Davies' specialities. He was a fantastic all-rounder on the farm. In the spring after the sowing, there was hoeing. Mangolds were sown, ridged up with a single plough drawn by a pair of horses and sown with a double drill. A lot of this kind of work was piece work because it was a chance for the men to earn a bit of extra money and it was a skilled job. Wages were then 26/-or 27/-a week and most men could double their wages at piece work. They worked from dawn until night and enjoyed it, but earned every penny they got.

Thistle dingling was another job that had to be done each spring. You had a weeding paddle on a long stale and a little hoe and a gang would walk all the corn field and cut the thistles off. After that job came hay harvest with eighty acres of hay to lug in. Father liked to get as much as possible in June — a ton of hay got in June was worth two afterwards because there would be more protein in young grass.

On the farm at that time we had two Dearing mowing machines which were 22 and 23 years old when we eventually sold them. They were good light machines for the horses to pull. The men would start at 5 am in June because it could be quite hot later. They cut 40 acres the second week in June, always on a Friday, and two days later it would be turned and it was aimed to get it into cocks within a week. To get it into the stack yard in nine days was good going. The whole process took a lot of labour and it was easy to make a mess of it. There had to be the right amount of room for the waggons to go between the cocks. If the cocks were not properly made, they would disintegrate when you stuck the forks into them. Bad weather caused extra work as the cocks had to be turned. Lugging the hay made use of three or four waggons, four men in the field loading, six in the stack yard, two on the waggon unloading, two on top of the stack and two men actually making the stack. Two lads would be driving home and one leading the horse in the field and the operation had to be keenly co-ordinated. Wrapping the ropes had to be done well as this was most important because badly-wrapped ropes wasted a lot of time. Loading was a skilled job — there would be one man loading at the front and one at the back, and, when the load got to the yard, the unloaders would know exactly how it was loaded so that they would start the opposite way to the loading. Any faults could cause trouble.

After hay harvest, which finished during the first or second week in July, there would be the tidying up. Tom Davies and his gang brushed the hedges perfectly very level. Careless brushing would not take account of the weak parts in the hedge thereby producing an up and down effect. But a hedge brushed by Tom Davies would be just as level as the hedges are today when they are done by machines. Part of the tidying up was cutting the thistles around the ground which had been grazed. A gang of eight or nine did this job which took up considerable time. There is an old saying: "A thistle cut in May will grow next day; cut in June is much too soon; cut in July is bound to die." Gates had to be mended and all sorts of other jobs done. The horses would be put out to grass for six weeks. They would return fat as pigs and wouldn't like the idea of starting work again.

Depending on the weather the corn harvest would start at the end of August or the beginning of September. For some years it was my job to ride the chain horse. There would be a bag of straw on its back and I would put my feet on the traces and hold on. There would be a rein onto his collar and I would guide him in a straight line. At the corners you had to turn right-handed and keep him steady or the horses at the back would get off their legs. There was an art in this too. As I said earlier, every job on the farm required some skill. When Father changed the system no-one had to ride the chain horse. A clever device was brought up using a big piece of wood with a hole in it attached to the binder involving three horses. Careful turning was essential because the horses could tread on each other's feet, hurt their coronets and lame themselves . The three horses worked a three-hour spell and they would be changed for three fresh horses while they were watered and fed,

Before we had an elevator at the farm it was difficult to load into the twenty-bay Dutch barn as they were very big bays, reputed to be the biggest in Shropshire. One man would have to make a sort of alcove and take loads from two men below. The alcove was called a madgehole. We once had a 6' 5" fellow doing this job and he kept putting hay under his feet and rising up the required level. He didn't have so high to pitch it. Father said to him once: 'Sam you want a longer pickle', to which he replied: 'No, boss, you want a longer man.'

The crop rotations at Uppington were a five-year plan. One hundred and sixty acres of grass seeds that you had to be very careful with — a mixture of 10lbs. of Italian rye grass, 4lbs. of S21 perennial rye grass and 4lbs. S23 perennial rye grass — the 21 was early ripening and the 23 later ripening — 4-5lbs. Montgomery red clover and ½lb. New Zealand Wild White. The reason for that was that the Italian rye grass would grow a tremendous crop the first year and you would get a lot of grazing but it would die out after that first year. The perennial rye grasses would then take over and the clovers would really become established in the second year so that you could get plenty of nitrogen through their leaves into the roots. I'm always telling farmers today that the best way to get nitrogen into their land is to grow a good crop of white clover in stubble and plough it into the land after it's flowered. In this case at the second year you could cut your choppers' hay — good quality hay with a lot of clover in it. The third year would be wheat which came to harvest fairly early and it would be stubbled, cleaned, cultivated and all the scutch taken out. It would be ploughed in the winter and set with mangolds, swedes, kale or some other root crop to feed the stock. Following the roots would be barley and oats sown with grass seed for the following year.

October would see the lugging of mangolds — a very tough job when done by hand. The swedes were next and on these the lambs would be put after weaning. Swedes were cut and put into hods in the fields for pulping in the spring. These were covered with straw and soil and kept until needed. Sheep troughs would be moved up so that the carrying of swedes was easier. The sheep also got so much corn to eat that they became very fat, up to 150lbs. dead weight — they were just like little donkeys!

My elder brother John had a totally different attitude towards farming. One day I asked him: "Are you aiming to be a millionaire?" He answered: "Yes, I've every intention of being so." And that's what he finished up as!

He was a very clever lad. When he was at home at Uppington he never went anywhere without a notebook and pencil in his pocket. If Father told us to go and do a job, he would cost it out. He would sit on a bank or gate and cost every job. I think he would have costed how much it entailed for us to go to the lavatory!

He became the first man to pay for hoeing roots, etc. by the 100 yards. Until then they were all paid for by the acre, or so much an acre. Then he started measuring the rows and would break it down this way to hundreds of yards per acre. He was the first man to start paying the men in this way for piecework. We were growing 113 acres of sugarbeet and one per cent of the throughput of the factory. But brother John had every field mapped out and whichever way we sowed he knew the length of every row. The men would do a full twenty rows each. John would then just have to go into his office, look at his maps and work out how much to pay them. He was a very clever man.

John went to Nottingham. In 1940 he had to buy his farm of 390 acres for £9,000 and to this day I don't know how he found the money. In 1943 the next farm came up for sale — 290 acres for £10,000. He had only two real friends, his accountant and his bank manager. So he went to his accountant and said: "Bernard, I'm going to buy Thorp Farm", to which the accountant replied: "What are you going to pay for it with — washers?"

John said: "No, I want you to come with me to see Ned Foster (the bank manager) and tell him that you have persuaded me to take out a £10,000 insurance policy for ten years. And that if I do that, I shall be able to have the money to buy the farm."

So off they went to the bank and he came out with the farm! That was in 1943 and then in 1947 he sold the two farms for £47,000 and £17,000 ingoing. He formed a company and had the ingoing paying over five years. Then he was away, off to South Africa and Kenya. He thought of settling there but decided to come home. On his return he bought an aerodrome. Then he sold the hangars and the land and made himself a lot of money. Thereafter he started buying farms all over the place, cleaning them up and selling them. He finished up having to live on the Isle of Man just to save tax!

CHAPTER IV

Growing Up

In the autumn of 1925 John went off to Harper Adams College, leaving me on my own to do all the odd jobs. Looking back now, these were the real formative years of my life. For the first twelve months after I left school, I had had very little social life chiefly because I had no transport. John had a push-bike but Father would not buy one for me and so I got around on horseback. I used to ride the cob who took the milk to Walcott station every morning. But in that autumn of 1925 when John went off to college he was given a motor cycle and I inherited his push-bike. In addition my cup was full when I was given my first horse, a thoroughbred who was suffering from navicular disease, by our neighbour Noel Wenman, a very well known farmer who kept a stallion and some decent mares on the stud which he had bought from Craig Tanner, the famous amateur rider. In those days navicular disease which occurs when the back of the navicular bone at the rear of the hoof becomes rough and lameness is attributed to painful friction between the flexor tendon and the rough surface, was looked upon as an incurable condition which could be alleviated by judicious management, the use of drugs and careful shoeing. Recently the admirable Equine Research Station at Newmarket has discovered that the disease can be quite successfully treated with Warfarin, but, as I say, in those days it was definitely incurable. However, you could put off the evil day.

Mr. Wenman gave me the horse on condition that I kept it sound for the hunting season and sent it to the kennels to be put down when the disease had really set in. So I dug up the cobbles in the middle of one of the stalls and filled it in with clay which I watered every morning. The horse stood on this wet clay all the

47

time he was in his box and throughout that season I kept him sound, hunting one day a week and having an immense amount of fun.

Mr. Wenman, a particularly fine horsemaster, was not only a good farmer but he was in the happy position of having a private income of £1,000 a year, which, at a recent estimate, was worth the equivalent of at least £35,000 a year today; an interesting man who made a young lad very happy by giving me this 16-hand hunter. The North Shropshire hounds were kennelled at Lea Bridge, fourteen miles away from Uppington and I became great friends with the hunt groom Arthur Espley, who would bring the hunt horses over and stay with us for the nights before nearby meets.

When I started riding Mr. Wenman's horse clothes were a great problem. The only breeches I had were my working cords but I would hunt in the clean pair of these, borrowing a pair of Father's leggings. Then an uncle Ben Bickley died and left me his breeches, boots and leggings which fitted perfectly. I still have them to this day. Colonel Sowerby, the land agent at Uppington, gave me a Whippy saddle and for my birthday I was given a hunting whip. I had Father's black hunting jacket which was almost green with age but wearable. My cap, which was also green, came from another uncle and I used it until it literally fell to pieces. I had some wonderful hunts, including one day when I finished up on my own with Billy Bromley, when we killed in the open and I had the great honour of being presented with the brush.

Hunting was different in those days. Most of the land belonged to the big estates, the tenant farmers were required to pull down any barbed wire or build jumping places in the fences with flags to indicate them. It was so easy galloping across the grassland and I still vividly remember the silence — no planes, cars or tractors. Sometimes you could hear a train in the distance and some times a distant saw or a dog barking. Standing on point at the back of a wood I could listen to hear the hounds speaking to a fox. Country people loved hunting. Wages were low and there was not much entertainment but they loved to follow on foot. To see hounds and a fox would provide conversation for weeks and in the pubs at night all classes of people became the greatest huntsmen in the world.

Now that I had my horse, I used to ride for an hour every evening after work — frequently in the dark — but how I loved it.

Bicycling to the local dances and functions I began to meet more girls. One little darling in particular used to ride and we would meet every Sunday morning on the Wrekin. I would be there before 10.30 in the morning and it was possible to hear ten sets of church bells ringing. It is a wonderful memory. No matter what I'd been doing the night before I went on this jaunt riding through the pines. The air seemed cleaner and fresher and sometimes I even thought I could see the sea. Of course meeting that girl gave it a special edge even though to enjoy ourselves we had to tie up our horses and had a certain amount of trouble with our riding clothes. Nevertheless, "where there's a will, there's a way!"

Sadly, at the end of that season my horse became so lame that he had to be sent to the kennels. I missed him terribly. Noel Wenman persuaded Father to buy me another for £12 but this was a little 15-hand thoroughbred/hackney cross mare and turned out to be the worst animal I've ever bought in my entire life. She was absolutely mad, nearly killed me on several occasions and we had to cash her in — at a loss!

In the summer of 1925 all the cowhouses were concreted with a nine-inch deep gutter at the back which helped enormously to keep the cows a lot cleaner.

At this time Father had to change his policy in many ways. The post-war depression had set in and trade was so bad that we had about four years wool in stock. You had a job to get £4 a ton for wheat. No-one seemed to want anything. It was a world slump.

Father decided now to sell the big Oxford sheep and, after weaning the lambs, we started to take the ewes to market, walking fifty a week to Shrewsbury. As I was a good walker and had a wonderful dog, I came in for a lot of this walking. When I went to Shrewsbury or Wellington walking the stock Father would give me 6d. to get a meal — I could buy three small sausages and a lot of mashed potato for 4d., so that I saved 2d.

My sheepdog was bought for me as a puppy for 5/-. He came from a family called Price at Cressage who are still there breeding some of the finest sheepdogs in the world. Only last year, indeed, they had the world champion.

So well bred was my dog that he needed no training. One day Father and my uncle Jack bought 400 Kerry ewes at Knighton leaving me and my dog to bring them back. I walked in front and he followed behind, keeping perfect order throughout and even allowing cars to come through on the odd occasions when they appeared. We stayed the first night with Bert Barker at Clungunford. The sheep were safe in his field and I was given a good meal before going to bed quite weary at 9 pm. Nevertheless before long I realised that someone was in the room, and, to my delight, one of the maids, a most attractive slim dark girl with a nice figure whom I had noticed at supper, slipped naked into bed beside me. She proved so passionate that my tiredness was soon forgotten and we had a wonderful night together which didn't end until she left for her own quarters at 5am. Soon afterwards, fortified by a good breakfast, my dog, the sheep and I set off again. We stayed the night with my uncle at Weston, leaving his hundred sheep there and completed the journey with Father's help. These ewes went to the ram on October 1 in order to lamb at the beginning of March and we found they were much more saleable than the Oxfords. As we had to have still more stock we bought 100 Cheviot yearling ewes which would lamb in April.

That spring I had the job of lambing on my own. It was a joy to lamb these smaller ewes even though they were somewhat wild and took a bit of catching. But I soon found out the right way to do so with hurdle funnels and pens. The Cheviots had a big fault in that they would give birth to a single lamb, suckle it and then get down to have another, which, as inexperienced young mothers, they were inclined to neglect in favour of the first. The following year they understood the procedure and the costings on these proved that they were a much better proposition than the old Oxfords.

Still, right through the twenties and thirties, horses remained a most important asset to the farm. The implements were geared to work at four miles an hour. If you ploughed with a pair of horses they would go at just that speed. If you went slower and were ploughing seven inches deep and nine to ten inches wide, it would not turn the soil right over and, if you went faster, the plough would throw the soil and you would miss parts of the ground.

Machines for cutting the hay had to be used at the right speed too as, if you went too slow it would cause chugging and too fast would bring breakages. We had old Shire horses which were slow but very strong. All sorts of stallions travelled the country and the best horse for any purpose was one got out of a Welsh cob mare. If you put a Shire on her you got what was called a Vanner, a light-legged horse with not much hair on its legs, valuable in the towns where they were wanted for pulling delivery vans. We used them for light jobs such as raking and harrowing. They were faster than the Shires. Second cross Shire/cob was a fine strong animal with cleaner legs, a wonderful temperament and particularly active.

The bushy, hairy legs of the shires were a nuisance because they had to be washed regularly, particularly those with white legs, who used to contract a disease called Grease, a horrid ailment which irritated them and sometimes caused them to throw themselves right down and get entangled in the chains. Many farmers used hackneys, which were quite spectacular with their high knee action, for driving traps. Covered by a thoroughbred they could produce good hunters and, although the first generation were inclined to be small, the second and third proved splendid good-sized animals. Of course there are all sorts of cross-breeds and there was a good market for a horse. Some farmers, indeed, made quite a lot of money from breeding but we usually bought from the regular sales at Shrewsbury or Craven Arms.

1926, the year when I was sixteen, was a disastrous year not only for Father but for farmers all over the country. On top of the depression we were saddled with the General Strike, crippling the railways at a time when motor cars were still in their infancy and we had to rely so much on transport by rail.

For example this was the first year that we started to grow sugar beet — ten acres of it to begin with — but the sugar beet factory was at Kidderminster. Then we had a regular order for 102 gallons of milk a day which had to be put on the train for Birmingham. No trains, so Father had to make lots of butter and cheese. Our fertilizers always came by rail, but luckily Father had just started making his own special feed mixture for the livestock which was taken up country-wide. This consisted of oats, barley, wheat and beans or, with the spring corn, peas mixed up in the right proportions. This constituted a beautifully balanced ration which became known by Father's initials as the "TJ Mixture" and was later marketed by Leightons of Whitchurch.

However, to add to our troubles, we suffered abortion that year. We had 74 pedigree Shorthorns. In September and October most of the cows calved and we had a few calving in the spring. During that year we had only 18 live calves and I walked the fat barren cows to Shrewsbury market to sell them. We bought big freshly-calved cows then and didn't bother to bull them but milked and fed them. I was regularly on the road to the various auctions. Walking freshly-calved cows who had left their calves was a nightmare .....So many of them seemed to go quite crazy. I had cows all over Shropshire — one even swam the river at Atcham and one got onto Charlton Hill. It was a hell of a job but with hindsight the experience was good for me.

Most farmers were struggling during that year and when rent day loomed the market at Wellington was swamped with animals with which they were trying to raise the rent money. At that time Wellington was the biggest fatstock auction in the whole country. About 500 to 600 fat cattle went through the market every week and butchers came from everywhere, including big buyers from London. Normally just before rent day the cattle would have to be sold and removed to the station to make room for others to get in the market to enable the huge volume to be dealt with. This year for the autumn rent day I started to take 32 to market which were destined to pay the rent. But I never got them there because the road was blocked and we came to a complete standstill at the top of Haygate Road.

Father came back to tell me that it was hopeless due to the overcrowding of stock. We had to take them to Shrewsbury the next morning but never got a bid and I took them back home. My feet were decidedly sore.

We fed the cattle intensely on barley and got them up to 8cwt. in just over twelve months. This was to stand me in good stead later in life.

They were good beasts and the following Friday a dealer called Simpson from Hodnet came and bought them. I remember Father saying that at that time if you got £1 a month for each animal you were doing well and so Simpson's price of just over £10 each was not too bad for that year. Of course the cattle had to go to Hodnet and guess who was detailed to take them there on Saturday morning! I went through Wrockwardine onto the Wellington/Market Drayton road. By late afternoon the cattle were so tired and footsore that they would not walk on the road so they walked on the grass verge and even up the hedge banks and, every time I stopped they just lay down. We arrived at Mr. Simpson's yard after 7.30 that evening and Father came to complete the transaction. Mr. Simpson said that he wanted the cattle in a field a mile down the road but I had to tell him that I just could not go any further and as, by then, all the cattle were lying down, he left them and opened a gate into a field by the side of the house. There they stayed and we were wined and dined. Even today I can clearly recall drinking about a gallon of lemonade! On the journey home I was utterly exhausted but we had the rent money with £8 to spare and so we were 'home and dried'.

Rabbiting was still my best way of making money. I could catch at least half a dozen on a Saturday afternoon before milking. At first I caught them with my lurcher dog, ferrets and nets. As I said earlier, my uncle Ernest in Wellington gave me 6d. a brace which seemed a fortune but as I grew up I was becoming quite a good shot and I soon found it was easier to shoot the rabbits. So I muzzled the ferrets to stop them biting and popped the rabbits as they came out of the holes. One night I shot a pheasant which had been sitting at the bottom of the hedge. Now the pheasants belonged to the estate, not to the farmer, but I kicked it under the hedge and retrieved it later, putting it in the bag with the rabbits. Uncle Ernest gave me 1/6 for that bird and offered to take any stray pheasants which I shot.

Most farmers had a withy bed where they made stakes for hedge-laying and thatching pegs for the stacks. We had one towards the Wrekin which was thick and normally held quite a few pheasants. My uncle gave me raisins and aniseed which I would put down every night and by Saturday the area was full of pheasants. On my Saturday evening expeditions I shot 28 birds before Christmas that winter. I know it was poaching, but when you have no money you've got to do something!

That was the winter when I finally grew up and took on the responsibilities of a farmer. One day in November when Father was helping with the ploughing he bent down and could not straighten up. He was crippled with sciatica, was very ill and remained in bed for four months. Looking back today I think that this must have been partly due to pressure on his nerves from the horrible summer we had suffered. With John at college, Father's enforced stay in bed put the bulk of the work on my shoulders and I had to go up and report to him every morning after breakfast.

With the Strike over things got back to normal and we started running the milk into Walcott Station every day. Six 17-gallon churns two and a half miles there and then the journey back eventually took its toll on the cob. One fine morning I went up to Father's room when I got back. "Father, I'm afraid the old cob won't stand any more. He's as lame as a cat."

Father said: "That means you'll have to go into Shrewsbury and get another one, Tom. Luckily it's the sales today in Shrewsbury Market so get onto Mr. Wenman and ask him to take you into town to buy something to run the milk."

I rang Mr. Wenman, popped my bridle and saddle into his car and away we went. We both looked round but couldn't find anything suitable and it looked as though I was in trouble. Then I saw a good-sized, well-bred mare standing about 15 hands 3 inches with plenty of bone and lovely lop ears which always mean a good, genuine sort. She looked a grand type of mare, so

I started to make some enquiries. I discovered that she had belonged to a man who was a very moderate horseman and who, about a fortnight earlier, had fallen off her out hunting and broken his leg. His wife had sent her to market to be sold without reserve. I couldn't resist her and bought her for 11 guineas, popped the saddle and bridle on her and rode her home across a bit of country where there were some nice fences. I just clicked to her and she really flew them.

Now we had a very good man who had come to us out of the Army after the war during which he'd been gassed, a great fellow called Jack Noakes. He was an outstanding horseman who looked after the garden and, when Father was hunting, the hunters, as well as taking the milk to the station. There would be about 40 horses with floats in those days meeting the train.

So, before going home, I went to see Jack and pulled up outside his cottage gate. He came out, looked at the mare and said: "Do you hope to win the National with that? Has she been in harness then?"

I said: "Buggered if I know, Jack!"

"You're not going to run the milk with that?" I pointed out that she was all we had. I asked him to come at four in the morning to start milking so that we would have plenty of time for her. The mare had a few marks on her which looked as though she might have worn a collar at some time.

I went upstairs to see the Old Man who said: "What have you bought?" I said: "I bought something for 11 guineas". "Ugh!", he said, "That wasn't very much. A good cob is worth 20." I reassured him: "It's a grand sort", I said. The next morning we finished the milking early and as soon as we'd cleaned up, we put the tack on this mare. Luckily she'd been well broken — but not to harness!

Although she winced a bit when we put the crupper under her tail, there was no real trouble and, after tying down their lids, we loaded the six big churns into the float. All the men were excited and came to watch as well as helping to load up. I got into the float while Jack held the mare's head and they pulled the float onto her. The tracings and britchings were both chains which the men hooked on. We had put a rope over her rump so that if she did kick she couldn't get her backside up. She was tied from shaft to shaft right over her quarters. Then came the moment. I said: "Let her go, Jack!" And she went straight up into the air, spilling some of the milk out of the churns. Somehow Jack managed to jump on the back and away we went at full gallop down the yard, through the yard gate, left-handed up by the estate yard and up a little hill before the downhill slope all the way to Walcott. We crossed the A5 at full gallop with no chance of stopping — it was a good job there were not many cars around in those days! I couldn't get her into a trot until we had got onto the bridge after two miles flat out. Nevertheless she was still running away at the trot into the station, right-handed..... Jack started shouting and everybody came out to see what was happening, saw we were in trouble and rushed to the rescue. I didn't try to back her up to the platform to unload the milk because I knew it would be hopeless. Many hands helped unload while Jack held her head.

We breathed a sigh of relief and decided that we should give her some exercise on the way back. So we called in on Craig Tanner who was, as I have said, one of the best amateur riders in the country and everybody's hero. An unmistakeable horseman, a lean, wiry man with twinkling eyes in a tough weather-beaten face, he was just finishing his breakfast when we raced in to his yard. "Good God, Tom, are you going to take that to Cheltenham?" He looked round her and felt her legs. "By God", he said, "that's a good sort! You shouldn't be running the milk with her."

When we got back at about half past ten her shoulders were a bit sore and so we gave them the usual treatment, dabbing maid's water, over those shoulders. Perhaps I should explain. Of all the old-fashioned remedies, piss, or urine, call it what you will, was one of the strangest. But it seemed to work. The cock fighting men used to bathe their birds' heads in piss between rounds to revive them. Now those large farmhouses which you'll see all over the country, had room for quite a few staff. For example, we would have four farm hands living in the house and always two or three maids. Those were the days before universal flush lavatories and there was always a bucket of maids' piss in the stables — to bathe the horses' shoulders with. If the horses came in sore at hay time or harvest time, particularly animals which hadn't worked for some time, their shoulders would be bathed with this maids' water. Their chamber pots would have been emptied into a bucket kept by the back door. It was supposed, by tradition, to be virgins' water, but I'm afraid that there weren't many of those in our house!

Then I went up to my father's room. "Father, we've got the best horse we've ever had, my luckiest buy. A real corker!" He got out of bed to have a look at her, grudgingly approved but said: "I'm afraid you'll still have to take the milk with her!" She lasted for years and proved to be a star turn, a wonderful hunter. I did not realise quite how good she was until one afternoon when we were lugging muck with three horses and carts out of the covered yard. At about 3 o'clock I was just taking out the last load when I heard hounds in the distance. I shouted to one of the men to come and take the horses, ran into the stable and put the saddle and bridle on the mare. Still wearing my old breeches, leggings and hob-nailed boots, I jumped on her, galloped out and caught them up as they came into the first field of our farm. I had a marvellous time leading them all the way to the Wrekin.

I then started her in gymkhanas and, even though she was a bit big, she learnt straight away. I taught her to pull up and turn on a sixpence. I could gallop down the field, jump off the saddle, hit the ground with my feet and vault straight back into the saddle on either the right or the left side. In musical chairs she was so good that she could hear the music stopping before I could. In those days they didn't jump off and run in but, as in the West Country, you had to gallop in. I won quite a few of those events on her. At Uppington Fete that year I won four first prizes of £1 each, which was big money for me! But she still ran the milk and I had to hunt Father's little mare who was nothing like as good. In fact she gave me a dreadful season with some awful falls because she would jump anything big and strong but go right through weak jumps.

Back on the farm in the spring of 1927, they were building the beet factory at Allcott which was to open in the last week of September and, as things were so bad, Father took the bull by the horns and grew 100 acres of sugar beet which, as it turned out, saved him. In June we had finished hoeing the sugar beet and established a regular plant of a very good crop. Father was so hard up that he went to the factory and obtained a sub. on his beet — so much an acre. This helped him out and I'm sure the factory did the same with many farmers who were in trouble at that time. That beet factory was the making of Shropshire farmers.

One day I had an inspiration. I decided to point-to-point the little mare and, with Father's permission, I got her fit riding up the Wrekin and schooling fast over fences. I entered her for the North Shropshire Members' race on Easter Monday. Today I am still proud to recall that I actually rode on that splendid course at Eyton-on-Severn in 1927.

In great excitement I took her to the course. There were ten starters including Craig Tanner, who advised me: "Always go the shortest way round, Tom".

We jumped the first three fences well and I was lying about half a length behind Craig as we came into the fourth fence right in front of the stands, when he suddenly turned his horse straight across and pushed me through the wing, giving me a dreadful fall. The bridle broke and the tree of the saddle was smashed as she turned a complete summersault throwing me for yards. I knew we hadn't a chance of winning but she'd been jumping well and I hadn't anticipated anything like this.

After the race I was sitting in the changing-tent feeling very sorry for myself when Craig Tanner came in, put his arm round me and apologised. He said that he hadn't realised it was me on his inside but thought that it was his greatest rival, George Ballard. "Never come up on anyone's inside, Tom", he said. "It's very dangerous". That day he went on to win five races out of the six. More words of wisdom from Craig — "If you ride a winner, it's a damn good horse, but if you lose, it's a bad jockey".

I thought of this day some years later when the Grand National-winning, swash-buckling jockey Dave Dick told of one of his first steeplechases after he had graduated as a young man from the Flat. Although all chance of winning had gone, he was coming happily into the last fence when that great wily professional Frenchy Nicholson, near the end of his career, came upsides and put him through the wing giving him a nasty fall. Rubbing his bruises, Dave walked back to the changing room ruefully where he found Frenchy sitting on a bench. "Why the hell did you do that?" he asked. Frenchy looked up with a crooked grin. "You've got to keep in practice!", he said.

In September, after running the milk one day, I decided to go to a big show quite a way away at Tillstock. I jumped a few stiles on the way, stopped at the Bear at Hodnet for a bite of bread and cheese and a pint of beer, made a tentative date for that evening with the pub keeper's daughter May and arrived in time for the first event at 2.30 pm, Musical Chairs (in this case, boxes) for which, surprisingly, there were forty two competitors. It proved to be something of a scramble but I managed to get into the last two. Connel and I galloped flat out into the last and I just beat him to the box, leapt off my horse landing so hard and fast that the box broke, running a nail into my backside. It ripped my breeches and made such a hole in my bottom that I had to have six stitches put in on a quick visit to hospital. I arrived back at the show to take part and win the last race, the walk, trot and gallop.

By now it was nearly six o'clock and I had to get back to Uppington. It was some journey. I walked and rode standing up in the irons to ease my sore back side. Nearly thirty miles, but I made it home by 2 am. Of course, I did tarry at the Bear at Hodnet, where not only did the horse and I have a good feed but I also managed to make love to May, despite my wound! Both the mare and I were very exhausted when we got back to Uppington. There was no rest for the wicked. Next morning I had to get up and milk as usual and the mare had to take the milk to the station.

Sadly, at the end of September, Father sold both horses to my uncle in Sussex, who sold the little one and hunted my good mare until she was twenty-two years old. Some time later I had a very good day on her with the Crawley and Horsham but now

I had no horses for three years. Father bought a Ford lorry instead. It was the start of mechanisation. It took the milk to the station and we lugged all the beet in it.

On my seventeenth birthday Father had given me a cheque for £20 which was to be my salary for twelve months providing all my clothes. It was quite a shock to be given my first wage and £20 seemed a lot of money but, believe me, in a few months I was flat broke and was back having to make money in any way I could. I was given a Post Office Savings Book containing £27 which had accrued from a christening present from an uncle. I cashed it and bought a Sprint Sunbeam 5 hp motor bike. I always seemed to be in financial trouble after that. My uncle Arthur who had come over from South Africa told me that if I ever bought a moving vehicle I would surely be hard up. He was absolutely right ....But I had a lot of girls with the help of that bike!

Indeed my social life had improved out of all recognition. There was the charming, co-operative daughter of a Wellington hotelier who accompanied me to dances and to all our local events. And then there was Miss Reynolds' establishment. Our neighbour Miss Reynolds, a spinster lady with a nice sense of humour and a wicked twinkle in her eye, was way ahead of her time. She was the most house-proud person I have ever known, insisting that her maids polish under the furniture as well as on top. As she was very strict most of them didn't stay very long but, as she paid and chose well there was a regular supply of comely lasses and for some reason she relied on me to keep them happy. I didn't disappoint her or them. And, looking back, I find it quite surprising how willing they all were to co-operate and enjoy themselves with me.

On the first Sunday a new girl arrived I was invited over for supper and then it was up to me. On winter evenings when I went round at about 8 o'clock to check that all was well on the farm there was usually one of the girls waiting for me and, in the summer, we went walking in the fields. I think I made love to them all. Life was very pleasant.

Father ploughed his land well and deep with four horses in single file. We had a wonderful old waggoner called John

Woodcock who made no mistakes. One year he put a young colt in the team when we started to plough a 53-acre field and before we were half way through he had him actually leading. The first day of ploughing John would take a lad along with him but after that he would manage the four horses on his own. It was sheer joy to watch this wonderful team working and one that I will always remember.

In the winter of 1927 we bought a Mallotte one-way plough which, drawn by four good horses, would turn everything over and all the muck from the animals would be ploughed in for the roots. We fetched lime from Much Wenlock with a seven-ton trailer behind a steam engine. This was put in little rucks which swelled with the dew and the rain until it was fit to spread. We added fertilizer which needed mixing on the slab floor and then had to be used almost immediately.

One year we grew 1% of all the beet that went to Alcott. At the time there was a world shortage of sugar and beet was grown all over England. The Alcott factory paid carriage for beet from as far away as Cornwall.

Father became known as an authority on beet and he judged all over the country. This brought him in touch with a man called Tucker who farmed a large acreage and had a lot of cattle at Wadebridge in Cornwall. He persuaded Father to buy 50 Exmoor "Galloways" which were sent to Wellington station. Now these were really wild cattle and we met them at the station and tried to drive them to Uppington but they went spare all over the county. Some of them got onto the Wrekin. They could go faster than deer. It was a week before we managed to get them all rounded up. When we went to feed them in the yard they'd go absolutely berserk, climbing up the walls. They never did any good in the yard and were obviously a breed which should have been fed outside.We didn't feed them too well in the winter, turned them out in the spring and they got fat quickly on our good grass. They topped the market at Wellington in July and August. Old man Tucker is dead now but his son has been my friend ever since. Father's judging even involved a whole week away in Germany.

CHAPTER V

The Chastity Belt

1927 was famous for Lindbergh's first solo flight of the Atlantic and, in 1928, the Pacific was flown by Captain Kingsford-Smith. The year was also remarkable for the victory in the Grand National of the sole finisher without a fall, the 100 − 1 chance Tipperary Tim, owned by Mr Kenyon and trained here in Shropshire by John Dodd.

This was the year when that wonderful steeplechaser Easter Hero jumped across the Canal Turn fence which he straddled almost stopping the entire field, allowing the moderate, sure-footed brown stayer to win. From my point of view, looking back on a lovely life of many loves, I can think of no occasion more extraordinary than that exciting night when I ventured to a dance at Wrockwardine and met a young lady from Little Wenlock. I have no idea how this delightful, vivacious, fair-haired girl with curves in all the right places, arrived at the dance nor did I care who had brought her. I only know that, after we had been locked in each other's arms on the dance floor throughout most of the evening and had consumed a number of drinks, I was the one who took her home on my motor bike. No sooner had we started with her arms clutched round my waist than her hand began to explore between my legs and, before long, we stopped at the Forest Glen for a stroll in the woods — just for a little walk! She was eager and most co-operative but I was in for a bit of a surprise. It was a lovely night and we were soon lying comfortably in each other's arms on a bank. But, as I started fumbling around to remove her knickers, I encountered a large, tough safety device of the kind used for holding knitting stitches, twisted all down the side through her vest, knickers and every-

63

thing, securely fastened with a large pin.

"What on earth is that for?" I asked.

"Oh", she said, "Mum put that on before I came out and when I get home I have to go into her bedroom to show that it's still there!" I think someone once said that love laughs at locksmiths and certainly Jones was not to be denied. As my love was now as aroused as I was I managed, with her help, to extract the pin, remove all the encumbrances and insert myself for a couple of hours of blissful enjoyment. I never saw that girl again. I can only imagine that when she got home she got into terrible trouble because it would have been well nigh impossible to get that pin back into its original hole.

On another occasion brother John and I rode our motor bikes to Iron Bridge where we met a couple of smashing girls whom we took on our pillions to the lovely bluebell woods at Brosley. We split up. My girl and I walked into the woods and were soon doing what comes naturally, when suddenly we heard John's bike starting up and a girl screaming. Running back to where we had left them, we found the girl standing on her own. Apparently she had repulsed the advances of John, who had taken off without her. I got both girls onto the back of my bike and dropped them off at Dawley, where they lived. Incidentally I ran out of petrol about a mile from home!

About a fortnight later, when my bike had a puncture, I borrowed John's AJS because I wanted to meet that girl again. I rode down to Ironbridge and was sitting there waiting when suddenly four lads came up, pulled me off my bike and beat me up. It turned out that one of them was the brother of the girl John had abandoned in the woods and, as I had his bike and looked like him, they had mistaken me for him. I never made that mistake again.

That Sunbeam bike would do 100 mph then, in 1928, but only 27 miles to the gallon. It had originally been built for a man called Tommy Spann for the Sprint Mile. I got an immense amount of pleasure out of it. One of my thrills was to go down the Avenue near the A5 on a Sunday afternoon and wait for my friend Jack Jones who rode a Norton at the Isle of Man TT races, to go by on his way to see his girl in Shrewsbury. After he'd passed I would rev. up my bike and overtake him before he got to Atcham.

One day I was doing 60 mph up the main road when I hit a sugar beet and came off, smashing the bike to pieces and I got a nasty hole in my head and knocked the ends off my fingers scraping them along the road. I was badly bruised and the bike had to be sent back to the Sunbeam works to be repaired. The insurance paid for it and, when I got it back, I sold it to Dave McCarthy, the son of a Ludlow auctioneer, in a nicely-weighted deal in which he gave me £25 and an Ariel 500, which was a big bike but far more economical and easier to ride than the Sunbeam. What's more, it had a very good seat on the back, ideal for my female passengers!

At the end of that year, when I was eighteen, I decided to go into business in a small way on my own.

There are so many things which now we take for granted which happened for the first time during my life. For example, I was already eighteen when women were finally granted the vote.

By now my father was actively teaching me to be a farmer. In his youth he had been a champion ploughman and now he was a famous judge of ploughing matches. One day when he was judging at Bishops Castle he introduced me to the invincible Tom the Lion, champion ploughman of the entire country, who was giving a demonstration at the show. I was shown the hundred-year-old wooden plough which Tom had used for forty years during all his championship matches. Made of ash, it was about 23 feet long and the shill board, which is the metal that turns the furrow over, was about 8 feet long. After Tom's demonstration Father and he adjourned to the tent where, over a few pints, they yarned back to the last century and the days when they used to compete against each other. Eventually old Tom said: "When I finish ploughing, I will give young Tom here this plough."

The very next year Tom came to see Father and said: "If you'd like to fetch that plough, young Tom can have it and I'll come and give him a lesson or two on how to use it."

So Tom arrived to spend three or four days at Uppington

giving me some intensive instruction. The method of ploughing required for these matches was one which went back a long way before the advent of drills to drill your corn. You were required to plough about 7½ in. wide and about 5½ in. deep and you would turn the furrow completely over, smoothing down the sides. The idea was that you would then broadcast the corn which would drop into the 7½ in. beads and then you would harrow it. That would be the corn sown and there would be no need for drills at all. But, believe me, it must have been a slow job. In those days, if you could plough an acre a day, you had done a very good job of work.

At the shows, when I was ploughing brother John was winning a few prizes hedge-laying. It was very good fun and grand experience. We would load my plough and John's tools into the cart pulled by one of my horses, the other horse tethered behind, and set off the day before. I did quite well and always managed to be in the first three but sadly that historic plough soon wore out and Father bought me a Ransome Match Plough. It was a great tool but I never ploughed quite as well as I had with the old wooden one that Tom had given me.

At the pubs in the evening old Tom the Lion would regale us with stories of his long life during which he could do anything on a farm. In the autumn he would go to every ploughing match and then in the spring of the year he would travel a Shire stallion. His proud boast was that every season he would have more women than his stallion had mares but, as in those days a stallion would cover anything up to a hundred mares this was perhaps a little bit of an exaggeration!

He would lead his stallion all round the country stopping at pubs which always had stables where mares used to come from the surrounding farms to be covered. He told us about one such Shire stallion which had the smallest tool he had ever seen in his life. "In fact it wasn't much bigger than my own", he said, "but it seemed to make no difference because he was the most virile horse I ever had. One season I gave him 120 mares and he got 101 of them in foal."

One evening he arrived at the pub where he was staying the night and found five mares waiting for him, all full in season.

66

The old horse had already had two mares earlier in the day and after he had covered two, he was starting to get a bit jaded. So Tom told the landlord:"You had better put him in the stable and give him a feed, but tell the men to stay with their mares while I have some grub too."

As he was leaving the bar about an hour later the barmaid gave him a look and he said to her: "I think you had better come out with me and we'll show that old stallion how it should be done!" Rather like the old Army instructor: "I will demonstrate and you will imitate!" So out she went with him into the box and, for the next hour, they performed so well together in the straw, that the stallion was rejuvenated and it wasn't long before he served the three mares. Tom laughed: "What's more, the only one not in foal was the barmaid!"

1929 saw the election of a second Labour administration under Ramsay Macdonald but it was to be short-lived. It was also the year of the Wall Street crash and the terrible American slump. But I knew little of these things. For me, 1929 was the year when the Young Farmers' Club started in Shrewsbury and it went so well that, within nine months, we had 74 members. I suddenly realised that since leaving school I had been more or less a farm labourer and had barely put pen to paper and so, to make up for all that I had missed, I took an active part in everything to do with the Young Farmers — in the debates, ploughing, judging stock and so on. I was also in the football team and in the drinking team!

Our football team was virtually unbeatable, even when we played the police, who were so much taller than most of us. We looked like midgets playing against them but we could run rings round them because we were so much faster. They were very good to us and every year gave our team free tickets for the Police Ball and plied us with free drink and free food, going out of their way to see we had a good time and usually succeeded in getting all of us, and our girls friends, good and pickled.

From the time when I was about nine my Father had always encouraged me to "guess the weight of the sheep" or "guess the weight of the pig" in the competitions at the local fetes. Father himself was very seldom far out and, indeed, on several occasions, won the prize. Under his tuition I improved steadily year after year and he was delighted when, at the age of thirteen, I won the prize at the High Ercall fete. This made me very keen on judging weights and, indeed, on judging stock like Father. So I was particularly interested in a fascinating lecture given to the Young Farmers one evening in June 1930 by County Livestock Officer Mr. R.O. Smith on Stock Judging. At the end he told us that if we really wanted to learn and put our names down he would be willing to teach us and that he would enter us in competitions at local fatstock shows at Birmingham and in London. 25 of us gave him our names and he was as good as his word. Right the way through June, July and August, once a fortnight we were taken to the best breeding farmers in the district and in September he started to look for a Shropshire team to judge at the big shows at Birmingham and Smithfield in London. Mr. Smith told us that when we went judging fatstock at these big shows we would be facing some of the best judges in the world and, if we wanted to win there, we would have to be very good indeed. He picked teams of three with two reserves and started competitions among ourselves to find out the final team in which I was lucky enough to be included. As he was a very clever man, a famous judge and an outstanding teacher, I will set down his instructions, which, fortified by my own experience, I have used and passed on successfully throughout the rest of my life.

First, the judge must be immaculately turned out, wearing a good, well-knotted tie under a spotless, beautifully-ironed, well-cut white kennel coat. The judges would ignore a dirty, long-haired young man slouching round the ring but, if you were clean, tidy and alert they would certainly remember you when you went up to give them your reasons for judgement. In the ring there would be four beasts paraded for you, each marked with a card A,B,Y and X. First, stand back and look at the beast over all. General impression is important and, particularly, you are looking for conformation, by which I mean you must find the animal which has the most tender meat on the most expensive joints, in other words since the most expensive joints are in the hind quarters, you must have big beasts with big quarters, heavier than the fore quarters, and it must be tender meat, not fat.

A beast has a thick hide covered with hair underneath which are the flesh and bones. Now there are tell-tale places all over the animal where you can feel the quality and depth of fleshing. Remember you are looking for the one with the most lean meat on the most expensive joints. So, when you stand behind it, you want an animal shaped roughly like a wedge with the bottom end towards you — in other words, a wide rump tapering off towards the fore quarters. Its back should be straight but tapering off towards the fore quarters. then go round the sides and, once again, you will assess the hind quarters against the fore quarters. You don't want a beast with a big belly. If it has, it will kill out very badly. The killing-out percentage of a beast varies from 56 lbs. to 70 lbs. to the hundredweight. A really deep-fleshed animal with a light belly is likely to kill out right up to 70 lbs. to the hundredweight, and that is how the retail and wholesale butchers who are buying them in the market will judge them. You want to see a straight back and a fine shoulder which should come down fairly straight, not too round or too prominent. If you have a great big lump of a shoulder it is too coarse. From the front take a good look at the brisket. A beast's brisket should come down in a V. If you get a rounded one it means that beast is fat. So, before you start to handle it, you will assess the conformation with the idea all the time in your mind that you've got to have a beast which, when it is killed, will contain a lot of expensive meat.

Now you must start to feel the animal, starting on the near side, placing your left hand on his hip because then you can feel if he's going to kick and you can push him away from you. So keep your left hand on the hip and your right hand by its tail. Bring your right hand gradually up to the left, feeling and handling that flesh. The part between the hip bone and the tail is called a plate and that plate should be level. It is where your most expensive meat comes from, your rump and hipbone steaks. When you touch it you will find right on the tail, on either side, a lump of fat. Get your fingers round that and gradually, very carefully, squeeze it. If it is soft, flabby and bubbly, that beast will be fat in nature all the way through. It should not be too big, but firm, and you will find that the lean, smooth flesh will just give under your fingers. If it doesn't, it is tough and hard. It wants to be just pliable and a bit spongey. That is nice, tender young beef. Now change hands and put your right hand on the hip and feel the loin, along the top of the backbone. The loin is the part between the hip bone and the last rib, with the short rib sticking out. Put your hand on that and once again let the loin come right in between your fingers and thumb. Bring your hand down and then once again, very gently with your fingers, feel the depth of flesh, which is very important. That is the amount of flesh between the skin and the bone. By putting your hand like that you can tell whether you have got a very deep-fleshed animal and a thick layer of flesh between the hide and the bone which is good. Continue with your left hand right along the top of the animal, along its chine but, before you get up to the shoulder, put your left hand on the first long rib which goes right round to the brisket and half way down, again you can assess the thickness of flesh. If the beast is fat you will find out around that first rib. Still keeping on top of the beast, the chine should be rounded and, on the top of the backbone there should be a little indentation of flesh on both sides, so that you can't really feel the backbone unless you push right into it. Still with your left hand going along the ribs, keep your right hand on the top of the shoulder and, if you look down, you will see a bone sticking out which is the point of the shoulder. From there is a muscle going up towards the shoulder and you can feel again whether it is lean or fat.

Now, you will have two cards for giving your reasons and, as you judge each beast, you will put its number and list the good or bad points of that particular beast. Then you go on and judge the other three in a similar fashion. By the time you have done that you will more or less have made up your mind how you are going to place them, first, second, third or fourth, and then you will have another look at them. If you are undecided about two of them, you could make a note of that and go over them once again to see if you can find any small point which makes one better than the other because, when you come to give your reason to the judge, he will know if two animals are pretty well equal and will give you very high marks if you can find the reason for the difference between them. In that case, even if you've got your animal wrong — the wrong way round — and give your reasons to the judge, it is quite likely that he could give you 100% and you could still win the competition.

When you go into the ring, walk straight up to the judge and stand anything up to ten or even fifteen yards away from him, looking just over his head. Don't look him in the eye because it might disconcert you because it is probably some time since you actually judged the animals and you must have your reasons in the forefront of your mind. You should really have remembered them but, when you make your notes, remember that you must abbreviate everything and make them as simple as possible. If you do have to glance down to refer to them, try to glance down only once between giving the reasons on each beast.

You start off giving your reasons by saying; "Mr. Judge, I place this class of four cattle in the following order — A,B,Y,X. The reasons for doing so are as follows... I place A first because..." then give your reasons, whatever they may be. If you find a fault in the first beast, a very small one, for example, you would give it now and then go on to your second beast "and I place B second ...."

When you have finished your assessments, then say "Thank you, sir" or "Thank you, sirs," away you go and hope that you have done well.

As a team we were very lucky. We won at Birmingham and in London two years running. The third year the same team was entered for Birmingham and London and we got right to December 1 when R.O.Smith realised that I wasn't eligible because you had to be under 23 years old on the 1st. December. So they had to pick someone else at the last minute and, with Jim Slater, they went on to win again.

Remember, when you are giving your reasons, don't waste the judges' time. You get two minutes and, in fact, you can do it in less and still get them right. My son Edward got 100%

marks in Birmingham which has never been done before or since. I taught him since he was a small lad and he became the best judge of stock in the country, winning at Birmingham, London and everywhere else.

R.O. Smith also taught us to judge dairy cows and sheep and during the summer we used to go all round the county shows judging dairy cattle. I remember judging the dairy class at the Royal Welsh and actually coming first out of sixty or seventy entries. I am often asked about the tricks of the trade. Of course, there are ways of putting flesh on animals with a weakness. Suppose a showman has a beast which is weak at the back of the shoulder, then all he does is to get a wire brush, starting months before the show and tap every day on this place with the wire brush, bruising the skin and increasing the blood flow to it. You can really change a beast with a wire brush. If you have an animal which is weak in its second thigh just tap, tap, tap and bruise the skin, perhaps for a week, and then it will heal up again. You can make flesh grow anywhere by increasing the blood flow. Yes, there are tricks in every trade. Once at the Fatstock Show someone had blown up his cattle — he put a needle underneath the skin and blew them up!

Another year a ram won all over the country at all the championship shows. He was indeed Britain's champion ram for that year ...until the very last show. Then, instead of automatically awarding the championship to this magnificent creature which dwarfed all the other rams, the judge, for some reason, put his hand between the sheep's hind legs and felt its balls. He squeezed and got no reaction. he squeezed again and found they were hard. It turned out that this champion of champions was not a ram at all, but a weather. It had been castrated and the owner had sewn a couple of potatoes into the sack! Of course there was a fair old scandal and it was disqualified from all its prizes.

But sheep are indeed more difficult because you have to contend with all their wool. Luckily I have terribly sensitive fingers which tell me what is underneath. Having sensitive fingers has made a big difference to my life in many ways. I can feel things which other people would never know were there.

Once you have learnt to judge properly you can judge anything. Indeed I think I have judged just about everything — ploughing, hedging, fatstock, dairy stock, sheep, horses of all kinds, even Land Girls and Beauty Queens. When you think about it, even with beauty queens, it is essential to have the meat in the right places! In other words, it is conformation that counts. The Young Farmers was a wonderful experience. We learnt about every branch of farm work and had all sorts of competitions — milking, hedge-laying, stack-making, sugar beet hoeing, pulling sugar beet and every other farming activity.

We had lectures on every aspect of farming too, given by some of the best men in the country. During the winter we would have a meeting every week and we had some fascinating debates. One of the most interesting I remember was "Should a farmer's son marry a farmer's daughter?" We had debates on farm work and on the social side. I learnt a lot from it and gained considerable confidence because I had to use my brain for the first since I had left school at the age of fourteen. I maintain that the Young Farmers is the best thing that has ever happened to agriculture in this country. It is very strong today and now there are fifty-two clubs in Shropshire. They have a club in many villages, even schools have their Young Farmers Club. There are rallies every year. In my day we had to leave at the age of twenty-three but now it is twenty-five.

The social side was wonderful, too. We had dances, tennis, cricket and every other sport, including football in which I was lucky enough, as I have said, to be a member of the unbeaten team.

We would have our dances in Shrewsbury, riding a horse in with a pair of overalls on top of our evening clothes, tie the animal up and go home on him at the end. Every pub in Shrewsbury had room for horses. You could get 70 horses into the Lion and Pheasant and 150 into the horse depot in Shrewsbury. It was a great life. One year we Young Farmers got up a team of Cowboys and Indians for the Shrewsbury Carnival. I had only a three-year-old which I had just broken in. Still, we entered for the Carnival, lined up in the quarry and had just got into the main street going towards the centre of the town with the first float in the carnival about half way up it, when people started throwing streamers and shouting. The streamers went round my horse's ears and he ran away with me so that I was leading the carnival right up to the top!

We had horses for everything at that time and it was great fun. There was nothing better than driving a good cob. You'd get the horse out to go to town on Tuesday and find about half a dozen others going up the same road. We could have a flat-out race all the way into town.

You would take a horse out everywhere, going to the pub, courting, to the pictures and so on. There's nothing like it today. We had a fantastic time. Many's the evening when I've finished up three parts pickled and jumped fences and gates, galloping back across country in the moonlight. Happy, happy days.

CHAPTER VI

Love — and Marriage

At the Young Farmers Dance at Market Drayton in January 1930 I met a marvellous girl called Betty Hawkesworth and fell madly in love with her. Now that winter of my twentieth year I was so busy at work and play that, looking back, I'm not quite sure how I stuck it out.

Vin Evans, one of our neighbours, had a very good young horse and, as he was not much of a horseman himself, I used to hunt it for him. At the same time I was going out with a nice girl called May Turner who lived at Erdington near Bridgnorth, staying with her family from time to time and hunting with the Wheatland on a splendid little thoroughbred/Welsh cob cross of theirs. Life was becoming somewhat complicated socially because every Saturday I was taking Betty out and every Sunday it was May Turner, with whom I would go to chapel. During the week I had another girl from Upton Magna. May was a nice girl, pure and holy, who kept her legs firmly crossed; Betty, lovely, tall fair-haired Betty with the beautiful figure not unlike my present sweet Rosemarie, was looking forward to marriage and, from the very start when we had fallen in love, we had decided firmly to save ourselves for that day, but Sally from Upton was a very different cup of tea. A young, healthy country girl, she was as randy as I was myself and regarded good, happy sex with no holds barred as an essential ingredient of life. We kept each other well satisfied. It was a pity that Sally had to describe our activities to Betty in the hairdressers. But then, it's extraordinary what women will confess under the drier and it made little difference.

My word, I must have been fit at that time. I reckon that from the autumn of 1928 right up until the time of my marriage in July 1934 I was making love regularly to twelve different girls. Dont forget there were always Cissy Reynolds' ever-changing assortment of home-helps to be obliged as well! Life would have been very different if I'd married Betty, which we both wanted badly. Her father, a farmer and timber merchant, drank himself to death and his wife soon followed him into the grave. Thereupon her uncle came over from Johannesburg and took her back to South Africa with him. Before they left I was invited to dine with them and Betty told me that she did not want to go at all. She wanted to stay in England and marry me. However her uncle said that I was no good for her; I had no prospects and was a dead loss. So off she went to South Africa, breaking my heart for the first time in my life and causing me to go very wild for quite a while. I visited her when I went over there in 1968 and took a number of photographs but sadly dropped my camera and ruined them all!

No prospects indeed? Losing my girl like that set me back on my heels and made me realise that it was time I started to make a proper living.

Out in the wide world events were moving inexorably towards the showdown of the Second World War. The ominous signs were ignored by people who were still haunted by the horror of the trenches and who just could not imagine another holocaust. So they skated on with a frenzied gaiety refusing to believe that the ice would ever break under their feet.

In 1928 a German airship with sixty people had crossed the Atlantic and the following year the Graf Zeppelin made numerous successful inter-continental flights. But in 1930 Britain lost interest in airships for ever when the much-vaunted R101 was destroyed in France on her first flight to India with the loss of 48 lives.

1931 saw the resignation of the Labour Government and the formation of a Coalition under Ramsay Macdonald. Unbeknown to any of us Germany was now re-arming fast. At the beginning of 1933 a little-known man with a ridiculous moustache and a loud voice called Adolph Hitler was appointed Chancellor by Hindenburg and step by step he gained supreme control of Germany. The Reichstag was set on fire almost immediately afterwards. The following year, 1934, saw the assassination by Austrian Nazis of Doffuss, the Austrian and, and on the death of Hindenburg a week later Hitler became Dictator of all Germany.

In addition to all my enjoyment with the girls by now I was hunting regularly every season. I owe much of my knowledge of horses and of farming to our neighbour Craig Tanner. By my early twenties I can say without boasting that I had become a good horseman and it was undoubtedly mainly due to Craig. A big cattle-man with a good herd of Herefords, he came from a family well-known locally as wine merchants and farmers. Tanners of Shrewsbury was a highly-successful, well-respected wine business. A hard man but a fair one and a wonderful friend, Craig was undoubtedly one of the finest amateur riders in the country, better than most of the professionals. Perhaps his best horse was Setti The First, on whom he won the 1927 Foxhunters' Chase at Aintree, which in those days was run over the full Grand National course and distance. Craig had a groom called Arthur Jones, who was first-class at his job but was always on the drink. Now Setti was a brilliant hunter but Craig and Arthur were worried stiff because they could never get any weight on him. Whatever Arthur did, the horse refused to eat. However, after Arthur had got very pickled one night and forgotten to look in on the horse, he discovered the next morning that Setti was a night feeder. He would eat nothing by day. Thereafter Arthur gave him a very large feed at night and before long the animal was big and round.

Craig sent cattle all over the world and on one occasion he wanted me to take some to Australia. All was arranged but at the last minute another farmer, who had been taken ill and advised to have a sea trip to recover, took my place.

Our hounds had been split in 1892 into the North and South Shropshire, divided by the river, but their point-to-point at Eyton has always been a joint one. In addition to riding the course on many occasions I have been heavily involved for most of my life, ending up as Chairman. It is undoubtedly, to my mind, the best point-to-point course in England. The point-to-point has always taken place on Bank Holiday Monday. Back in 1932 Jack Savage, Vin Evans and I were entered in the Members' Race and decided to ride round the course the day before, on the Sunday. In those days they had a boat across the river to ferry the people over. So we tied the horses up to a hedge at about mid-day and did not come out of the pub over the river until about half past two, by which time we were paralytic. It took us about twenty five minutes to ride round the course!

Now, as I said, losing Betty because I was alleged to have "no prospects" had begun to worry me. Help came from an unexpected quarter. A neighbour, Harry Lea, who farmed the Charlton Farm, had become a confirmed alcoholic who had to be sent away periodically to dry out. Noel Wenman, the other neighbour who had helped me so well with the horses in my boyhood, looked after Harry's farm for him on these occasions but by June 1930, fed up with the regularity of these visits to "the funny farm", he refused to do it again. He felt it was high time Harry pulled himself together. As there appeared to be not much chance of this Mrs. Lea came to see Father and asked if I, now 20 years old, would look after the 300-acre farm until Harry came back. It was a good farm and, when he was sober, Mr. Lea was a good farmer. He milked 60 cows, reared all the calves, kept the heifers on and sold the steers for beef. He kept 20 sows, reared the pigs and sold them as bacons. He lambed 200 ewes, feeding all the sheep out on the roots in the winter. In addition there was a fair bit of arable land; he grew sugar beet, wheat and a very good sample of quality malting barley — it was outstanding barley land. Moreover he was a good man with horses but just before I went he had taken every sound horse to Shrewsbury market, sold them and gone on an almighty binge for a fortnight until he was completely paralytic. This was the reason for his enforced sojourn in the home at Church Stretton.

When sober he was not only a good farmer but an excellent employer with a fine gang of men who, by the time I went there, had finished hoeing all the sugar beet and been paid so much on account by Mrs. Lea. I had to reckon up the rest. I put them on to brushing the hedges which had to be paid at 4d. a rood. A crafty Irishman called Donnelly, seeing me running the tape measure along the hedge on the road side, said:"Hey! Ya haven't measured the other side yet!" Of course the payment was 4d a rood for both sides and the top!

There were three mares left on the farm of which one had already foaled and two were in foal as well as a nice dark brown, three-quarter-bred horse who was lame. Even at that early age I seemed to have acquired already the instinctive gift of diagnosis and healing which has been such a wonderful asset throughout my life. The vet had not been able to find out where this horse was lame but I suspected that it was in the foot. I have always held that any vet worthy of the name will, in these circumstances, always call in the blacksmith who inevitably knows more about feet than anyone else because, after all, this is his life's work. So I called in Jack the blacksmith who, as soon as he bent down to look at the foot, was kicked unceremoniously out of the box. I got him back to hold the horse because I could see a swelling on the coronet, took out my knife and just touched the spot whereupon puss shot out in a jet, hitting the horse on the belly. This relieved him considerably and I kept an eye on it every morning. Eventually I got him so that I could pick the foot up and cut out the poison until there was hole right through the foot. In fact, when he trod on mud it would seep up through that hole like a sausage but, nevertheless, we got the horse fit to work again. This was the first of my little treatments for which I have ever since been in constant demand and have been happy to perform.

We cut the hay and got it all in by the second week in July before Harry returned.

When he did come home the trouble began. His wife fed me well and every morning, after a good breakfast, I would visit Harry in bed. My days were filled, from 5.45 am to 8 in the evening and I was paid 30/-a week — the equivalent of about £48 in today's money. Every morning when I went in I found that Harry was completely pickled. When this happened every morning for a week Mrs. Lea and I began to get worried. Where was he getting it? One morning by chance I solved the problem. Entering the Dutch barn I saw the glint of bottles between the two bays and started to make enquiries. It transpired that every evening old Donnelly had been going down to the pub and bringing back bottles of whiskey and beer which he stuck between the bays and then Harry had been getting up in the night, creeping down secretly and drinking the supplies.

Sober again with his supplies cut off, Harry got up from his bed one morning and asked me to take him to Wellington Market to buy 200 ewes for himself and 100 for his son Jim who farmed at High Offley. Leaving me to bid for the sheep Harry went off to the pub. I duly bought 300 good Kerry ewes at 27/4 each, told the auctioneer that Mr. Lea would pay for them and walked them back to Charlton. All that night there was no sign of Harry and we did not see him for a week. Then we instituted a search, found him and brought him home where he retired to bed for a further week. This kind of thing continued all the time until one day in September, when he announced that he was taking a busload of people to Aberystwyth and he wanted me to get onto the farm early to get on with the milking because two of the men would be absent ... We didn't see Harry again for many days.

By now I was the boss and was organising the farm in the way that I wanted it. On the day after the outing I was giving my orders to one of the men who told me that Mr. Lea wanted that particular job done in a different way. I told him that while I was in charge things would be done in the way that I ordered but I took the precaution of going in to see Mrs. Lea because Harry was still not back. Some days later we heard that Harry was in a house at Walcott and I went to pick him up. He was in a terrible state. He hadn't shaved for a week and his clothes were filthy because he had been rolling about all over the place inside and out. I got him home and into bed before telling him in no uncertain terms that I'd had enough. I would not put up with it any longer. I told him that I would do everything he asked but if I was in charge I would do it my way and, once a job was started I would brook no interference from him. He apologised but I was very unhappy. So it continued through the busiest farming time of the year until late October when all the sowing was done and the work was well forward on the farm. Then I told Mrs. Lea that I was leaving. I did not even go upstairs to see Harry. During my life I have met many boozy doctors who claim that alcoholism is an occupational hazard of the medical profession. Be that as it may, I have also known a great many farmers who were heavy drinkers, either celebrating good times or, like my grandfather, drowning their sorrows in the bottle. As far as the West Country in concerned I lay much of the blame on those traditional quarts of immensely potent cider in the early morning and throughout the working day. Many farm workers in those days lived in a constant happy haze, a short life perhaps, but a good one!

When I went home Father was quietly very proud of my first experience as a farmer on my own and sympathetically asked me to work on the farm again. This I did for a few days but, before long, I decided that having tasted independence, I would start up on my own. Father was sorry that he could not afford to start me. He had started John and no longer had enough money to finance me too at that particular moment. Sugar beet was the only thing that was paying. It was quite a year — Father had lost £1,000 — the equivalent of £32,000 today and farming was very tricky all round. However I had another string to my bow. The general slump was over and the meat trade was now quite good. I reckoned I knew something about meat and decided to become a butcher.

My worldly wealth was £20 but I had fair hopes of some cash for my birthday in November. I still had my old motor bike with its well-worn pillion whose vibration between their legs had excited so many young ladies over the past few years, but this was not enough. I spotted a van for sale at the Ryton Stores in Dorrington, a good little runner which I bought for £11 10/- (about £360), and, loading the motor bike in the back, set off for Shrewsbury. There, from the Salop Timber Company I bought enough boards to erect shelves in the van, a good chopping block, scales, choppers, knives, saw and everything I wanted for the butchery trade. I also bought some tins of paint. I got up early on Sunday morning and spent the whole day equipping and painting that little van — a nice smart maroon on the outside and a good, hygienic white throughout the interior. Next morning, bright and early, I went into Wellington

Market and bought a 52lb. lamb for 25/- (£36) which I took
home to Uppington, killed, skinned and butchered in the old
dairy. Then I killed one of my own pigs which I had been
keeping for just such an occasion and I was ready for business.

When preparing the pig I made one very big mistake. I
scalded it to get the hair off without knowing that you had to let
the water go just off the boil before scalding. I had achieved
what was locally called "missing the scald". The hairs should
have come off easily but it took me nearly all day. I had learnt
another lesson the hard way! To make matters worse this was a
black and white pig and in the end I "borrowed" Father's open
razor to finish shaving off the pig's hairs. To his dying day he
never forgave me because that was his favourite razor and I'd
blunted it for ever.

Now, with my van well loaded with bits and pieces of lamb
and pork I drove round the village and, as they had always
known me and I was asking competitive prices, practically
everyone bought something from me although most of them
were asking for beef. By the time I'd gone through Rushton to
Aston I had sold out. Mrs. Rogers, my last customer at Aston,
asked for beef. I raced off to Davies' shop in Shrewsbury.
George Davies and I had been friends for many years and still
are. We had judged together with the Young Farmers and I
thought that he would find me some good meat. I ordered two
sheep, a small pig and a good piece of beef. George was not as
green in his side of the business as I was in mine. I can still see
that beef on the counter — a great big piece with a little bit of
bone showing in it, weighing about 30lb. which he sold to me
for 10/-. But I didn't realise that it was an 'H' bone — half of it
turned out to be bone. Nevertheless I returned to Mrs. Rogers
and cut her a nice joint off it. After cutting four more nice
joints I began to run into trouble with the bone. Another lesson
learnt! Undeterred I drove on to Burcott and Wrockwardine
and sold out. When I went back to Mrs. Rogers the next week,
she called me everything under the sun. She said the beef was so
tough she couldn't get her knife through the gravy! I lost more
customers with that beef than all through my business life as a
butcher. It was obviously an old cow or bull.

Next day after telephoning first, I drove to Davies and collected more meat which I took round the various hotels in Wellington. Much to my surprise I did very well and by the end of that week I had collected quite a nice little sum of money. Next Monday back to Wellington market to buy five sheep; I killed two of my own pigs and bought some more beef from Davies. Off on my travels again, business thrived so that by Easter I was killing a little beast a week and about twenty sheep as well as two or three pigs and a calf. Once a month I went to Shrewsbury cheese sale and bought half a ton a 4d a pound. Before long I had built up a turnover of £100 a week on which I was making a profit of £30 with no trouble at all. When you think that the men on the farms were working 60 hours a week at that time for £1.10/-, this was fair money.

Feeling flush for the first time I went back to old Harry Lea and bought a grand little unbroken 15.1 hand gelding with three white socks from him for £14. He was a little topper, very easy to break and school and one morning he really surprised me by jumping a five-bar gate in cold blood as I went to open it.

I hunted him first on Boxing Day 1931. There was a great Christmas atmosphere and a number of us North Shropshire people gathered for the South Shropshire Meet at the Oak Inn, Cantlop. Quite a little gang, Noel Wenman, Harry Lea, Ted Turner, Vin Evans, Jack Savage and myself. The drink was flowing from the pub and it was quite a long time before we eventually moved off — in very good order!

Apart from that gate my little horse had not jumped a fence but he was soon to be put to the test today. We found a fox very soon in Pitchford Big Wood and started a lovely run. I was following Mr. Wenman who always had a good horse. He jumped an iron hurdle on the edge of the wood. Nothing daunted, my horse hit the hurdle and although we did not come down, it shook him. He, too, had learnt a lesson. It was the best thing that could have happened to him because he was bold enough to take that rap and afterwards he always jumped like a stag. We ran the fox from Pitchford Wood, right-handed for Row Covert, straight through that as if he was going for Lodge Hill, left at Frodesley, through the Obelisk over some splendid fences and turned for Kenley Gorse before they bowled him over just before he got into Lords Coppice.

Hacking back, hounds found again at Cantlop Coverts and away we went to Condover. By now my little horse was getting really tired and when we came to a very big fence I turned him left-handed rather than overface him. Vin Evans who was following close behind on his great big hunter, hit us right in the ribs and knocked us over the fence. We both came down on the other side. By this time horse and rider were quite done and we made our way home after a wonderful day.

He really was a wonderful little horse and he gave me tremendous fun for many years. A very light bay with a white, almost clown, face, three white stockings and a white sock, he was know throughout Shropshire as "the Hereford". The old rhyme goes something like "One white sock, try him; two white socks, buy him; three white socks, give him to your wife; four white socks, keep him all his life".

But, like Robert Sangster's The Minstrel, who won the Derby nearly fifty years later, this little horse was the exception to the rule. He was a wonderful character, all guts and, when I sold him eventually, he went on to become one of the best show-jumpers in the Cheshire countryside. That rap on the iron hurdle which did him so much good, taught me a lesson too. Every year the opening meet of the North Shropshire Hounds was held at the house of the Master, Mr. Jim Everall. They would draw the Marl, a good covert, and always found a fox that would run to the Plantation, passing the back of the Master's farm. He had divided one of his paddocks with a split oak post and rails fence. I would always follow one of the best horsemen on a good horse. Most of my horses hit it but only one came down, a horse I bought in Ireland. He was never any good, so I sold him but the others never looked back and all became first-class performers over any country. That, of course, is why American horses, who have raced over timber in their native country, are such splendid jumpers. I always broke two three-year-olds every summer, showed them hounds cubbing, turned them out until January and then got them in and hunted them after I had qualified the point-to-point horses.

I am often asked why I am so fond of pigs, which seems strange for a horseman, because horses detest the animals almost as much as they loathe camels. Good stables will always keep in a bucket a solution of pig dung to spread on bandages and rugs to stop young horses from biting them. I've known many young horses shy badly, terrified of pigs.

The answer goes back to my eighteenth birthday when I was absolutely broke and my father gave me a present of £20 (£640 certainly in today's money but it was expected to last me for a year!) I harnessed up the horse to the bull float which we used for carrying animals and drove into Wellington market where I bought a sow and ten sucking pigs about a week old for £7. I bought six little buckets from Bromleys and 1cwt. of sharps from Turners, drove off home and put my new pigs in the orchard. I fed the sow for a month on the sharps and the swill from six houses in the village, then took her and the pigs back to Wellington market and she made £11. £4 was a hell of a profit in those days. Then I bought another sow and ten pigs for £10, kept her for a month and sold her for £15. When I got another £20 on my nineteenth birthday, I asked the vicar to let me use a little cowhouse and stable behind the vicarage — you couldn't see it for nettles and brambles — and I gave him £1 a year rent for it. Then I bought some more pigs and filled the building up. By my twentieth birthday when I received a further £20 I had no money because it was entirely invested in pigs. But I was making a very nice living and keeping going with them, selling them, breeding and keeping them, those I wanted, until by the time I started butchering I had about 50 pigs. No wonder I'm fond of the animals. They kept me going all that time when I badly needed money to enjoy myself, the hunting, the dances and the girls. What's more, you can get very fond of them because they are genuinely brainy animals. Tests have proved over the years that pigs are more intelligent than Alsations, for example.

July 1932 saw the opening of the The Mytton Mermaid, our famous local hostelry, which has remained the centre point of our lives ever since, over more than sixty years. Originally called Atcham House, it was part of the Attingham Estate and was then rented to a man called Budass, who owned Trouncers Brewery. There were stables at the back for eight horses with a flat above them and these were rented out to George Lucas, formerly head groom at the Hardwicke Estate, who kept a livery stable. He had married the delectable daughter of a farmer called Inions and they had two sons. George was always immaculately dressed, particularly out hunting when he wore white buckskin breeches as though he was a "highflyer" with the Quorn. Now the whole place had been taken on a twenty-one year lease and completely refurbished by Clough William Ellis, the millionaire who earned fame by building the popular Welsh seaside resort of Port Merion. He used the Mytton Mermaid as a half-way house between Birmingham and Port Merion, deliberately kept his prices down, put on a very good show at all times and provided first-class food and drink. By the time he had finished the dining-room, for example, was quite superb, with its parquet floor, panelled walls, oak antique tables and furniture. The two chief waiters were splendid fellows who remained there for years. Ellis's efforts were greatly appreciated. Ever since "The Mytton", as we call it, has remained the acknowledged centre for so many county activities and festivities, dinners, dancers, wedding receptions and so on. A lovely place where everyone who came to Shropshire called, because Ellis did everything in his power to advertise it. He had a life-sized giraffe made out of wood placed on the lawn, which could be seen from the road and proved a genuine "show-stopper" because passers-by, inevitably slowing down to look at it, would almost certainly call in. It has always had a very happy atmosphere.

This opening evening in July 1932 I called in on my way back from a Gymkhana at Berrington where Peter, my dashing little horse, and I had won £2 in prizes (nearly £70 today). When we arrived at "The Mytton" at about 9 pm the place was obviously crowded and there were sounds of merriment from within. I took Peter round the back, watered him and gave him a bucket of George's oats before going into the bar to find the place thronged with all my local friends being plied with free strong beer by old Lucas himself acting as barman. What an evening!

By midnight the barman was "legless" and I was pretty well gone myself when I staggered out, climbed on my horse and set off on the five-mile ride home. I don't recall much about that journey but I do know that at 5 o'clock next morning my father came into the stables and found me fast asleep still on the horse's back!

By 1933 I was definitely becoming broody. I had become reconciled to the lovely idea of marriage with Betty and now, devastated at having lost her, trying to get over it by making love to more and more different girls — and make no mistake, they were nearly all wonderful fun — I still felt that I needed a home and a wife. Without in any way boasting I can say that there was no shortage of applicants for the job. With plenty of money now from my butchery, hunting, showing, dancing, loving the local ladies, fit and fancy-free, I suppose I was quite a popular little chap. Maybe I was even regarded as an eligible bachelor, a bit of a catch!

Now I've always had great respect for marriage as an institution, but perhaps those branches of the Services are right which insist that an officer should not tie the knot until he is at least 28 years old. It would certainly have made a great deal of difference to my life if I had obeyed that rule. Moreover, in a poor marriage, there is nearly always fault on both sides and I don't believe that you are entitled to criticise anyone else's marriage unless you have been a fly on the wall in every room in the house. In my early twenties I was very vulnerable and Freda Hunt, the tall, dark, handsome chemist's daughter from Wellington, who was older than I, was, as I later discovered, a woman for whom the grass is always greener on the other side of the fence. She would go all out for something she wanted and then, when she had got it, she would be looking for something else. During 1933, while still enjoying other young ladies on the side, I went out quite a lot with Freda. Her father bought her a very nice little Riley motor car in which she would drive me to the pictures in Shrewsbury, theatres in Wolverhampton and sometimes, in the summer, away for a day at the seaside — which was really living it up in those days!

We were still fairly puritan regarding the serious business of marriage — don't forget, "the swinging sixties" were still thirty years ahead on the other side of a six-years wartime revolution — and men in our walk of life expected their future wives to be virgins until the wedding night. My beloved Betty and May Turner were good examples of what I mean.

So either Freda was chancing her arm or she was pretty sure of me when we went on that first week-end to Llanbrynmair. Her brother Ken, Barbara, Freda and I stayed at the pub, the Wynnstay Arms, which was kept by the former butler to Sir Watkyn-Wynn. As soon as we arrived Ken jumped out of the car and ran in to register. He booked us two double bedrooms and, in my innocence, I assumed that I would be sharing a room with him. It must be hard for today's reader to appreciate that, despite all my romps with other girls, I was acutely embarrassed to find that this was not to be. Needless to say, young and randy as I was, I soon recovered and, after an excellent dinner with plenty to drink, made the most of the arrangement. It wasn't until 4 o'clock in the morning, as she slept beside me, that I suddenly broke out in a cold sweat, got up quietly and went outside for a long walk by the brook. Jones had finally burnt his boats. I had compromised Freda in front of her brother so that I was inescapably bound to marry her. So be it. Resigned to the situation, I went back to bed to carry on where we'd left off.

After a good breakfast, we had a lovely day driving on to Aberystwyth and Borth — all along the coast. We bathed several times and laughed a lot. I remember being completely stumped when Freda posed the old riddle "As I was walking to St. Ives,I met a man with seven wives; each wife had a bag and in each bag she had a cat. Each cat had seven kittens — kits, cats, bags, wives, how many were there going to St. Ives?" As we drove, the others laughed and laughed while I tried to figure out this problem. In the end it had to be explained to me that the private life of this hag-ridden, cat-cursed moron was totally irrelevant. That was his problem. There was still only one man going to St. Ives!

Of course we became engaged and during that winter I took my fiancee to all the dances, including those organised by the Young Farmers and, on successive nights, the Hunt Ball, The

Farmers Ball and the Pengwern Boat Club Dance at the Music Hall in Shrewsbury. Traditionally we celebrated New Year's Eve with a particularly festive dance at the Forest Glen — I think I went there for forty years from the age of sixteen.

1934 was the year when I graduated from the Young Farmers to the NFU, became a Steward at the West Midland Show and got married.

Although I was making plenty of money from my butchery Father wanted me to get married and settle down on a farm. One day in February he said: "Tom, that farm at Atcham is to let. It's in a fairly bad state but it has a lot of potential and I think we'll get it cheap. I want you to come and have a look at it with me."

I was not too keen because I really wanted to have a house and a butcher's shop with a bit of land attached but Father insisted that I was a farmer and not a butcher.

"I'm going hunting, Dad", I said.

"Right, but be back at half past two."

They were meeting at Shawbury, ten miles away and it was 10 o'clock in the morning before I got away on my little horse, Peter. But, knowing my way across country, I arrived in time for the meet at 11 o'clock. After hounds had messed about in Shawbury Big Wood (200 acres) for three hours, my date with Father went by the board when we found an old dog fox returning home from a night's courting who went away towards Morton Corbett. Craig Tanner and I were in front when we came to a field from which the only way out was an iron gate firmly secured with a padlock. Craig and I took the gate but no-one else followed and we kept going right-handed to Stanton, left through Betsford by the kennels at Lea Bridge and through the wood at the back. Our quarry took us on across some wonderful country, practically all grass with good fences, very little wire and a few big ditches to Loppington Big Wood where we ran him to ground at 3.25 pm. We had covered ten miles practically straight in fifty-five minutes.

Having decided to leave him, we heard a holla at the back of the hall and immediately found a fox going towards Tilley, who turned round Wem, through Soulton again on the main Wem/ Lea Brockhurst road just before we got to Preston Brockhurst; another marvellous run over good land and splendid fences before we ran him to ground at The Rocks at Grinshill just as it was getting dark. There were only twelve of us left with hounds and not only was my Peter very tired but he had lost two shoes. Keeping on the grass as much as possible I called in on the blacksmith at Shawbury for two new shoes and buying some biscuits and a bottle of pop at the local shop, arrived home after 8.30 to find Father not best pleased. He had looked round the farm, considered it suitable for me and had taken it. When he showed me round on Saturday afternoon, I found it in a hell of a mess but agreed that it would be a start to my farming career. On Sunday I took Freda round. The house was so filthy that she cried and said that under no circumstances could she live there. But Father had taken it and that was that. We had to go. Moreover that was the first week in February and I had to start farming it from 26th March. Although he could not lay his hands on the money at the time, Father said he would give me the equivalent of £500 (£16,000 of today's money) and presented me with a couple of old horses as well as sending some fat sheep into Davies' in Shrewsbury for which they paid me. In the end, with the money, the sheep and the two horses, which were valued at £10 each, plus my own small savings, I ended up with £780. This doesn't sound much but it was a considerable sum in those days. Atcham Farm comprised 209 acres and the rent was £300 a year, including the coarse fishing.

"1991/1994 Value of Pound in"

1800 – 1819	£350
1820 – 1839	£230
1840 – 1859	£170
1860 – 1879	£120
1880 – 1899	£80
1900 – 1919	£44
1920 – 1939	£32
1940's	£17
1950's	£13
1960's	£8
1970's	£5

CHAPTER VII

Cleaning the Augaean Stables

Ordered chaos reigned for the next four months. With Father's invaluable help and the universal credit which his name carried throughout the county I was working flat out preparing the farm and so, in her own department, was Freda whom I was due to marry in July.

Father had been offered the farm in the first place by the Longnor Estate because old Bromley had had the farm for 26 years. So, I had to get rid of Bromley who was still farming seven acres of glebe land and had no intention of giving it up unless I made it worth his while. I had to give him £100 compensation. Now of my 216 acres, 80 were plough — all good flat land by the main road but heavy, because none of it was drained. Beside the river were meadows which had never been grazed properly. No fences and great bogs of stickle grass which it took me years to clear. There were no drains at all on the farm, just ditches which had never been cleaned out and, after heavy rain, which we had at the end of "Fill-dyke" February, much of it was just like a bog.

Father guaranteed the rent but as far as all the little items left on the farm, like grates in the house, barbed wire and all kinds of unforeseen things, Bromley was not a sharp dealer for nothing. The valuation came to £1,100 which I did not have but his agents gave me twelve months to pay.

As soon as the sales started in March I started to buy equipment. First I had to sell my little horse Peter, which almost broke my heart, but I got £85 for him, a fantastic profit, particularly as I had had so many years of pleasure from him and I knew that the girl from Cheshire who bought him would give him a really good home.

I took some buildings from Colonel Sowerby and a little patch of land behind the house, bought two cows and started rearing calves; three carts for a fiver each, three waggons for £7 each, a Massey-Harris mowing machine for a fiver, which was actually useless because it was too light to cut that strong grass at Atcham. Three nice working horses for £45 and a really good cob for £22, a grand little all-purpose mare who would work with the team, drive me in the trap to town and to Shrewsbury Market, do all the odd jobs about the farm and still give me the odd day's hunting, which was a rare treat in those hectic days, as well as proving a first-class hack. I called her Nelly and, although she may not have been the star performer that Peter was, she was a fair substitute and an excellent companion.On March 25, take-over date, I moved my cows, calves and pigs from Uppington and on the first Tuesday after that date bought 21 cattle for £52. The mistakes of youth! The nine little black ones which I thought were Welsh Blacks, turned out to be Dexters which would, of course, never grow any more! The lot included a big bullock Hereford which I sold in the autumn for £21. As I was paying for them the auctioneer, an old friend of my family, looked at the bill and said: "They look cheap. Give me that cheque and I won't put it in for a fortnight. As long as I'm here you can always have a fortnight's credit." This was typical as, although I had very little money myself, my Father's reputation and credit was so good that wherever I went I was greeted as Tom Jones' son — alright. Putting in drains instead of trying to clear the ditches, fencing the whole place — the cattle came into the garden — what a mess! Farm buildings full of muck; drains blocked until the cobbled yard was like a lake of slurry; the once beautiful garden with box hedges all round had gone completely wild back to nature; nettles head-high where the front gate to the drive should have been; old duck pens full of rats by the back door and a pig trough full of just about everything you can imagine. The pig styes, only twelve yards from the back door, were piled with filthy old clothes, rags, cans and bottles. The oven was full of indescribable things while the scullery and pantry were littered with old boots, leggings, dirty wellingtons, stinking socks and so on. In fact the smell in and around the house was disgusting — the only water was a hand pump in the middle of the back kitchen and there was no bathroom or inside lavatory — the only "convenience" was a privy down the garden. The hot water came from an old washing boiler in a corner of the back kitchen with a pipe running to the corner of one of the bedrooms. A rotary pump struggled to get water into a bath surrounded by ragged curtains in the corner of a bedroom. The cold water had to be carried up.

Fortunately Father and I had known Gordon Miller, the agent to the estate, well for many years with the result that new grates were put in, a bedroom was turned into a bathroom with a lavatory and a downstairs lavatory was also installed — all free of charge. I should think so too!

Electricity was brought down the lane; points, lights and switches were installed in the house and buildings; interior decorating — after scraping off all those layers of revolting paper and paint we found lovely oak woodwork underneath; cleaning, cleaning, cleaning. All accomplished in double quick time with the help of my own man Bill Tart and some more splendid local people. Meanwhile I was keeping going by wheeling and dealing with cows, calves and sheep.

The three cottages on the farm were in such a mess that they were not fit to put a man in but Gordon Miller promised to do them up as quickly as possible. He got the estate workmen in and managed to get one cottage shipshape by the end of August and another by the end of September. I took on another man called Joby Watkins who came every morning from Charlton to help Bill Tart. I also had a lad and a man for the butchery. I managed to make 20 acres of hay but the arable land was nothing but scutch, docks and weeds so no autumn corn had been planted. We put in 10 acres of sugar beet, 9 acres of swedes, 10 acres of oats and 47 acres of barley. Luckily it was quite an early year and Father sent his tractor and a man to plough in all the rubbish. He ploughed about 50 acres and although we were late starting, we got the sugar beet in as well as 10 acres of oats by the main road. By the last week in April we had ploughed and sown the lot. Father helped me with the

95

ploughing lending me implements that I could not afford to buy. I used his corn drill and sugar beet drill and, indeed, got on exceptionally well. We cleaned, ploughed and mucked the land so well with our own horses that I eventually had a marvellous crop.

Once all this work was in train I moved myself into the house. I bought a small table and a couple of chairs, took an old seat out of a Daimler car and put them in the kitchens. Add an old bed in one bedroom and my furniture was complete. I ate all my meals at The Mytton for 30/- a week, went home to Uppington for the weekends and thoroughly enjoyed my life.

Freda had eventually made up her mind that she would live in the farmhouse, which she now set about cleaning and tidying. Her father gave her £100 and she drove round the sales buying furniture, bits and pieces. After I had, by the standards of the times, committed myself irrevocably during that weekend in Wales with her brother, she became, although outwardly loving and possessive, more and more the modest, chaste, engaged lady, saving it for the great day. She seemed to lose much of her sense of fun and to become rather straight-laced. Without being unkind, it was as though, having landed her fish, there was no point in playing it any longer. I remember telling her one day the story of brother John's and my most successful escapade a few years earlier when two of our maids were being courted by a pair of brothers. We discovered that every Wednesday night, regular as clockwork, they would return from an evening in the village and make love in the cart shed. After work every day the carts would be backed up against the sleepers at the end of the barn, tipped so that they could be swept out and held in that tipped position by pegs attached to bits of string. In the morning those pegs would be withdrawn and the carts would bump down to their normal position. Having often used the carts myself with the Reynolds girls for the same purpose I knew that the angle of the tip was ideal for love-making. Get the girl in the back of a cart, brace the feet against the sleepers ... perfect! After watching them on several occasions John and I made our plan. On this particular Wednesday having made sure that the strings were firmly attached to the pegs, we hid in the barn until the brothers and the girls were really on the job, hard at it, with the carts rattling. Then, timing it to a nicety, just as we reckoned that they were reaching their climax with the grunting and the moaning, we pulled out the pegs. Crash, down came the carts. We had succeeded beyond our wildest dreams. Both girls became pregnant and nine months, almost to the day, produced babies!

Freda was not amused. So, I'm afraid that in the few weeks remaining to me as a bachelor I made the most of my freedom, with the utmost discretion, of course. Although they teased me mercilessly about my forthcoming nuptials and the approach of respectability, Sally from Upton and several of my other best-loved girl friends were genuinely sad and determined to make the most of what was left. There was also a very attractive, amusing horsey girl called Jenny whom I used to meet riding on the Wrekin in the early morning just as I had some years earlier with another little lady in a boyhood romance. This time there was no clumsy frustrated fumbling with clothes...

Concentrating on the farm had interfered with the butchery which was the main source of my income. The man I had engaged as a butcher turned out to be no good and after about two months he had lost about a quarter of my customers. So I sacked him and found a another much better man who even managed to get some of my old customers back. Freda and I were married on July 6 and I determined to be faithful. But it was a losing battle because from the very outset that marriage appeared doomed to failure. Even on our honeymoon at Watchet near Minehead we had rows and on our very first night, just as I had done that weekend in Wales, I got up and left the bridal bed at four in the morning. That was not a good omen.

I had drawn £50 to go on honeymoon and when I returned, received a letter from the bank manager informing me that I was £26 overdrawn and refusing me any further credit. Freda had spent her £100 very wisely so that we had all the bare essentials in the house but, as I hadn't even the money to pay for the meals at The Mytton, I had to sell some ewes and fat lambs.

By the first week in August Gordon Miller had finished one of the cottages and I was able to take on an excellent man who had just got married called Bert Lowe. I put him in complete charge of the stock. He was so good with calves that from the time he took over we reared 100 calves a year. In September I employed another first-class man, Bill Lightfoot, who looked after the horses.

We managed the harvest very well that season. Thanks to Father's help in the spring I did well with barley, wheat and sugar beet. Things began to look a lot better. That year, as I said earlier, I was asked to be a Steward at the West Midland Show for the first time. I was Steward of the Angus cattle on the Wednesday and of the Welsh Mountain ponies on Thursday. I was to enjoy this for the next fifty years and have happily lived to see my darling wife Rosemarie take over as a Steward in my place.

By now I was buying and selling cattle, sheep, pigs and horses on an ever-increasing scale, privately and at auction. I only bought beasts that were ready, or almost ready to kill. I was sending ten to twenty a week to Wellington and sometimes a load to Shrewsbury on a Tuesday. I was moving a lot of cattle and I had a big turnover. I started to do the same thing with sheep at £3 or £4 each and I would sell them the next week. t meant that I was away from the farm quite a lot but I had three very good men. I looked after them, paid them a bit over the odds and gave them all the milk, sticks, etc. that they wanted, as well as letting them catch rabbits. They were happy and I trusted them implicitly. All my life I've had good men and they've been my friends.

My first daughter Bobby was born on August 21, 1935. It must have been a very early harvest because I remember I was unloading the last load of wheat when Nanna Dodd, who always looked after our children for us, came running out to tell me that I had a daughter. And what a lovely daughter. I have always been so fond and proud of my children of whom the other three, Judy, Edward and Patricia ('Wooty') were born at intervals during the next ten years.

A little later I bought the best car I ever had in my life, an American Hudson Terraplane, which was a treat to drive and very powerful although heavy on petrol. She would not do more than about 18 mpg but it's interesting to look back and think that nearly sixty years ago here was a really comfortable car which would happily do 100 mph. It was a marvellous engine which was used in several other vehicles including that classic English car, the Railton. She had a bench seat in front so that, if necessary, you could have two passengers beside the driver and a 3-speed gearbox with a very high top gear.

I drove all round the country in that car, particularly with my neighbour Harry Jones, who was already a big cattle dealer. One of the many sales we attended was in Shaftesbury, where they had a practice I had never known before. Until a heifer had had a second calf she would be described as a bullock and, when she came into the ring to be sold, they would throw in the skin of her calf to show that she had not aborted. On these occasions we used to spend the night in Andover. Wherever we went Harry seemed to know the landladies and, a gay bachelor, slept with most of them! I was now a respectable married man determined to stick to my marriage vows, but finding this increasingly difficult because Freda, having got what she wanted, no longer appeared to have any enthusiasm for love-making. In the nine years from that first experience with the milkmaid up to my wedding day I had made love to very many women. Now, being forced to go without was becoming a terrible strain. On the old Army principle of "Send them to bed tired!" I was trying to take my mind off it by working flat out, farming, cattle-dealing, hunting, showing, driving all over the place and, incidentally, making quite a bit of money. Undoubtedly it all helped, but the mental and physical strain was almost unbearable at times.

At that time you could often buy cattle cheaply privately on a farm because many of the people in Wales did not know the true value of their animals. Sometime in 1937 the BBC started to broadcast the prices of cattle, sheep and pigs on the wireless every morning. They would quote a price per score for the pigs, per pound for the sheep and per cwt. for the cattle. After that, the Welsh farmers would think nothing of walking their cattle up to ten miles to a railway station to find out their value by weighing them on the weighbridge. Nevertheless there were still a lot of good bargains to be had for anyone who really knew his animals as I did by now. Very early in life I had learnt one of the greatest lessons, never turn down a profit. One day I was riding along the main road on my good chesnut mare when man pulled up in a car, admired her and asked if I would sell. Having paid only £15 for her originally and had an immense amount of fun out of her, I asked £100. He offered £70 and we settled for £80. He turned out to be Bill Craven who kept the Royal Lion Hotel at Aberystwyth and I sent her there on the train from Shrewsbury station.

I was doing particularly well with my sugar beet and, in addition to my pigs, was handling an amazing number of sheep. I was averaging around 2,000 sheep at a time in those years up to the war. At nearby Harnage Grange Colonel Pollitt farmed 1,000 acres, of which most was grass. I persuaded him to let me rent his grass for £200, at the same time pointing out that my sheep would do the land a power of good. He would want far less fertilizer next year to grow the grass because there was more potash in the water of a sheep than in any other animal. As he had originally asked me £1,000, I gave him an extra £50 for the grazing of all his sugar beet tops!

In the outside world, after Hitler had become Dictator of all Germany, Baldwin had ousted Macdonald and taken over as Prime Minister in June 1935 just before the start of the war between Italy and Abyssinia. The following year, on the death of his father King George V, Edward VIII took over the throne but reigned for only 325 days before his abdication through his infatuation with and insistence on marrying the divorced American Mrs. Simpson. What a bonanza today's tabloids would have had! Just before Christmas his brother the Duke of York succeeded him.

In 1937 Neville Chamberlain took over as Prime Minister of a coalition ministry. In 1938 Austria was annexed by Germany and the British Navy was mobilised. But a near-fatal year was lost when Chamberlain returned from Munich at the end of September, waving his bit of paper, claiming that he had made peace with Herr Hitler and Mussolini.

This ridiculous respite was short-lived, as any thinking person knew it would be. During 1939 the two dictators broke every treaty and agreement and, after the German invasion of Poland on the first day of September, war was inevitable. Like millions of others, listening to that ultimatum and declaration of war on Sunday September 3, I wondered just what the future would bring. I drove down to The Mytton where the atmosphere was mixed. There was the general patriotic "let's get at the bastards" and "The only good German is a dead one!", but there were grim faces and some tears in the eyes of the 40-year-olds and upwards, who, only twenty-one years earlier had had such high hopes when they were released from the tragedy and horror of those stinking trenches.

After lunch I saddled my horse and rode up onto the Wrekin. A good horseman knows that one of the best ways of settling a nervous, excitable animal is to let him stand and "count cattle". On this beautiful, sunny afternoon my beloved Shropshire looked wonderful as the cattle and sheep grazed and the corn stood in stooks, waiting to be gathered in. I had no more knowledge than anyone else of what the future would hold but I knew in my heart of hearts that life could never, under any circumstances, be the same again.

CHAPTER VIII

Dig For Victory

Winston Churchill, the greatest wartime leader of all time, was to put it in a nutshell. He said: "Every endeavour must be made to produce the greatest volume of food of which this fertile island land is capable."

And the man who was to inspire us all with his oratory as Prime Minister in May 1940 declared "The U boat and the bomber versus the farmer and the gardener. Torpedo and bombs against wheat, the potato and their many allies. The land is a vital war weapon — it's in your hands. You can defeat both submarine and bomber. Every seed placed in the ground is a bullet sped on its way to the black heart of Germany. The potato has come into its own; every root of every kind, for winter storage, is a shell destined to find its mark. Do your bit to provide these munitions of war. Plenty of food and you can provide it easily to spell certain and complete victory. Go to it — dig, sow, plant and cultivate for victory."

For once Britain was not caught with her trousers down. It was discovered that in the First World War, which had, after all, ended only 21 years earlier, Germany produced enough food on every 100 acres to feed 85 people, whereas our country was feeding only 40 people on the same area. This situation was to be reversed with a vengeance.

The Minister of Agriculture immediately appointed a War Agricultural Executive Committee (WAEC), which was soon to be known as the War Ag, for each county and made the Cultivation of Lands Order 1939 authorising the Committees to exercise powers conferred on them by the Defence Regulations to increase home food production in time of war. The aim was to increase an additional 1½ million acres of tillage area in

103

England and Wales compared with that of June 1939 and each county was allotted its share of that total.

Now I had already studied these plans with Captain Foster and Lady Boyne, who, like me, were realists and knew that war was inevitable. Moreover, as my father was far from well, I had to help him with his farm at Uppington as well as running my own.

On the other hand, at 29, I was fitter than most of the other men of Shropshire who, from early on Monday morning, would be queuing to join up in the Services. Born in 1910, I had been raised with a built-in hatred of Germans and everything German. The long sad lists of brave happy friends and acquaintances on War Memorials and Rolls of Honour in every village Church bore witness to those who had paid the ultimate price of fighting for freedom against that evil nation. Worse still, perhaps, were those many men who still lived among us, gassed, maimed, wounded and shell-shocked. The phrase "made in Germany" symbolised everything that was rotten and contemptible. Furthermore, at that stage of my life, I had never had cause to be afraid of anything. I would not call myself a brave man but I did not know the meaning of the word fear. Moreover, joining up and going off to war with so many of my good friends would be infinitely preferable to staying with a marriage which was steadily deteriorating from bad to worse. Realising that this could well be the most important decision of my entire life I suddenly had an inspiration. I would ask our Lord Lieutenant. I have always had enormous admiration for these wonderful, quiet, firm, dedicated men who, with no thought for themselves, devote their time and energy to serving their counties and people in every conceivable way.

The Earl of Powis, a great man already in his seventies, who was to be Lord Lieutenant of Shropshire for a record number of years, was a great friend of my grandfather and father. Grandfather and he were both on the committee of the Welshpool Show; I had met him many times with them both. In March 1938 he had asked me to buy him 30 Short-horn heifers and 5 Suffolk rams in September. He would be in Shrewsbury on Monday morning. So I hurried home, telephoned and arranged to meet him.

He didn't waste time. "I know why you've come to see me, young Tom," he said, "and I admire you for it. But I've made up your mind for you. I don't want you to join the Army. It would not be in the best interests of Shropshire or of England for you to do so. Although I have no doubt that you would have made an excellent officer, there are tens of thousands of others. On the other hand, with your knowledge and experience you are the equivalent of a general in the world of agriculture. We need you not just as a farmer in your own right and on your father's farm but as an administrator. This is going to be total war, young Tom, and you are a vital part of Shropshire's war effort. During the next few years you will have to take some tough decisions from time to time and you won't always be popular but I know you can do it. As you know, your father, along with a number of the other best farmers in the county, are on the new War Agricultural Committee under Captain Foster's chairmanship. I want you to help your father with a view to taking over if necessary. Get to know Captain Foster, Lady Boyne and the other members. The Committee will have very far reaching powers. You can forget all about peacetime farming.

"Moreover, with rationing which, as you know, has come into force immediately, all meat slaughtering, marketing and distribution will be centralised and you will be one of the most important men in the county, responsible for grading meat for human consumption. We'll also need you to help keep up morale on the leisure side which, as the war goes on, may not be all that easy. And there'll be a fair bit of work needed on the welfare side as well. For a start, with so many men away in the forces, some of the families are going to find it hard to adjust and, of course, we are having to welcome quite a few children who are being evacuated from Liverpool.

"So that's where your duty lies, Tom. Go to it and good luck. You're a farmer not a soldier — and that's an order, young Tom!"

So now I knew just where I stood and, with a feeling of great relief, returned to inform Freda who, for some reason, did not appear overjoyed at the prospect of having me at home throughout the war rather than away in the forces. Despite all my efforts, we seemed to be drifting further and further apart every day. All work and no play ... sexually I had become desperately frustrated so that it actually began to interfere with my work.

Whatever mistakes were made on other counts during the war — and, considering the circumstances, they were comparatively few — agriculture was something of which we can always be proud. For the first time all the farmers pulled together even though some essential measures, such as ploughing up much of their lovely grassland, nearly broke their hearts. At the very beginning the Duke of Beaufort set a fine example by ploughing 150 acres of his Park at Badminton. My father put the same amount of grassland under the plough. The 'War Ag' was supremely efficient. The aim was to ensure that the county was correctly farmed to further the war effort by producing the maximum amount of food. For this purpose they were given draconian powers. Anyone who was farming badly could be turned out. Farmers were divided into three categories, A, B and C. An A farmer was given instructions to grow certain things but was otherwise more or less left alone. For example, with the food shortage, it was necessary for farmers to grow more potatoes and those with the good land were given this responsibility.

A B farmer would be told what was wrong with his farm and his farming methods and was told in no uncertain manner that, unless he improved and did what the Committee told him, he was likely to be downgraded to a C farmer. A C farmer was given 12 months to put his farm in order. If he complied he would then be upgraded to B but, if he failed, he could be turned out of his farm. These were drastic measures but it was essential if we were to grow the food that we needed. Yes, Britain's farmers were marvellous.

Sadly, you couldn't say the same for all sections of the community. If the farmers' patriotism had been shared by all our countrymen it is probable that thousands of lives could have been saved and the war could have been ended earlier. As I drove round the country in my Hudson Terraplane on essential business I used to wonder at the vast acreage of unused tanks sitting packed like sardines in enormous parks. The trade unions were probably as guilty as anyone. Under the dictatorship of Germany, the production line could be stopped at once. A Mark IV would replace a Mark III; a Mark V and then a Mark VI would be made to order. But in England, it was alleged that the unions refused to stop the production lines even though there was a desperate war in progress. These huge stocks of unused Matildas and Valentines, all equipped with those ludicrous two pounder pea-shooter guns, costing at least £30,000 each and never even used, gave credence to that story.

Farmers and country people generally were different. We accepted the rations, the constant shortages, the blackout and so on as a normal part of our effort to defeat Germany. "Don't you know there's a war on?" had meaning for us.

The War Ag took 80 acres off a man who farmed at Kenley, next door to Colonel Pollit's land at Harnage Grange. When I inspected it I found it in a hell of a mess but Mr Sinnit, who had succeeded the late Colonel Sowerby as agent for the Uppington Estate, told me that I could have that land rent free for two years on condition that I cleaned it up. Mind, there were at least 20 acres of solid gorse and bracken. Nevertheless I took the land, and I cut all the gorse and planted. I bought an Allis Chalmers Model U Tractor with a single-furrow Hornesby plough convertible to single or double, ploughing 14 in. deep and 18 in. wide. My man, Jack Williams, a good ploughman, made an excellent job of it but in the gorse part after ploughing, all the roots were sticking up in the air. Not knowing too much about very poor land I planted oats but it was such a mess that the operation was a disaster. I don't think we had ½ ton to the acre. There were more thistles and rubbish than anything else. So the next year we ploughed it very lightly, 5 in. deep, limed it (2 tons to the acre) and planted wheat. I used 2 cwt. of fertiliser and in the Spring gave it 1 cwt. of nitrogen (sulphate of ammonia in fact) and we had a grand crop of wheat. After 10 days threshing from those 80 acres I was able to sell 1,200 bags of wheat. We cut down the high hedges, laid them and tidied up the whole place. That was a typical little wartime operation. While doing this I thought back to one of my last successful operations in February 1935. In early Spring I bought, for a gamble, 100 barren cows for £308, took them home and put them on some rough grass round the farm. I kept them moving from field to field and they pulled the old grass nicely. They were in the field by the river one day while the farmers were going along the road to market and on the next Tuesday morning a farmer asked me in Shrewsbury "Young man, you've got a hell of a good herd of cows there. You're getting some milk, aren't you?" He didn't know they were only feeding cows. So on the second Tuesday in June when the cows had done exceptionally well, I asked my cattle dealer friend, George Holland in Shrewsbury, "Will you come and buy 20 cows, George?" and he said he'd be there at four o'clock. I rushed home, got these 100 cows in, picked out the 20 worst and took the others as far away as I could so that he couldn't see them. Our friend George appeared at four o'clock to inspect the cows, he asked "How much do you want for them?" "A fiver apiece" I said. "They've done pretty badly haven't they? I'll give you four apiece for them." In the end we settled at £4 10/- for each cow. After that I sold all the better ones and by the second week of July those 100 cows had made me a net profit of £840!

But now with the war, I could see there was no chance of keeping my butchery business going. Wholesale butchers and the auctions were finished. Instead of being sold by auction all fat stock was graded in the market, allocated to abattoirs, killed and distributed to all the butchers so that there was no hope for a retail butcher unless you happened to be well in with one of the big allocators. So I sold my business for what was then a fair price of £150 to Davies and that was the end of my butchering for a time so that I was able to concentrate on my farming, started a dairy herd and gave up dealing. But 1939 was definitely a turning point in my life. Because of my butchery experience I was made Sheep Grader at Shrewsbury. There were three panels of graded sheep and between 2,000 and 3,000 animals were graded every Tuesday. Indeed we got so many sheep that they had to have a second grading day on Thursday as well.

The criterion was that the Ministry only paid a price on animals fit for human consumption, in good nick, with enough meat on them to kill. So I had to estimate the dead weight of the animals and certify that they were fit for killing. Up until 1941 they were produced for me in pens of 10. I had to estimate the dead weight of the animals and pull out the few, possibly 2 out of 10, who were not fit to grade. Believe it or not, by the end I got to the stage where if I was a pound out on average, I reckoned I'd done badly.

On the cattle side, farmers were only permitted to grade two-year-old heifers who had had one calf. These could be distinguished by the fact that they had just two broad teeth, which would increase to four as three-year-olds. The racket was to pass three-year-olds off as two-year-olds by pulling out two of the four front teeth and shrivelling the bags. They made a lot of money but woe-betide them when they were caught. Like black marketeers, they were rightly regarded as traitors to the war effort. Patriotism and hatred of the Germans ran high. "Don't you know there's a war on?" was the constant cry.

As soon as war broke out 43 children from the Docks area of Liverpool were evacuated into our area. It was a good scheme, which in general worked out extremely well and it's value was proved many times over by the subsequent bombing of Merseyside. We had some fun with them because they had never seen the countryside. One child picked a large bunch of dandelions for his favourite teacher and another, seeing the lovely apples on the trees in the orchard, asked Evelyn: "You're not going to leave them out all night are you?"

Evelyn? In the early summer of 1939 two very rich, prominent, youngish Birmingham business men came to ask me whether I would allow them to put two caravans in one of my fields so that they and their families could get away from the city from time to time, particularly if there was any bombing when the war started. After I gave them permission and they had installed their caravans, they came most weekends and turned out to be very nice families indeed. We would meet in the Mytton on Saturday and Sunday evenings and before long became good friends. One of the wives, 24-year-old Evelyn, was a very attractive young woman. Small, dark and slim with saucy twinkling eyes, a pert little nose and generous mouth, she had excellent legs and a lovely figure of which she was fully aware. As time went by our eyes were constantly meeting and one evening over a drink she asked: "What time do you get up in the morning Tom?"

"About six o'clock — I always walk round the farm before breakfast."

"Which way do you go?"

"Down the main road".

"I like to go for a walk in the morning", she said. I thought no more about it and went home to the usual unfriendliness of my own bed.

When I went out at six o'clock, I found another beautiful morning in that glorious summer of 1939, with the sun breaking through the haze and the corn standing nearly waist high. There, to my surprise, sitting on a fence waiting for me, was Evelyn, wearing a cool summer frock that left little to the imagination, the hard nipples in her firm little breasts showing clearly in a manner which was very daring for those days. As we walked together right across the fields she said "Oh, this corn does tickle up my legs in a funny place." She laughed, "It makes me feel very odd!"

When we came to a stile I climbed over, turned round and held out my arms to catch her. She never hesitated and leapt straight into them so that I rolled onto my back with her on top of me. As we landed laughing happily and I clasped her, I discovered that she was wearing nothing at all under her dress. Excitement took hold of me such as I hadn't known for five years. "Oh Eve!" I cried.

"Oh my Tom!" she replied. "This is what I've been waiting for."

She wasted no time and, for the first time in my life, I was raped! I couldn't believe my luck. Deliverance had come at last and I believed that Eve was the most wonderful woman in the world.

For her part, Eve genuinely loved me, believed that we were indeed made for each other and, as soon as her husband Norman left to join the RAF, moved into the caravan permanently and signed on as my Land Girl. She was a good worker and became very useful to me — in more ways than one! I had to teach her everything about farming but she was a quick learner and in return she taught me a great deal about love and life.

After selling my business and finishing dealing as well as butchering, I was able to concentrate on farming. I bought a hundred Friesian heifer calves which Bert Low reared for me. In addition I bought a few cheap cows which we milked by hand and, by the end of 1940 with a herd of fifty, I had a milking machine installed with all the usual sterilising equipment and so on. Mrs Low and another woman came to milk every day.

One day I discovered that Ernie Wheelsby, the scrap dealer, had two very good mares which he wanted to sell. The War was a funny time for those of us who were left at home. With racing heavily curtailed, little or no hunting or showing and forage at a premium, owners, breeders and riders away in the Forces or otherwise engaged, stallion services were stolen or given away and good horses languished at grass or drifted about waiting to be picked up for next to nothing. I took Eve with me to inspect these two horses in a field down by the river on the other side of Frankwell. They could have been made for the two of us. One was a fine big hunter, good enough to show, and the other was a small 15.2 hands thoroughbred mare. Ernie was one of nature's real gentlemen, a really good scrap dealer and the most honest rogue I have ever met. A splendid fellow. I let him have some bags of scrap iron and bought the two horses for £27.

I never discovered where they came from but they had obviously been done the living best. Both perfectly broken with excellent manners. Eve and I would often ride to Kenley and back in the morning. The South Shropshire Hounds still met very occasionally and an old kennel huntsman called George kept ten couples going. No-one could afford to lose poultry, particularly during the War, and every now and then we were called out to deal with a fox who had been doing a considerable amount of damage. Mr. Clapham, who looked after them through the War, would often telephone me and ask whether I would take the hounds out as he was otherwise engaged. We had some very good days. Both these mares that I had bought were very useful. I imagined that they had probably belonged to a hunting couple up in Cheshire. The big mare would jump anything and, when I rode round the farm, she would fly over all the gates and fences. As petrol was rationed, I would ride her to Shrewsbury and to farm sales all over the county. Eve, with her perfectly mannered little mare, and I thought nothing of going fifteen or twenty miles at a time.

In January 1940 my father was taken very ill with diabetes and rushed into hospital, where he had to stay for three months before he could be stabilised. On a number of occasions during this period we thought he was going to die and he had asked me to look after the farm. He had also taken a farm at Hordley near Ellesmere for my brother George which was to be taken over in March 1940 but he had the rights to go in during the winter to plough. So George spent the entire winter on that farm and by the time Father came out of hospital in April I had been extremely busy looking after his farm and helping George, on top of all my other commitments. Father had been farming the Deer Park at Acton Burnell — two hundred acres which I took off his hands; I had my ground at Kenley and I took Father's place on the War Agricultural Committee which, of course, entailed inspecting farms one day a week and attending important meetings.

Acton Burnell was an old Deer Park which had held deer until the end of the First War when the fence fell down and the deer got out. Father turned fifty cattle out onto it when he took it over in 1939. Out of the two hundred acres about half were covered in bracken five-six feet high so that quite often he could not see his beasts when he went to find them. It was really a lovely spot with two beautiful lakes in the middle but sentiment belonged to peacetime. There was a war on and we were digging for victory. In the Spring of 1940 I decided to plough the eighty-acre field which had the most fern on it. We burnt the bracken and with the help of Frank Hyles' tractor, ploughed it in.

Although we had any number of problems, Frank's man Felix eventually got the whole acreage ploughed. It was light land and we kept the roller going behind the plough before harrowing it and testing it for lime. It wanted twelve tons an acre and so we put two tons on to start with before sowing the grass seed. We were lucky with the weather and by the end of May we had good grass on which I put some ewes and lambs that I had bought. One evening in the Mytton, Eve and I worked out my commitments. I had 200 acres at Acton Burnell, 80 acres at Kenley, 224 acres at Atcham and over eighty acres of that hill land in addition to a thousand acres of grass keep rented off Colonel Pollit for winter. I had my cattle, sheep and pigs. Not only was I heavily involved with the War Agricultural Committee and the National Farmers' Union but in January 1940 I was made Chairman of the Red Cross Committee, which meant a great deal more work. No wonder the Lord Lieutenant had forbidden me to join the Forces!

CHAPTER IX

"There's A War On"

In the outside world the war was hotting up at last. The Germans invaded Denmark and Norway, soon driving the newly-arrived British troops out of that country. May saw Hitler's Forces marching into the Low Countries and on the 11th of that month Winston Churchill formed a National Government.

When Anthony Eden broadcast an appeal on 14th May, 1940 for men between the ages of 15 and 65 to join up as Local Defence Volunteers (LDV) he warned: "You will not be paid, but you will receive uniform and be armed". The response was phenomenal. Walking, biking and hobbling, the menfolk of Britain turned up at their local Police Stations to register. Within twenty four hours the country as a whole had enrolled some 250,000 volunteers equalling the strength of a peacetime Regular Army. I was made Intelligence Officer of the Atcham Squad. This entailed very hard work indeed. In addition to all our other work — and don't forget the best men had gone from the farms — I had to be on guard on the bridge two nights a week from 1 a.m. to 6 a.m., the time to start a new day.

Initially we had no rifles, only brooms tails but, when I look back, I believe that it really was the Home Guard who stopped the Germans invading. Unlike all the other countries, we had a properly organised Resistance Force. It was really rather marvellous because we were totally untrained at first but we took it all very seriously. Our headquarters was The Mytton — you couldn't have a better place! — and, in addition to our military duties, we had a lot of fun with many social functions. Although, in the security of nearly half a century of peace, the Home Guard has come to be thought of as a laughable, loveable, bungling Dad's Army, you have to remember that our duties were usually carried out in very difficult circumstances after a long day's work. Moreover, we were living in an atmosphere of war, surrounded by aerodromes from which bombers and fighters set forth, all kinds of uniforms on men and women, rigidly-enforced blackout, strict rationing of petrol, food and all other commodities, grave but usually depressing reports from the battle zones and the constant daily threat of a marauding German aircraft going to and returning home from their deadly missions on Liverpool and Manchester. So fear and the increasing threat and talk of invasion stretched tighter the already taut nerves of a country at war and made us take our duties ever more seriously.

Acton Burnell is historically famous as the place where the first Parliament is said to have assembled in a barn in 1283, the eleventh year of King Edward I's reign, in order to pass the Statute of Acton Burnell, which was indicative of the growing importance of England's mercantile class. Its object, as set forth in the preamble, was to make provision for the more speedy recovery of debts. Amongst other matters this Statute ominously made arrangements for the restraint of the debtor's goods and so can be said to have laid the foundation for the sinister, interminable rise of bailiffs, accountants, lawyers and civil servants. I had cause to curse that Statute when the taxman attacked me in 1960!

The two lakes at Acton Burnell had been created by the monks from the nearby monastery and still contained fish including tench weighing up to 10lbs. On the side of the hill the monks had built a 'larder' dug into the rock twenty feet deep and twenty feet square with a roof over the top covered with soil and a big wooden door. Ice had been cut in blocks from the lake and put in the bottom of this 'ice house'. They would slaughter the deer from the Park and store the venison which would provide food for months. We ploughed the 30-acre field rather late but it was a beautiful field of soil and, with the oats we sold, resulted in a tremendous crop.

At the beginning of March I bought a cottage at Cound Moor for £200 quite near the Deer Park and put a good old farm worker called Bill Ward into it.

Just to show you the sort of restrictions we were up against, I reckoned that I needed two miles of barbed wire and a great many posts to fence off this land at Acton Burnell. So I went to the agent, Gordon Miller, who said that I could cut down any oak trees and split them into posts, which was fair enough, but it was difficult to obtain anything else for fencing without permission from the War Agricultural Committee. George Etoff was the man whom the War Ag allowed to hand out permits for such requirements. Going to his office in the Square in Shrewsbury I saw one of his secretaries, a most attractive girl, and told her that I wanted two miles of barbed wire, at which she laughed and said I would be lucky to be allowed one roll. I told her that I had taken the Park at Acton Burnell which had never been fenced and that if I was to farm it properly it had to be fenced strongly. "Perhaps I'd better have a look," she said.

"Perhaps you had," I said. "I'll pick you up when you finish at five o'clock and take you over."

We made friends on the way over in the Hudson in which I always kept a few rugs. After a short walk together through the bracken on that glorious warm summer evening in the splendid isolation of Acton Burnell, it somehow seemed only natural to take off our clothes, lie down and get to know each other a lot better. We made love for several happy hours ... I got my wire alright! Thereafter Joan became a regular visitor to the Park to see how the erection was progressing! We went to see Sid and George Warren, who could tackle any farm jobs, and arranged for them to cut down an oak tree and split it for posts and put up the barbed wire. It took them the whole of the summer. I sent up all my Wessex sows and carefully selected the boars to put on them — the longest, leanest boars I could find. I had forty sows at Acton Burnell. All very well and splendid for the war effort as well as my pocket, but I had a problem getting rations for the pigs' feed. You were allocated permits for feed stuff according to the amount of stock you had on the June 1939 returns. So, having increased my pig and dairy herds, I was desperately short of feed and had to do something about it.

117

We ground a lot of our own barley, started growing oats and then I bought grains from the Wrekin Brewery. Then from the Milk Marketing Board at Minsterley I raised a supply of whey and skimmed milk from the creamery where they made a lot of cheese and butter. We converted the outbuilding and yards for feeding purposes and from two tanks filtered the whey through into troughs into which we added the barley mixture. I had acquired a hammer mill and also a Nissen hut which held 15 tons of barley. The hammer mill blew the corn into a mixing space next door to the shed in which I kept my pigs. So everything was fairly handy.

At about this time a man called Don Goodwin from Bibby's called on his way round every farm helping the farmers to fill in their forms for ration coupons. He queried whether I was claiming for my dogs and so on, putting down all sorts of things when he found that I had not been getting my right amount of rations. He said that even if I did not buy my corn from him he would call and fill in the forms once a month. So I gave my business to Bibby's and have dealt with them ever since. I bought all my seed and feeding stocks from them and also my corn. I never asked what Don was charging and what he would give me because I knew that I would get a fair deal. Throughout the rest of the war I had my rations from him and I used to send a lorry to Liverpool for them. Five tons a week at first, soon increasing to seven tons, and when I got another farm it became 14 tons and the journey had to be made twice. I would send him all my coupons and I never knew how he managed to supply me. Only once was I not able to get what I wanted and that was when he had some Inspectors in checking coupons and books. He sent me 3 tons every other day until they had finished. Of course I could not tell anyone that I was getting that amount of corn.

By the time that I had fifty sows at Acton Burnell I obtained a contract for ten bacon pigs a week from Beddards of Shrewsbury. It was an excellent order and, because I was producing very good pigs, they gave me a little bit above the odds — about £22 each. As I said earlier, on top of all my other activities, while Father was ill I looked after his farm. He came home in April 1940 but one day in June I was summoned from Kenley urgently because he had had an accident. The egg man had called at Uppington, collected the eggs and Father walked down to the gate with him, expecting him to drive on with the wagon but, instead, he apparently reversed knocking Father down and luckily, as he drove off, he looked back and saw my father lying in the road. Broken arm, ribs, dislocated shoulder, broken jaw. When I arrived the ambulance was there and I really thought I would never see him again. I travelled to the hospital in the ambulance and arranged for someone to collect me later on.

So I had to take on Uppington again. Uppington which I loved so much and my father was now growing 50 acres of potatoes to help the war effort. It was a wonderful farm but taking it over again on top of all my other commitments was almost the straw that broke the camel's back. Consider. I was never idle. As a member of the War Agricultural Committee, County Executive of the National Farmers Union, Grader at Shrewsbury Market, while at the same time handling up to 2,000 of my own sheep and farming a thousand acres of my own, I had more than enough on my plate.

Add to that the Home Guard, the South Shropshire Foxhounds and countless other activities, including the organisation of Attingham Fair, Chairman of the Shrewsbury NFU Red Cross Committee, organising 'Flapping' meetings (unlicensed race meetings) at Bayston Hill, 'Most Beautiful Land Girl' Dances at every Village Hall with the final at the Music Hall in Shrewsbury and so on. Raising so much money that Shropshire collected a larger sum than any other NFU in the UK and we received the Florence Nightingale Lamp for our efforts. Moreover, now in war time, there was another consideration. No day was long enough, particularly in the winter months when the strictly-enforced blackout frustrated so many essential activities. At harvest time and in the autumn there was no question of beating our fickle climate by reaping, ploughing or sowing at night. All lights were out — by law. Woe-betide the transgressor. Any doubts were removed by the odd stray bombs as German aircraft, temporarily 'lost' when returning from raids on Liverpool or Manchester, unloosed their evil cargo haphazardly. Besides, we knew that what the bastards had done to harmless Exeter they could do to Shrewsbury just as cruelly if they wished.

My brother Arthur had been at school until he was 17 — not like the rest of us who had had to leave earlier for financial reasons — and then he was articled to auctioneers for three years. My sister Mary had contracted tuberculosis and died. We were all vetted for TB and when Arthur was pronounced doubtful he was sent to South Africa to work for my uncle Arthur's friend, a stockbroker who had started a business in Johannesburg. For a time Arthur did very well but then he started gambling on the Stock Exchange and in 1938 lost all his money. Everything went — his beautiful flat, big car and all. He started peddling insurance hopelessly and returned to England in 1940 trying to join up. Turned down by all the Forces because of his flat feet and eyes, he eventually got a job at the beet factory, making Uppington his home base.

My routine involved a six o'clock start when the men arrived for milking and I would go to Uppington before 7 a.m. returning there each afternoon. One morning when Paddy O'Neill and 42 women were picking potatoes, the tractor kept stopping. To my annoyance Paddy had not cleared the fluff in the carburettor as I had taught him and so I took off the carburettor myself, a boring, hot job which made me particularly mad. Eventually when I got the tractor going again I found it was nearly nine o'clock. Imagine my fury when I heard Arthur, who had obviously been enjoying a nice lie-in and a good breakfast, starting up his old car which had no silencer, on his way to 'work'. I ran to the gate and stopped him.

My father had long been asking me to go into partnership with him but I did not want to forego my independence although I would dearly have loved to have had the farm. All these thoughts rushed through my mind when I stopped Arthur and really let fly at him — telling him in no uncertain terms that he was a selfish bugger who had never done a thing in his life to help Father. I said it was high time he left his cushy job at the factory and came home to help run the farm. To my surprise and to his eternal credit he took it all in, went to the factory, gave in his notice and started work at home the following week. He knew nothing about farming but he had had a fair business training. As a result he did everything Father told him and made the old man very happy. This was just as well because I have always been my own man and would have done things my way — not Father's way.

My father never made a fortune, probably because he was too good a farmer. He kept too many men and was perhaps over-meticulous about the property which was always absolutely spick and span. He still employed men who had started with him in 1903 who stayed and died at Uppington. Their sons are still working on the farm. After Arthur joined him he made money as he had not done before. Arthur would drive him round the farm when he felt better and he would issue all the instructions.

I have often wished since that I had taken over at Uppington but at the time it was just not possible.

I was getting on very well with Acton Burnell. We harvested the oats, made sheep pens, prepared a sheep-dipping bath, turned the stables into boxes for horses and farrowing sows. I bought and erected a Dutch barn and became very friendly with Mr. Bruce the landlord, who had married the last of the Smyths, owners of Acton Burnell for hundreds of years. The last male Smyth was in a mental home but Miss Smyth, who had married Mr. Bruce, was a wonderful lady and he was a great old man, a real gentleman, who was interested to see what I was doing with the former derelict land and often came to help me. Whenever I was doing anything interesting I had to telephone to tell him and he would always turn up to help with every kind of job. In those days I castrated all my own Stock. With the sheep I would do them as fast as the three men could catch them and Mr. Bruce loved holding them for me. I spent many happy hours round that historic Park. There was the old castle there and the gable ends of the building which had housed that first parliament. Those monks who created the lakes and lived at the castle, had laid on water from the spring into a big

121

well and piped it right through the castle. They actually had indoor sanitation which went under the castle through a channel made out of stone blocks. On each floor, in the Norman style, they had built a garde robe, or toilet, from which all the waste was washed away by the underground water.

I had four men and three Land Girls, including Eve. Early in 1940 I had applied for a Land Girl and collected a very quiet girl called Connie whom I picked up at Shrewsbury station and took to the depot at Abbey Foregate where they fitted her up with her clothes. We went home, where she had a meal and went to bed. Although I knew she had come from Liverpool, I somehow expected that she would have known something about farming. I called her at 6 am the next morning and she came down looking very tired. With a Hurricane lamp to light our way I took her across to the cowhouse but, when I switched on the electric light and she saw the cows, she started to scream and scream. I quietened her down and asked whatever was the matter. She said: "I don't want to go anywhere near animals. I put my name down for dairy work and thought I would be working in a dairy. I've never seen a cow before!"

So, to start with, she was utterly useless but, as time went by, she gradually improved until she could help Bert Lowe with the cows. Bert's wife had been marvellous but she was pregnant and the reason why I got the Land Girl was because she could no longer do the work. It was autumn before Connie was of any use. At that time I harvested 80 acres of oats at Kenley and we arranged our dairy herd to start calving in the middle of September. We had very little milk in the summer — there was a lot of work to do — but through the winter we would get quite a lot of milk from the cows and soon as the grass came in the spring they would have another flush so that we would get considerably more out of them. Through all the harvesting in August and with the cows calving from the middle to the end of September, Connie was left to milk ten cows and feed calves on her own. It was the making of her. She gained confidence and thereafter was better than any man at the job. She was as strong as a horse and stayed with me until the end of the war when she married the son of Frank Parry, who had the threshing machine and did a lot of work for me. When Eve left Hilda joined us and also stayed until the end of the war. She was very good, married a local lad and still lives in the village. We put sheep on about fifty acres in front of the Hall to pull all the 'keep' off the ground. Around the village there were about fifteen acres of paddocks which belonged to the church and which I now rented. They were very useful when we started to lamb the ewes. It was in 1941 that we ran into all sorts of trouble with lambing. Despite looking healthy, lambs were dying after twenty four hours. I took two of them to the Research Station at Tettenhall in Wolverhampton where they carried out tests and advised me that the little creatures were short of animal protein. They suggested that I gave the in-lamb ewes 2 oz. of fish meal a day. Now this was very expensive and difficult to obtain but Mr. Ken Redfern, manager of Bibby's, got me some white fishmeal right away. We fed this to the ewes with corn and beet pulp as well as a few oats and within days the lambs were coming healthy. That problem was solved. The re-seeding had done well but was short of lime and needed 12 tons to the acre. A man called Jim Jarrett started in the first week of April putting factory lime onto it with his 5-ton Bedford lorry. We had ploughed 68 of the 80 acres which was all sloping down to the lake. It was quite an operation but it was really worth while. Jim delivered the factory lime at 2/6 a ton and we received a 2/4d subsidy on it, so that there was no too much of a strain on the exchequer. We put 15 to 20 tons to the acre. After Jim and his young lad had delivered it, we would harrow it up and down and across with the tractor and chain harrows. Here we had 420 lambs from the 300 ewes turned out on the keep. They did very well.

In the middle was the 30-acre Belvedere field which had had oats on the year before and which we ploughed now before sowing with Arran Pilot potatoes. It had to be ridged and the women would drop the potatoes, we then split the ridges and covered them. We chain-harrowed the weeds until the potatoes came through the top of the ground — we had no sprays in those days. When they were nine inches high we ridged again.

One day I arrived to find potatoes with holes in them covering the ground. I dug up a few to find they were full of wireworm. As I said earlier, there were a lot of oak trees in the park and the jackdaws and rooks roosting in them were picking out the potatoes to get at the wireworm. The emergency action I took now was typical of what we had to do to further our desperate war effort. Those potatoes were vital supplies. I soaked some barley in strychnine and put it in tin cans, trickling the barley down the rows. Next morning at daybreak I collected and buried about 150 jackdaws, rooks, pigeons and pheasants, all lying dead. I was terrified because, even in wartime, if anyone had found out that I had killed all those birds there would have been hell to pay.

I instructed three of the women to reset the potatoes with trowels and we started digging the crop in June. With a group of twelve local women who were the best workers I ever had, we dug until the first week in August beginning at five tons a day and working up to ten tons. The lorries collected them at night. I was paid well, the 30 acres earning a profit of £1,300 and, of course, those spuds had really cleaned up the ground.

During these hectic months Acton Burnell was my escape. I had been given, all to myself, a timewarp in which I was always discovering fresh excitements that had been left untouched for years. Now, in this fascinating place, I was able to use my farming skills to help the war effort at the same time enjoying this oasis of peace while the world outside was in turmoil. If I never found the Sleeping Beauty I expected, I was able to introduce several of my own!

Before I bought the cottage at Cound Moor and installed Bill Ward, I discovered a roundhouse in the middle of the 80 acres, a lovely place, completely round with two stories. There was one room and a larder downstairs and one great big round room upstairs. It was beautifully built, dating back to Regency times with Adam fireplaces. Although the downstairs room had been somewhat knocked about because the door had been left open, allowing people and animals to enter, the big room upstairs remained intact with its four windows from which you could see all round the park. Not only had it an Adam fireplace but also a lovely ornamented stucco ceiling. I don't think I've ever seen such a beautiful room.

The little house had been built originally as a shooting lodge and the squire had used it for a number of different purposes, particularly using his *Droit de Seigneur* to make love to the young girls from the village. Legend had it that the Squire always had the first night with a girl after her marriage. The house had fallen into disrepair and it was a shame to see it deteriorate. So I took on another man and put him in to do it up. I installed a cooker and had the little room at the back made into a lavatory. As soon as he had decorated it and was making it fairly shipshape, this man brought his wife and his old father, a man of about seventy, to help him install a proper drainage system in the Park. One day he took off with his wife leaving the old man all alone, just a bed. I provided him with food and employed him doing the draining.

By that time I had started rearing heifer calves and turned 70 of these heifers out at Acton Burnell with a bull who was not the best-tempered beast. One day I arrived to find the bull bellowing. I could not see the old man anywhere but after hunting around I discovered him lying in one of the drains that he had dug while the old bull, who had gone for him, was scraping the ground in fury and almost had succeeded in covering up the old man. In those days I was not afraid of anything and set about the bull with my walking stick. I caught hold of his tail and he turned. I clouted him with the stick so hard that the stick broke but he ran away. I got the old man out as gently as I could, cleaned him up and put him to bed in the little house. Then, realising that I must get someone to look after him, I rushed to enlist the help of the local policeman but, when we got back to the house, the old man was dead. We managed to find the son, who came back and gave his father a decent burial. After that I decided not to put any more workers into the little round house.

Having ploughed the 80 acres and re-seeded it, I weaned the 400 lambs and turned them out on the re-seeded ground. I would go every morning at 7 am to see them, accompanied by my old dog Scot. We would go through the double doors into the park at Acton Burnell and Scot would work right round through all the hollows. By the time I had walked along the side of the lake he would have the sheep in the corner where we had a pen under three big trees on a corner fence. One morning he got them into the corner and, when I got there, he gave a yap and went running back up the field to one of the hollows. I followed him as he obviously wanted and discovered that he had located a dead sheep and was trying to pull it towards me.

The magic of Acton Burnell was working and now, after all those years of lying fallow, my sex life was becoming as complicated as it was in the days before my marriage. A neighbouring farmer had two daughters who took it in turns to help me with the sheep; the sweet secretary-girl often came out in her own car to inspect the wire; and best of all was Becky, lovely Land Girl of another farmer friend who had been bombed out of the Home Counties and bought a place nearby. We met one summer evening when I was walking round the place and found this gorgeous girl doing the same. The weather was warm, the birds were singing, the fish were plopping as they rose in the lake and the leaves in the trees were rustling in the gentle breeze. It was love at first sight and, once again, the bracken made a beautiful bed. Here, in grateful tribute to her memory, I must point out that my three-year love affair with Eve, which had started so passionately in the Atcham cornfields during the summer of 1939 and continued so happily for so long, had come to an end almost inevitably because, particularly in those days, in the cool light of day, there was no way that we could ever have been married. She was a lovely woman and a wonderful companion. In the circumstances it was best that we parted. She had broken the spell and I will always be grateful to her.

My love for Becky who became my mistress for the rest of the war was different. She was a free spirit. With no ties or recriminations we enjoyed each other mentally and physically as often as possible in a happy, carefree relationship. Right at the beginning, however, this beautiful friendship nearly came to an abrupt end when Becky caught me with the 'wire' girl. It took me a month to persuade her back into a good humour.

Thereafter there was no further trouble because she knew that she was number one.

We found some lovely places in the heather for making love but one night a thunderstorm broke and we rushed into the old roundhouse to complete our lovemaking, only to find the following day we were both covered in fleas! On another occasion we dodged the showers in a tin shed in which I used to keep corn and a few bales of hay. After thoroughly enjoying ourselves we tried to get out only to find that the door was locked. Bill Ward, whom I had installed in the cottage at Cound Moor, had seen the dog sitting outside, realised that we were there, come along quietly and fastened the catch putting the peg in it. As it was still raining and we found that we still had quite a lot of unfinished business, we didn't bother for a while but, when the rain finally stopped, I had to lunge into the door quite a few times before I could break it open. It was not long before I decided to dispense with the services of Bill Ward.

All those lovely oak trees — about 150 of them — around the outside were another bonus at Acton Burnell. In the autumn, however, as acorns are poison to cattle, we had to move the beasts for calving. Owing to flies from the lakes we were plagued with summer mastitis and usually lost about half a dozen heifers from this. Every day in the autumn we would run the pigs out into the park and let them graze to eat the acorns. Inevitably we had to let the sheep pick up some of them but, if there was a strong wind and a lot of acorns fell, the sheep would be ill from eating too many.

During the winter of 1942/43 I had rather a rough time with sore throats and the doctor decided to remove my tonsils. At thirty-two years of age, it was quite a rough operation and I was the exception. It was bitterly cold when I was admitted to the Eye, Ear and Throat Hospital at Shrewsbury in February. After the operation I was given a sleeping tablet and, when I awoke, everything around me looked yellow. Of course during war time there was very little heating, even in the hospital, and the pretty nurse standing by my bed in her starched apron and uniform was blue with cold. The whole experience was like some strange dream. "You're shivering", I said. "Come into bed with me."

"What a very good idea!", she replied and, taking off her shoes, did just that. To begin with she made me feel colder still but it wasn't long before we got warm! Nothing more was said about it and I felt much better next morning!

In 1942 we had planted Kenley, where I rented 80 acres, with wheat and had a good crop. I sold the corn to Bates and Hunt and every morning Ken Hunt would send a lorry for the wheat and the straw, which we had made into bales and stacked. The bugbear was the chaff. One morning when we had finished threshing Bates and Hunt had arranged to send a lorry to fetch ten tons of wheat. I asked for volunteers from the men to be there at 5.30 am to load the wheat but only one turned up. The two of us managed to get the wheat loaded but I had a nasty pain in my stomach and felt quite ill when I got home. Taking my temperature I found that it was 104F, went straight to bed and called the doctor, who diagnosed appendicitis and rushed me into Quarry Place Nursing Home. When a young girl, who looked only about fifteen, came with a shaving mug and brush and an open razor, I asked her what she was going to do. "Shave you", she said.

"But I had a shave this morning", I said.

"Not there", she said, "down below." I certainly wasn't trusting her with an open razor round that part of me, and insisted on doing it myself until an older nurse came to finish it off. Seven days in the nursing home and ten days rest did me a lot of good. I needed it.

There was so much work to do at this time that I needed quite a lot of capital. So I asked the new bank manager in Wellington, Claud Ball and he offered to lend me £1,500 out of his own pocket. Accepting that loan was one of the worst things that I ever did. He wrote out the cheque for £1,500, told me he wanted no interest but that I could pay him back by doing odd jobs for him. Stupidly I agreed and he found me a lot of work. I even had to buy sixty dairy Shorthorn heifers for him to satisfy and order from the Duke of Richmond and Gordon. Father and I went down to Goodwood to see them settled. It took me two years to pay back that £1,500 and of course there had been nothing in writing. Four years later, Ball had a heart attack and

I was particularly worried in case he had not shown the repayments in his record. He asked me to write on a piece of paper that "I had been so good to him and done so much for him that he had decided to make me a gift of the £1,500". Luckily I kept that bit of paper because in 1960 the income tax people got onto my back and went right back to 1943. Of course, working almost every hour of every day all through the war at so many different things I had been unable to keep many records and a lot of transactions were in cash. What I didn't realise when the tax people got going was that my accountant Cecil Stubbs was Claud Ball's accountant too and so, of course, up came this debt. I thought I was going to be put into gaol. I had to go before the Commissioners and it was a most alarming experience. Cecil Stubbs was no help to me at all so I changed to Whitting Ridell in Shrewsbury and am still with them.

Every year I had signed the Income Tax form saying that it was a true state of my affairs and I never told them that I'd paid the money back. Luckily Claud Ball was one of the Commissioners and I got away with it, although it cost me £8,500 and nearly broke me. That was the end of my dealings with Claud Ball.

There was an empty house on the corner at Acton Burnell which I now acquired. The outside had been plastered and it looked terrible because all the plaster was falling off. So my carpenter set to work removing it and found that underneath it was all lovely stone. Indeed it looked so nice that most of the surrounding houses, which were plastered, had their plastering removed. At about this time I advertised for a man and Bill Davies applied. He had been working for Jack Dakin at Newport who had another farm near Ludlow where Bill had been bailiff. He had a boy and a little girl and a newborn baby. So, when I was engaging him, I arranged to send them a cow. They milked her, made butter for me and had milk and butter for themselves. The two men, Davies and Ward, got on well together. We lambed 300 ewes. I always liked a good Suffolk-cross ewe, so I had bought some Suffolk rams to put on them.

We ploughed Kenley and used the straw. We grew barley and mixed corn and kept the grain to feed the pigs and animals at

Acton Burnell. In 1942 we ploughed as much of the big field in front of the house at Acton Burnell as we could and re-seeded it. In June I took Father for a ride. I had turned fifty young heifers out there who had just come out of the yards. The grass was apparently too strong for them and they were scouring badly. They grazed the ground we had not ploughed into the ground and even started to bark the trees. Father, with his wealth of experience, told me that there was only one thing to do — get some bales of wheat straw and spread it around. We did just that and the heifers went mad for it. They were obviously short of fibre and the wheat straw was the best thing for them, stopping their scouring and teaching me yet another lesson to remember. We grew kale and swedes for feed at this time, two rows of swedes and six of kale. We put the electric fence down the rows of swedes so that we could feed them to the cattle, moving it over and giving them a fresh strip every day.

Now during this period we fenced the 80 acres into three fields, leaving 12 acres that was unploughable. We devoted a great deal of time and hard work to organising a satisfactory water system, digging wells, laying pipes and so on. I insisted that the water must always be clean and fresh for the cattle. In front of the house there was a wet place in the park, for example, and at some time the water that had run under the castle had been diverted, before the days of making pipes, through stone culverts into the lake. Over the years the diversion had got dislodged, allowing the water from the hill to run free. The well was made but we did not make it deep enough. We put a pipe from it down to the trough which was ten yards away but, when we were laying it through the main drain we encountered running sand into which the pipes sank. We dug deeper and filled it up with oak slabs. We had to get it level and. indeed, it worked alright but, of course, the well filled up with sand as did the pipe from the well. So every few weeks we had to scoop all the sand out of the well to keep it free. We brought in a concrete mixer and laid a slab of concrete right across the front of the trough so that it was always clean and tidy. There is nothing worse than having cattle up to their knees in mud when they go to drink.

130

When I hear people prattling on about the socialist dream of a "classless society" I remind them that even in the animal world such an ideal is just as impossible. Some thoroughbred colts and stallions hate common geldings and have a particular aversion to hacks. Even if that hack is itself thoroughbred, they seem to smell something wrong about it and want to kill it. In 1942 I bought a chesnut show cob for 45 guineas. He was a really good sort who would stand anywhere unattended for as long as you wanted. Bill Davies did all the shepherding with him. The only time we had any trouble was after Charlie Birch had been to Newmarket and bought two thoroughbred colts for £40 each. When he brought them home and did not know what to do with them, I gave him £100 for the pair and turned them out at Acton Burnell. Next morning when Bill, all unawares, was driving across the park to feed the sheep, the colts attacked the cob and poor old Bill had the devil of a job to fight them off. He almost left there and then.

I was reminded of this twelve years later when Lester Piggott's first Derby winner Never Say Die, a big brave, powerful, savage son of Nasrullah, was in training with Joe Lawson at Newmarket. One morning on the Heath the late Sam Armstrong, immaculate in boots and breeches, was sitting importantly on his beautifully turned-out hack, waiting for his string, when he heard the sound of galloping hooves coming towards him and a desperate cry "Get out of the way!"

Turning round indignantly Sam shouted: "Who do you think you're talking to? Do you know who I am?"

Back came the frantic reply: "I don't care who you fucking well are, you'll be killed if you don't get out of the way now!"

Sam did just that, very smartly.

Amazing how horses hate pigs, as indeed they loathe camels. In any good yard you'll find a solution of pig dung to plaster on the bandages will prevent young horses from biting them. At Acton Burnell things were now going well. We made a tremendous amount of pig muck, which is the strongest you can get, and lugged in onto the fields. We limed the lot and grew a lot of grass. The ploughed land gave extra good crops. We had a good yield of hay and with just the right amount of fertilizer as well as farmyard manure, we soon got all the land into good condition.

When Bill Ward left I replaced him with Charlie Jones from Pitchford, a good tractor driver, who was particularly useful because Bill Davies had never liked driving the tractor. Charlie had a council house so I sold my cottage for £1,000.

CHAPTER X

1943 — Work and Play

The great idea came to me in 1943, the year which was, in retrospect, the first year of victory in the bitter struggle of total war against the forces of evil. The previous autumn we had begun to see a glimmer of light at the end of the tunnel. We listened to wireless news bulletins no longer in dread but in hopeful anticipation.

American forces were inflicting losses on the Japanese; the RAF had started to bomb Germany in retaliation for the cruel 'blitz' on our cities; the enemy had been halted at Stalingrad; and, after the battle of Alamein, Rommel's army was in full retreat across the Libyan sands with his rear now threatened by our invasion of Tunisia. All this we welcomed in patriotic optimism, still tempered with trepidation. Unknown at the time to all but the very few who realised its terrible significance, December had witnessed on a Chicago tennis court the first self-sustained controlled nuclear reaction in uranium.

More military triumphs for the Allies ushered in the New Year. Crushing German defeats, first at Leningrad, where the 16-month siege was finally lifted and then at Stalingrad, coincided with our own 8th. Army occupying Tripoli and the first bombing of Germany by the Americans, whose increasing presence, smart uniforms, winning ways and open-handed generosity to the ladies were not always appreciated by the indigenous male population. "Over-paid, over-sexed and over here!" was the complaint of many Britons in and out of uniform, frustrated by enforced absences from loved ones and the constant struggle of working for victory amid the oppressive austerities of total war.

Yes, as I have said, total war. Only Britain, who had stood

alone against the might of Germany, Italy and their allies, genuinely knew the meaning of that phrase, which meant that everyone, from duke to dustman, suffered the same shortages and restrictions as we battled shoulder to shoulder with dogged patriotic pride to save our beloved green and pleasant land from the heel of the jackboot. Friends, who later fought their way through Northern Europe, relieving horror camps like Belsen, were flabbergasted to discover that the perpetrators of these unforgivable atrocities, the German people, had right up to the end been living in luxury compared with the folk at home.

Although, of course, we in the country were much better off than the people in towns, every commodity, all the essentials of life, food, clothing, fuel, etc. were strictly rationed. The communal spirit of the British people in adversity was quite wonderful and looking back now the whole wartime period seems like an unreal dream for those of us who lived through it.

Inevitably, in town and country, the traditional pleasures were limited, including, of course, most spectator sports because too many people, crowding into one place at the same time, would have presented an inviting target for marauding enemy airmen. So, from 1942, steeplechasing was completely banned and fox-hunting virtually closed, for the added reason that essential foodstuffs should not be wasted on sporting animals. Such was the fervour that, but for the intervention of the King himself, the breed of the thoroughbred would have been damaged irreparably. After all, pasture was needed for breeding cattle and sheep to supply milk and meat. Nobody today, who did not know the English countryside before 1939, can fully comprehend the transformation that was wrought. Right up to the outbreak of war there had been so much wonderful grassland particularly in the Midlands. That famous Meltonian Monica Sheriffe, later to own good Classic racehorses, said: "If you ever saw a ploughed field in Leicestershire, you would stop and say 'Good God, there's a ploughed field!'"

By 1943 we, in our little area of Shropshire, had a likely military target too, in the American aerodrome at Attingham, a fighter base of some consequence. Initially those Yanks pranged a record number of priceless Spitfire fighters as they landed after sorties. Their pilots were trained on US fighters which touched down at about 100 mph. It took them some time to appreciate that the Spitfire landed at 170-180 mph.

Still, they were good, brave lads supplied with a ready source of enjoyment from the ATS base in Attingham Hall. One dark night, returning from an NFU meeting with my lights fully dimmed as usual, I was driving into my garage when I stopped suddenly in the nick of time. On the floor of the garage, right in front of my wheels, was an American airman on top of an ATS girl. After a few minutes, not in the least embarrassed, he dismounted and, pulling up his trousers, said: "Thank you, guy. I was coming, she was coming and you were coming. But you were the only one with brakes!"

Shortages were real. Wherever they went, whatever they asked for, however humble, people inevitably answered with the dreaded cliche: "Don't you know there's a war on?" So, when I started Attingham Show, we did everything possible to make our people happy. We even had clowns and, one year, managed to secure a Cossack ride which cost us £250. Wales and the Borders had always been famous for 'Flapping', unauthorised race meetings which, incidentally, were the nursery of many famous professional jockeys. Little, lithe gypsy lads with light racing saddles and nimble Welsh half-breds or thoroughbred weeds, galloping round a sharp track with rails of rope stretched between hundreds of well driven-in stakes. A two-mile course with Open races and some confined to ponies standing under 14.2 hands; strange how many contestants sunk down at the withers when they were being measured beforehand. A measuring-stick with a few nails in the cross-section works wonders in training for such events! Even at Attingham Fair during the war we had quite a few bookies. Betting was heavy and in the races no quarter was asked for or given. Devil take the hindmost; it was dangerous but tremendous fun!

We put on show-jumping, clay pigeon shooting, a fancy dress show and boxing run by Dick Burton, one of the best amateur boxers in the country. The highlight was always the steer-riding, which gave all the local lads a chance to show their metal on these 'bucking broncos'. I still have some wonderful film of these events.

Among the most popular side-show competitions, particularly in those days of tight rationing when we were not allowed 'bowling for the pig', consisted of hanging a dead cockerel by its neck and supplying each contestant with a sharp carving knife. Then, blindfolded, he or she would be turned round a few times before attempting to walk five yards and slash the bird's head off. Very few succeeded, particularly after sessions in the beer tent!

There were plenty of badges and lots of cups for the winners. Dr. Polland and I gave a cup every year for the best children's exhibit in the Flower Show. We made a lot of money from the Show for churches, village halls and other charities. That particular year, 1943, we gave £1,500 to the Red Cross. Amid all the austerity it was a truly wonderful, happy day out for all.

Throughout my life I have never been a very lucky gambler — perhaps because I have been so lucky in love! However this year, as a lover of steeplechasing, I had two good bets. Flat racing was zoned and the Epsom Classic races, the Derby and the Oaks, were staged at Newmarket. There was no steeplechasing in the UK, although the sport was carried on in neutral Ireland where a number of potentially top-class horses, confined to their Emerald Isle, competed against each other for 'peanuts'. One, who was too old by the end of the war, will always be numbered among the greatest jumpers of all time, the mighty Prince Regent, owned by the flour king, J.V.(Jimmy) Rank, from whom I was later to buy my stallion Distinctive. The hoardings in this country were plastered with the magnificent, nostalgic picture of 'the Prince' jumping in the Rank blue and primrose-quartered colours over the slogan 'Bread for Energy'. Those famous silks were to be carried by the filly Why Hurry in the Oaks.

The other famous National Hunt owner at the time was that eccentric lady, the Hon. Dorothy Paget, whose Golden Miller had been undisputed champion of the jumping world in the 30's. 'DP's' interest in the Flat up to that time had not been

My father surveying one of his fields of sugar beet in 1937.
One of the men on the tractor is my brother

My parents with their young family in 1916
(That's me in the middle!)

The start of my years of racing – leading in Little Pipp in 1946

Cable Home coming down after the water jump in a foxhunter's national event at the Grand National course at Aintree, 1949

Den Thomas, Attingham Show 1950 with Prince, who won 18 prizes

Bert Price and Bill Davies who worked for me for many years.
They are rescuing two of my sheep caught in the flood after
being chased by dogs. We lost 34

1950 – The first crop of barley to yield two tons to the acre

Market Day in Welshpool – 1956
(Self 3rd from right)

With my three brothers and sister – 1974
(From left to right) George, Tom, Self, Margaret Arthur and John

The Master coming home with Rosie – 1975

November 1977 – before all the fuss about fox hunting...
David Herring and self

Wellington Market Board 1972
A Presentation to Percy after 60 years' service at the Market
From left to right: Peter Ross, Tom Jones, Percy, Bert Owen,
C__ M__ln (Chairman) and David Lanyon (Secretary)

1980 – The golden years spent with Rosie
are reflected in this photograph at John O'Groats

December 13, 1982, Young Farmers Dinner at Mytton Mermaid
The survivors of the original YFC started in 1929 at Shrewsbury.
There are still 29 left out of 74 starters

West Midland Show 1981 Farmer Giles and daughter (or is it?)

This young heifer
was christened
'Gaffer'

I think the knees had
something to do with it...

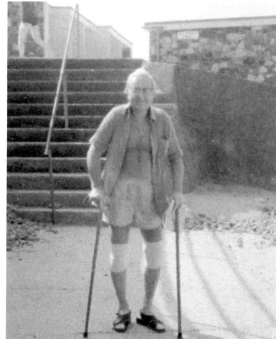

Malton Hospital – July 1989 - Tom with his usual bevy of girls
(but it's Rosie's hand he's holding!)

Rosie and self at my 80th Birthday Party with Richard Breeze, who
became an important member of our family in 1977 at the age of 15

This ewe was once badly savaged by a dog and nursed back to health, to become the founder of a 37-strong flock, all of which were direct descendants, while she was still alive. She died aged about 17.

1990 – Tom and Rosie on a VIP visit to Cheltenham where Richard Pitman signed a drawing of Pendil who won 17 of his 19 races

All the family at granddaughter's wedding in 1991

Tom and Rosie with Caroline and Susan,
Rosie's two daughters – 1993

substantial — she had paid the record price for a yearling who had got his own back for being named Tuppence by proving himself worth no more than that! — but she had a runner in the 1943 Derby called Straight Deal.

So I had decided to have a double; I backed them singly and coupled. It was a thrilling triumph. In a tremendous finish Straight Deal, starting at 100 – 6, beat the Aga Khan's pair, Umiddad and Nasrullah, by a head and half a length and Why Hurry obliged by a neck at 7 to 1. I had landed a 140 – 1 double.

News from the outside world continued to improve. Before the end of May we rejoiced to learn that Rommel had been finally defeated and all organised German resistance in North Africa had been crushed. The same month we thrilled to the exploits of the RAF Dambusters who, with their bouncing bombs, had breached the great dams and flooded the Ruhr. By August Sicily was in Allied hands and the following month after the Salerno invasion, which lead speedily to the capture of Naples, the Italians, as despicable in defeat as they had been cruel and cocky in victory, had surrendered. Nasty people, who had been the subject of ribald, derogatory remarks since the start of hostilities.

Nevertheless the Germans were by no means defeated and when Churchill, Roosevelt and Stalin met in Teheran, they knew that there was still a bit of a struggle ahead.

Back on the home front I was becoming increasingly disturbed about the meat trade at a time when all should have been going smoothly. After all, meat and milk had been controlled since 1939. As I explained earlier, all cattle and sheep, graded by experts like myself, were bought by the Ministry of Agriculture at a guaranteed price to the farmers, slaughtered and then allocated to the butchers, many of whom were saddled with a lot of rubbish as became apparent at a later date.

Now, there were always time of gluts and shortages of meat and milk. When meat was dear, the farmers would kill off old cows and any heifers which did not look too promising. This, as in 1943, caused a glut in meat. Inevitably, however, it soon resulted in a shortage of milk. Then, as night follows day, this would result in a shortage of meat because the calves were not coming along. But, when the milk shortage came, the farmers would bull every available cow and heifer and the three-year cycle would continue. There was no co-ordination at all.

The situation was so disastrous and indeed ridiculous that I could stand it no longer. At an Executive Meeting of the NFU, when J.C. Morgan of Upton Magna was chairman, I made an impassioned speech. The Government, on taking over control of meat in 1939, had promised the meat traders that when the Ministry eventually gave up control, the auctioneers, and wholesale butchers, would have their businesses returned to them. From my experience, I had now learned that this would be catastrophic. So I proposed that, as soon as meat was de-controlled, a Meat Marketing Board should be established to run alongside, and in harness with, the Milk Marketing Board. Meat and milk would thus be co-ordinated to the benefit of all.

The meeting, which included Bill Williams, later Sir Gwyllum Williams, and Jim Turner, who was later to become Lord Netherthorpe, applauded my idea and my motion was carried.

Nine years later that idea was to raise its head again at a time when we all knew that meet was soon to be de-controlled. It was such a good plan, but I had reckoned without all the hard, tough vested interests and it nearly ruined me.

But that was for the future and meanwhile, it was back to the war effort. Amongst our many visitors were some nuns and a convent of 150 girls, the Convent of Our Lady of Zion, which had been bombed out of London and now leased the Hall for ten years. I got to know the people very well and would be asked to escort groups of girls explaining farming methods to them. General de Gaulle's two daughters, two lovely blond girls, were among the students. One day when I was walking over the dam between the two lakes during the holidays, those two girls and some friends were fishing in the top lake. One of them caught a big yellow tench weighing over 8lbs. She was screaming in fright and I had to get it out for her. When I had landed the fish they refused to go near it and so I threw it back.

Though subordinated to the war effort, my interest in and love of horses was as strong as ever. On an expedition to

Newmarket my brother-in-law Ken Hunt paid 90 guineas for a big, lop-eared colt foal by Son-in-Law out of Idle Lady. We turned him out with another, which Ted Turner had bought, in a little field at Wellington behind Pearce's the builders. Tom Taylor looked after them there for twelve months. Now the yearling named Morning Sun, the Son-in-Law colt was sent into training with Atty Persse, the famous trainer of stars like The Tetrarch, Tetratema, etc. Staying bred and constructed, he obviously needed time but this was a commodity which the greatest-ever trainer of two-year-olds was not inclined to allow horses, particularly if their class enabled them to show a little speed as a juvenile. With races few and far between and hard to win as well as Ken being a small owner, it was a case of get what you can when you can. Atty put up the greatest champion jockey Gordon Richards, and told him to win. The wonderful little man with the big man's head and small, powerful legs, who rode thousands more winners than anyone else and was to become the only jockey ever to be knighted, needed no second bidding. Obeying orders, he galvanised Morning Sun to produce even more than he was capable of at that stage of his life, and, in a driving finish, forced him into second place. Geoffrey Brooke, Atty's brother-in-law and assistant, used to boast 'They never win after they leave the Guv'nor!' Morning Sun was no exception. His career as a Flat racehorse was finished. Moreover, he now resented training so much that whenever anyone got on his back he ran backwards. He just would not go forwards. We had to have him home and Kengave him to me on condition that I paid the horsebox.

I turned him out and fed him well all winter and then, in the spring when he was a three-year-old, I thought I'd better start riding him. He just would not go forward. Instead of knocking him about, trying to force him, I would just sit there. Every Sunday morning I would just sit on his back for half an hour. Suddenly one day he decided to go forward. He walked up the lane and I turned him quietly into the yard at The Mytton. The public bar was absolutely crowded and I shouted for them to bring me a pint of beer on a tray. I just kept as quiet as I possibly could and, when my order arrived, I told them to pour some of the beer onto the tray for the horse and I drank the rest. Morning Sun licked the tray clean. With the help of a man at his head I turned him round, we went out over the bridge to The Bell at Crosshouses where we did exactly the same before coming home. After that I rode him every morning and he gradually got better and better.

The following winter I put him in Bill's care at Acton Burnell and whenever I had time I would ride him round the farm. He grew to love it and, when hounds met at Acton Burnell in March of his four-year-old season, I took him out hunting. There were upwards of 40 people out, which was quite a field for wartime. Hounds drew Acton Burnell Hill and immediately found a fox who went round the hill three or four times and then up the hill towards Kenley. There were paths all round the hill and a very small fence into a grass field. I waited until all the field had jumped it and there was quite a hole in the fence. I could have walked him over. But, as Morning Sun had never jumped a fence, I thought this was a chance. A pretty little girl gave me a lead and he just popped over it. We were quite a way behind when we came to some posts and rails into Lodge Hill and found that the top rail had been taken off. The young lady jumped and Morning Sun followed. We eventually caught up and I stayed out until one o'clock.

After that I brought Morning Sun home, rode him two or three days a week and hunted him whenever hounds were called out to deal with any serious claims for fox damage. By now he had really settled down. He was a happy horse and a good one.

One day we were invited to a meet by Charlie Edwards at his farm at Causeway Wood two miles the other side of Acton Burnell. At 70 he was now one of the great chacters of the county; a big sporting landowner who refused to plough up his land when ordered to do so by the War Ag and was sent to gaol for two months for disobedience. Whenever hounds met at his home at Elsage Manor, he always invited me down there.

On this occasion Charlie, wearing a long frock coat which was hanging over the horse's rump and a three-quarter top hat, was riding a magnificent five-year-old thoroughbred heavyweight hunter called Elsage which was to become famous.

We found a horse for my old friend Dick Minton, who was on leave from the Army, and there were twenty-two mounted Home Guards, who used to patrol at night in the hilly country. If the enemy had dropped paratroops they could have been very important. In addition there were George the kennelman and myself when Charlie's car turned up full of booze. He was always winning cups for his livestock and on this occasion he produced a huge silver trophy in which he mixed all the drink, cider, brandy, whisky, home-made wine etc. By the time we moved off at half past twelve everyone was three parts pickled. We found a fox immediately which ran right across his land and, after four good fences we came to a high hedge with a brook in front of it and in one place blackberry briars which had grown right across the brook — twelve feet wide and 6 ft 6 in. high. Charlie on his big horse took it like a bird but no-one would follow him and the last we saw of him was jumping a gate to get onto Lodge Hill. Hounds took the fox round the hill two or three times and eventually they killed her — an old vixen who had been doing a lot of damage.

Another day during the war Charlie invited six of us to shoot at Causeway Wood. After a fair few drinks at a time when one would normally have been having breakfast we set off at 10 am and walked all round Lodge Hill but by lunchtime we had shot only one brace of partridge. However we had been walking the partridge into a field of swedes. Charlie himself was riding a horse with a bag over its head and shooting off the horse. After a snack lunch — more liquid than snack — we walked this root field, about thirty yards between each of us with Charlie, three spaniels, two sheep dogs and a lurcher. We finished up with about a hundred brace of partridge, three brace of pheasants all day, thirty rabbits and two hares. This was a rare treat for wartime and it wasn't over yet. We went back to the house where we tucked in to an enormous feed. Charlie had killed a sheep, which his bailiff's wife, an excellent cook, had prepared for us. After the meal, still drinking, we played cards until midnight. His Jewish Land Girl Rachel had a broken leg in plaster and, when she wanted to visit the outside lavatory down the garden, I was given a hurricane lamp and asked if I would take her there. With her arm round my neck she hopped along on one leg and I, being a perfect gentleman, waited outside until she came out and then gave her a very comprehensive kiss and cuddle before returning her to the house. She had a wonderful figure and I arranged to meet her the following Saturday. We played cards until 4 am when I had lost £6 and we decided to pack it in. I came home over the level crossing at Crosshouses. The gates were shut and, after tooting my horn, I fell fast asleep only to wake up at 7 o'clock to find someone behind me blowing his horn. The gates were open and away I went. Once again, unlucky at cards, lucky in love. For two years I met Rachel every Saturday afternoon. She was the most passionate girl I had met in a very long time.

One evening after I had taken a load of cattle in the lorry to Acton Burnell I got back to The Bell at Crosshouses where a lot of ATS from Attingham Park were celebrating a 21st birthday party. I joined in and it was some party. When it was over, they asked to take them back to the gates of the Hall. Two sat in the front with me but all the others piled into the back of the lorry which, of course, was still covered with muck from the cattle. When we stopped and I pulled the back of the lorry down you never saw such a mess as those girls were in. As drunk as lords, they had lain down in this muck and were absolutely plastered with it. They almost lynched me. Indeed I was lucky to get away. Every time I saw any of them afterwards they shouted after me: ''The shit farmer''!

My men and my father's men from Uppington worked so well that I decided to give them a Harvest Supper every year. The first couple of years we held it at The Horseshoe where we were very well looked after and then I became friendly with Mrs. Wingfield who was the landlady at The Bell at Crosshouses. I would take her rooks which I had shot and she always made the most splendid rook pie. One year I arranged to hold the Harvest Supper there for all the men, their wives and girlfriends. It was a great success.

On one of these occasions at about one in the morning two drunken Yanks walked in, one of whom was a very bad sort, chatting up the girls and roughing them up as well. He started to make a play for the girlfriend of one of my men. When I told him to get out he refused. I lost my temper and hit him. He was standing at the top of eight steps. He grabbed me by the lapel and, as we went down the steps, I landed my knee on top of him. I put him in hospital for a long time and for a while it was even thought he might die. He recovered, sure enough, but it taught me a lesson never to lose my temper again.

The name of my bank manager in those days, Claude Ball, always made me chuckle even when I was most annoyed with him. Perhaps you remember those schoolboy jokes about the titles of books — "The Broken Window" by Eva Brick or "The Tomcat's Revenge" by Claude Balls. Some parents need their heads examining.

One day Ball asked my help for a farmer at Claverley who was badly in debt to the bank and wanted some sheep on halves. I sent him 200 Cheviot ewes and visited them from time to time. They had a good crop of lambs. But on a Tuesday in June I had a call from my friend Phil Wall of Claverley who told me that the bailiffs were on this man's farm trying to confiscate all the stock and so he had moved my ewes and lambs into his own field, mixing them with his sheep. When I arrived in the dark — there was a tight blackout, remember — I bumped into a horse in a field some way from the house which must have been missed by the bailiffs. I looked at it by matchlight, discovered it was a good carthorse and bought it for a nominal sum which I paid to Claude Ball. I led it to Phil Wall's farm at 11 pm and sent a lorry for it next morning. When I got it home I found it had a long tail and as all working horses had to be docked in those days, I realised it had not been used overmuch. It proved to be a good sound animal and a bargain. Next morning I went back to Phil Wall and we tried to sort out our sheep. Luckily all mine were marked. In the middle of his farm he had a great big stone building with an open covered yard where, in the old days, cattle would be left to make muck which could be spread on the surrounding land. We put all my ewes in this place and made hurdles so that the lambs could get through into the yard but the ewes would be kept back. When I counted the lambs I found I was short of only six. We moved them all back home the next day. As the farmer was obviously going bust and needed some spare cash badly, I paid him for several acres of good cabbage and took six women there at 9.30 to cut cabbages all day. We put them in sacks, took them away in a lorry at teatime and I made about £100 on that deal.

I wanted to repay Phil Wall for doing me such a great favour by removing my animals. So, as he was one of the top Flapping men in the country, I let him have my little mare Jean, who turned out to be very good. I also let him have two of the horses I had bought from Tony Jones, a mare and a gelding. He broke them in and I let him keep them for three years. Eventually he had to leave the farm at Claverley and he took one at The Spode, Newcastle, Clun. As he had not enough money to buy sheep I used to send him 200 North Country Cheviots, which I would buy in the south of England. Jean proved unbeatable at distances from a mile to a mile and a half. To go to the big Flapping meeting at St. Asaph in North Wales, he would walk the mare eight miles to Craven Arms where he would put her on the train. People outside Wales have never really understood Flapping, the importance of it or the money which it engenders. At St. Asaph even in those days they were giving £100 first prize, which was more than some of the National Hunt meetings had been giving before the war. Jean won one and a half mile Flat and the same distance over hurdles. As the track was half a mile round and there was only one hurdle she had to jump it four times. We couldn't back her because the bookmakers would not take a penny. That evening Phil would walk her home from Craven Arms to The Spode and it would be practically daybreak before they arrived home.

The two colts I had bought from Charlie Birch had done exceptionally well and so I entered them for sale at Newmarket in 1944. I had the bigger of the two, a beautiful colt by Blenheim, offered for what was then the very good price of £500 but one morning before the sale I found him dead, killed by rat poisoning.

Travelling in wartime was not particularly easy. To go to Newmarket I booked a horsebox from Berrington Station at 3pm. Since I couldn't spare any of my men from their work on the farm, I travelled with him. We changed at Shrewsbury and got to Crewe at 8 o'clock. As we would be leaving at midnight I went into the town for a meal and a few drinks but, when I returned to the station, I found the box had gone. I saw the Station Master who said it had been moved to the sidings. Well, at Crewe in those days there were about 20 acres of sidings. They sent a man with me to find my horsebox and eventually we discovered it at the very far end. We traipsed over about 300 rails to get there with trains going in all directions, shunting and pushing trucks about. I got into my box, lay down on the seat with my overcoat over me and went to sleep, only to be rudely awakened by a loud clunk when they hooked us onto the London train. This turned out to be a slow goods train and it was after 6am when we got to London where, with a great deal more shunting we were quickly transferred to another train, which performed equally slowly, stopping at every station all the way to Cambridge to deliver newspapers. Once we got to Cambridge I had time to go to a hotel for a wash, shave and breakfast and we arrived at Newmarket at about midday. I shall always remember my first sight of that wonderful long platform specially designed for horses going to the races by rail. Eventually we arrived at Tattersalls' sales yard, where their splendid major domo Charlton welcomed me, showed me to a box beautifully set fair and bedded down with straw right up the sides of the walls, and provided me with water and hay. I put my horse in there and gave him a feed from the corn which I had carried on my back for him. Tattersalls were most helpful as I've always found ever since.

After settling my horse I went into Newmarket town, which sadly was not as lovely as I had always believed it to be. Quite recently a German aircraft with typical cruel arrogance and disregard for civilian life had bombed this completely non-military target and every few yards shopfronts seemed to have disappeared, leaving gaps in that lovely High Street. I spent the afternoon looking round and returned to groom and feed my horse before going out for a pint or two, only to discover that accommodation was non-existent. The White Hart had been almost completely demolished by bombs and, however hard I tried, I couldn't even find a bed and breakfast so I went back to the sales yard and told Charlton my plight. He took me to a horsebox, opened up a couple of bales of straw, gave me a horse blanket to lie on and a couple more to cover myself with and left me to sleep like a top until waking at 5 am to find myself very cold. However, an hour later Charlton arrived with a pint mug of hot, sweet coffee, one of the most welcome drinks of my entire life.

There was a morning sale from 10am to midday followed by racing in the afternoon and then the evening sale at which my horse was to be sold. 100 lots in the day, divided into the two sessions and my horse was towards the end of the evening.

I enjoyed the morning sale and talked to a number of people who took me to the races in the afternoon. When I went to place a bet on the first race I found Wylie Taylor, a drover from Bridgnorth who made a book at the Flapping meetings, standing up and taking bets there at the Headquarters of racing. The favourite for the first was an even money chance, at which price I backed it, but Wylie chalked it up on his board at 2/1 and was almost knocked off his stand with people backing it. The favourite won alright and so did I but luckily I had not backed it with Wylie Taylor because, as I walked by his stand, I saw it was empty. There was no sign of him. He had just disappeared, done a real Welsher — and at Newmarket, too. This was asking for trouble in a big way. I strolled down the side of the course to watch the five-furlong start and saw someone lying in a bit of a hollow with a coat over him. There was Wylie Taylor with his pockets full of money which he should have been paying out to the favourite backers. He got away with it and they never caught him. I wouldn't have liked to have been in his shoes if they had.

The main race of the day, a mile and a quarter event, was won by Lord Rosebery's Ocean Swell, so easily that I thought he must have a good chance of winning the Derby which he eventually did. Funnily enough the day he won the Derby which, in those wartime years, was run at Newmarket, I had gone to look at my sheep with Phil Wall and we went to a pub to listen to the Derby on the wireless. We nearly broke the local bookmaker in Clun. I backed it, Phil backed it and we told everyone in the pub to get on. They rushed out to do so and when Ocean Swell duly won at 28/1 we had a monumental celebration all that afternoon and night so that I didn't get home until the next morning!

But that was later. At the evening sale my horse made 320 guineas, an excellent price for those days, which made me regret the loss of the other one even more. Charlton had found me a bed in a small house near the sale ring and, after a memorable first trip to Newmarket, I arrived home in the late afternoon of the following day. My horse went to a trainer in Cheshire who won a few races with him. After that first adventure I hardly missed a sale at Newmarket for thiry-five years. I have had some great times there and made a lot of friends.

Back home, in addition to all my other commitments, I was busy organising the first of the annual Attingham Shows. For a couple of days I let all my men off the farm to prepare everything at the show and of course we had to clean up afterwards. On August 1 we formed a committee from the Home Guard to arrange the show with prizes for young stock, hunters, ponies and everything and prize money generously donated by the local merchants. Because of the shortage of petrol we arranged buses from Wellington and Shrewsbury and attracted 2,500 people. It was such a success that we made it an annual affair and it lasted until 1954. We had some of the best judges in the country and, with large entries, made a fantastic day of entertainment for the public. We divided the funds equally between the local parishes and the Red Cross, for whom we set up several records.

CHAPTER XI

Guarding The Coast

By the middle of 1944 the tide had finally turned. Although Hitler's secret weapon the Flying Bombs were now landing spasmodically on London, our own 1,000-bomber raids were tearing the heart out of industrial Germany in fair retribution for the Blitz. D-Day on June 6 saw an invasion fleet of 4,00 ships landing Allied troops on the Normandy beaches and, although it was still a little way off, the end was now surely in sight.

In December, just as the Germans were making their last offensive of the war in the Ardennes, the Wellington and Atcham Home Guard were sent to Dover to take over from the Regulars for a fortnight. We had so much fun and to this day I don't know how we stuck it out. Not for nothing has Dad's Army, repeated over and over again, been one of the most popular programmes ever screened on television. Among other friends my brother-in-law Ken Hunt was Commanding Officer, Billy Minton was a sergeant and I was the Intelligence Officer. I'm not sure why, but I was!

We were all paraded at Wellington and 'entrained' down to St. Margaret's Bay near Dover, where we were divided up into billets in private houses along the front. The first night we went down to the pub, imbibed a considerable amount of beer and staggered up to bed at about 11 o'clock only to be called out almost immediately on guard duty, watching a road from the top of a hill on a bitterly cold night until 6am. Seldom have I enjoyed breakfast more — piles of bread, porridge, as much tea as we could drink and whalemeat sausages. No respite on Sunday morning, when we were ordered to attack a house over some really rough ground, lying in ditches or crawling along,

149

jumping through the windows of the house and out the other side until the exercise was over. I'm afraid I got into trouble for not cleaning my rifle!

After another visit to the pub, we had to guard the coast again. This meant that Hedley Brown and Pip Lucas, who was a real comedian, were sent to look after the flame thrower in which they had been instructed. One of them turned the wrong wheel, the oil came back and they were smothered from head to foot in black diesel oil. Then four of us were ordered to run down a narrow path between the sea wall and the defence barbed wire which was curled all along the coastline up to seven feet high. I tripped and fell head first into the wire. I got my bayonet and my clothes all caught up properly and only just managed to extricate myself before the officers arrived.

We stayed on duty right by the sea and, as dawn broke, we saw someone walking up the beach. The four of us asked him what he was doing. As he didn't produce a very good answer, we captured him and took him to headquarters. He turned out to be the man detailed to patrol the beach every morning to see whether there were any strange things like mines, buoys, bodies or anything else washed up overnight.

After ten glorious days at Dover we were very fit but, by the time that we were loaded onto lorries to leave, we wore denim overalls over our uniforms which were in a pretty grim state. Next stop Salisbury Plain. The old saying says: "'Tis a terrible thing to be caught in the rain when night's coming down on Salisbury Plain." In our case it wasn't rain but snow. The whole Plain was covered with the stuff and we, shivering in the backs of our lorries were covered with our greatcoats. However we'd done ourselves well in Dover and were well fortified for inner warmth!

First we were taken to see the big guns — "big Berthas" — which could fire shells to the other side of the Channel, aimed by radar, which was pretty new in those days, Of course they weren't much good now because the enemy had already been driven out of France.

Then we were taken to the top of a hill and told to dig in. We had to dig a trench five feet deep, twelve feet long and four feet wide. It was hard going and the officers came round measuring with their sticks. Mind, we were getting through my bottle of rum at a fair rate and, when we were called out at 1am, there was Army issue rum as well. We sat down in the snow and I fell asleep until just before dawn when we were lined up and marched four abreast for an hour into a valley. I marched fast asleep, bumping into people, waking up and going to sleep again. We were halted for ten minutes and then ordered to attack the hill where we had previously dug in. Some Regulars were installed up there by then and they were firing at us. Because I was three parts pickled I was second up the hill, beaten by my younger brother Arthur much to my disgust because I had always rated myself fitter then him. It's just possible that the drink slowed me up!

When we got back to Wellington the mayor and half the town were out waiting to greet us. We made the headlines in the paper over an article stating that Wellington and Atcham platoon had taken over from the Regulars. We had been playing cards and drinking on the way back and were exhausted when we were inspected by a general. I was on the end of the platoon, dropped my rifle, was reprimanded again and felt a fair old fool. My reputation in the Home Guard was not too good, I'm afraid.

With the start of 1945, although the fighting war against Germany and Japan was nearly over and it was once again a pleasure to listen to the encouraging news bulletins on the wireless, the situation at home was still as fraught with difficulties as ever. Nearly five and a half years of all out effort on my ever-increasing commitments on top of the unremitting pressure of constant rows with Freda at home had taken their toll. I was under considerable strain and now I came to a pretty pass. One day I awoke to find that I could not hold my water and was unable to walk down the fields without collapsing. My doctor arranged for me to have every imaginable test and the results pointed to the fact that I was completely worn out mentally and physically. It appeared that even I, who had always believed that only wet people suffered from nervous breakdowns, had temporarily reached the end of my tether. I was ordered to go away to recuperate. So I telephoned my very good friend Phil Wall up at Newcastle near Clun and arranged to stay with him. You will remember that he had 200 of my ewes at his farm. The doctor told me to drink stout to build me up and I obeyed quite happily but it was nearly a fortnight before I felt that I could even get on a horse. Then most days I would exercise his Flapping horses. I would ride from about 10am and stop at a neighbouring pub for some bread and cheese washed down by a bottle of Guinness. Then I would return in time for tea. Luckily a most attractive friend of the family, who had been evacuated from Birmingham, found that she, too, was lonely and was only too happy to share my bed at nights. One morning when my horse needed shoeing I arrived at the blacksmiths at 11 in the morning to find 20 horses already there waiting. So I tied him up and went into the pub, where, as it was a wet day, a number of farmers had already congregated. I knocked back several bottles of Guinness and, when the blacksmith sent word that my horse had been shod and was ready to take home, I was paralytic, legless. The other farmers were pretty merry too, but they managed to push me home in a wheelbarrow while someone led the horse. I felt terrible the next morning but those weeks away had done the trick. I was once again my own man and the cure was complete.

Back home we had the best hunt of the war when we were asked to take hounds to a fox which was doing a lot of damage at Shady Moor by Netley. There were only five of us, George with his ten couple of hounds, Charlie Foulkes, Geoff Foulkes and a man called Ralphs who worked for them, as well as myself on old Cable Home, who was now going pretty well for me. When the rogue fox came out into a small wood with a few big oak trees, I galloped round the far side while hounds went round and round but eventually gave up suddenly. It was a glorious sunny morning and I was standing under an oak tree. I looked up and there was the fox in the boughs of the tree. Seeing me, he jumped down, frightened my horse and away we went. I holla'd, hounds came and, in full cry, we crossed the Rattling Hope road into a dingle with a boundary fence. I dismounted, discovered that the posts were a bit rotten and uprooted two of them lowering the wire so that the others could jump the fence. Then Charlie jumped off his horse and stood on the wire to enable me to go forward. We galloped on to the Long Mynd very, very fast. Then a thick cloud came down so that we could not see a hand in front of us but luckily the victorious hounds came back to us and home we went. We arrived back at Dorrington before they closed at 2.30pm and were able to have a good drink there. When I got home at 3.45pm my daughter Pat had been born.

At the end of April, as the British and American troops from the West and the Russians from the East rounded up the Germans, Mussolini and his mistress were shot by the Italians and two days later Hitler killed himself and his mistress. On May 8 the end of World War II against Germany was officially declared to be at one minute past midnight. In August after atomic bombs had been dropped on Hiroshima and Nagasaki, the Japanese surrendered unconditionally and September 2 saw the official end of the war.

CHAPTER XII

Peace Again

Amid great celebrations the lights came on again all over Europe. Men and women gradually came back from the war into civilian life. Racing, hunting and point-to-pointing got going again and so on, but, although the fighting war was over, the restrictions on our lives, including, of course, rationing, had to remain for some years to come. For example, it would be nine more years before the Government decided to change its wartime measures in the meat trade — and I was to be one of the chief sufferers.

When the war ended Reverend Mother Edwards from the convent at Acton Burnell Hall summoned me, took me round the beautiful gardens and asked if I would cultivate them for her. They had not been touched for five years and so I sent Jack Williams with a single plough. We burnt a lot of the rubbish, ploughed and planted five acres with potatoes. There was still a guaranteed price for potatoes and you had to have a permit to grow them. We grew enough potatoes to feed 180 people and I sold £320 worth at the end of the year, so it was quite a successful operation.

Jack Williams, my tractor driver, was a brilliant ploughman who ploughed land which others could not manage. I remember two particular pieces of land where previous attempts to plough had been unsuccessful. Jack learnt a lot from Tom Price, an outstanding mechanic, who helped me to overcome petrol rationing (somewhat illegally!) by manipulating engines to enable cars to run half on petrol and half on tractor fuel.

Now of all the names in my life the best has undoubtedly been Rosemary. In the autumn of 1945, 25 years before I was to meet my lovely wife, I was blessed with the company of another, when I engaged a girl groom of that name. A sweet, neat young redhead with eyes set wide apart over a turned-up nose in an impish freckled face and the slim, superb figure of the born horsewoman. Admiring those firm breasts under her sweaters did my pulse no good at all! But somehow I restrained myself because, ever since Eve, I had determined not to make love to my employees. She was a marvellous groom, looking after eight mares and three point-to-point horses whom she got really fit. My good resolutions lasted only until the Hunt Ball at the Morris Ballroom following a very liquid happy dinner at The Mytton. Pleading a headache as usual, Freda got someone to take her home early and I started to dance with Rosemary. I was conscious of a strange musky smell as she danced very close, rubbing up against me. She was wearing a dark blue button-through dress.

When we left, before getting into the big V8 with its bench front seat, I threw my dinner jacket and bow tie into the back. Driving with one hand, I had my left arm round her when, as we were coming down Emstry Bank she suddenly bit my neck. I jammed on the brakes, stopped in the middle of the road and kissed her. It was a long, incredible kiss, during which the buttons on her dress mysteriously became undone. As my hand wandered upwards I realised that beneath the dress she was naked. Later she told me that she loved the freedom of not wearing underclothes when she was dancing and, as any other red-blooded male would, I found the thought very exciting... For the next five years we were almost inseparable, riding, hunting, racing, showing, horse and cattle dealing, making love whenever we could all over the country. She was a wonderful lover and, after five years, we had grown to love each other so much that we either had to part or break up my family with a divorce and my children at that time were much too young for that to happen. It broke both our hearts and I shall never forget her face when, after making love all night, I had to leave her having breakfast at the Grosvenor Hotel in London. However hard I tried I have never heard anything of her since. For twenty years I regretted my Rosemary until I was lucky enough to sink into the arms of her even lovelier namesake.

One of my immediate post-war highlights was the 1946 Dublin Show when England won the Aga Khan Cup, the chief show-jumping trophy. Our winning team included Wilf White with his grand horse Nizefella which I had helped him to buy at St. George's Show for £150. There was a hunt ball every evening at the Gresham Hotel and the whole of Dublin seemed to go mad. I have never seen so much alcohol consumed in one week. Frank Davies and I certainly did our share!

In 1946 combine harvesters were still comparatively rare in this country but Charlie Foulkes bought one and did most of my combining for me. I bought 1,000 sulphate of ammonia bags which were very strong and would hold 2cwt. of corn. I tied them on ropes, left them in the river for a few days and then dried them out. I sent Freda and the children off to Black Rock in North Wales for a fortnight so that I could organise the harvest and help Charlie to drive the combine. Charlie had a lady friend and I had my Rosemary so we had a wonderful fortnight working and playing hard. One day when Charlie was combining his own farm at Wheathill we had managed 180 bags of wheat by the time we packed up at 8 pm. We arrived at the Red Lion on the main road at Wellington, where Ken Hunt was giving a party, at about 10 o'clock and proceeded to get fairly pickled. Ken bet us £20 that next day we would not be able to combine 200 bags. We got home at 2 am and at 5 am Charlie got me up to help him move the combine to Billy Brooke's place at Eaton Constantine. By mid-day fifty people had assembled in the field to watch our attempt on 200 bags. The trouble was that the field was only 15 acres of wheat and by 6 pm we could see that we were not going to get the 200 bags off it. However Charlie, who had been plied with drink all day and was as drunk as a lord, drove the combine straight over the hedge into the next field, where we won our bet!

When the war ended I realised that despite my many commitments I would now be able to fulfil my life's ambition by concentrating on horses in my spare time. I employed a man called Den Thomas as a lorry driver because I was sending a lot of potatoes into Wolverhampton Market — a seven-ton load every morning — and also moving a great deal of stock about the country. Not only was he a very good driver but I also found that he was a wonderful feeder of horses. Although he had been used to cart horses, not thoroughbreds, I installed him as feeder while Rosemary and I did the exercising. Remember that at that time, we had three point-to-pointers and eleven other horses including in-foal mares and followers.

Reaction to the end of the war took different people in different ways. With me it was horses, which had always been the second great love of my life. Now the intense pressure, the traumas and responsibility were relaxed. I had good men at home, land all over the place and plenty of cattle and sheep. So, as hunting, point-to-pointing and NH racing got going again, I threw myself wholeheartedly into the world of the horse, making up for the six years which I had lost.

I have already described how I managed to tame the bay Son-in-Law horse which had been soured off on the Flat. Now I was hunting him hard and schooled him for point-to-pointing as a six-year-old. I entered him for the Open Race at the Harkaway in which the favourite was one of those Holland-Martin stars and Martin Tate, later to become so well known as the first-class Worcestershire farmer-trainer, was also, like me, having his first ride in a point-to-point. His horse, which had finished third at Cheltenham, was second favourite and I was the outsider at any old price. Nevertheless, after a very exciting race, I beat the favourite and will always be grateful to Morning Sun for my first winner. What a party we had that night!

My season ended when Morning Sun broke down three fences from home in the Open at our own Eyton point-to-point. It was one of the hottest races of the season and I am certain I would have beaten the favourite and eventual winner Marquess, who was later sold for £3,00 to Lord Bicester.

During the summer Rosemary and I got Morning Sun sound again and I rode him in a novice chase at Wolverhampton on the day after Boxing Day. Always up with the leaders I finished second to Jack Moloney on the favourite Young Hero with the great champion jockey Fred Rimell third on Chance Shot.

On the strength of that performance I sold him to Sonny Hall and Tom Yates for £800, a fair price in those days. But he was no good in a big stable. He had fallen in love with Rosemary (he wasn't the only one!) and, like so many entire horses, wanted a woman to train him. They eventually sold him on to a girl who won a lot of point-to-points with him. A grand old horse.

A little earlier I had acquired a very good-looking, well-named five-year-old gelding called Cable Home, by Express Delivery out of Blighty. His owner Mrs. Ffrench-Blake, wife of the Master of the South Shropshire, told me: "Tom, I have a beautiful horse which I want you to have. £45 if you can ride him and he's yours. But if you can't ride him I want him back at the kennels to have him put down."

He had apparently smashed up four people who had tried to break him and the fifth was still in hospital. He was a real brute who used to rear up and come over backwards. I had him home and the first morning, after lungeing him for an hour with the saddle on, I jumped on his back. He gave a few bucks but I am always somewhat difficult to dislodge. No sooner had I got him into the front field when he reared up. I slipped off him, led him back to the yard, went in and got a large bottle of water. No sooner had I remounted than he reared up again but this time, before he could go backwards, I smashed the bottle of water right between his ears. It frightened him to death and he never reared again. He was so shaken that it took me about two hours to get him going. He was undoubtedly a real brute at this stage of his life but was determined to get the better of him. I took him over to Acton Burnell and galloped him three times round the 88-acre field. He still wouldn't give in and, when I arrived home eventually at about half past eight in the evening, I had never been off his back. He stood in Pitchford village with his ears flat on his neck and sweat pouring off him. Physically completely fatigued but still undefeated mentally.

As soon as they started cub hunting that autumn I took him out with the South Shropshire and, when a hound came out of covert behind him, he took off through the brook, through all the bushes, lacerating the backs of my hands, face and neck. I didn't lose him but he almost skinned me!

In November I started hunting him and took him out three days a week, giving him no peace. I would hack him ten miles to a meet; nine days in three weeks. I would leave at nine in the morning and arrive back home as late as eight o'clock at night. Finally I got to the bottom of him and thereafter he was a nailing good horse. We became the best of friends but he always had a mind of his own. He soon settled down, however, became a wonderful jumper and got to love hunting so much that, if he saw a pink coat, he wanted to be with it. Once near the front of the field he was a perfect hunter and I jumped some impossible places on him.

When Morning Sun, who had been point-to-pointing so well, went lame I entered Cable Home for the South Staffordshire point-to-point, intending to give him a schooling race and pull him up because I didn't believe that he would be racing fit. So I started off behind them, just cantering along but soon I found that I was passing them up one after the other until I was fourth, full of running, with only three fences to jump. It was then that the third horse, tiring fast, jumped right across me, came down and brought me down with him. Like a fool, instead of lying there curled in a ball, I stood up and was knocked down by a following horse who kicked me and broke three ribs. Now I knew I had a racehorse.

I turned him away for the summer and, when we started again next season, I had a top-class hunter, apart from the steering. He loved it so much that one day on my way to a North Shropshire meet for which I was late, he heard hounds away on the left while I was just lighting a cigarette. Next thing I knew he had turned violently left, over the fence by the side of the road, across a field and I was lucky to recover my reins. I hunted him hard that season and got him very fit. The first point-to-point was the Golden Valley at Clifton-on-Teme, a tricky little course, in which Ted Dorrell was riding Noel Wenman's good horse, Tricky Lad. As usual, hunt servants were acting as mounted officials. We jumped off nicely but as soon as we got to the first bend Cable Home saw a pink coat and, taking charge, aimed straight for him. somehow I managed to get him back onto the course but the second time round he did exactly the same thing and, of course, I lost a lot of ground. However I eventually got him going again and finished second to Tricky Lad. That week I entered him for the Aintree Foxhunters' Chase which was then run over the full 4½-mile Grand National course. Nevertheless I knew I had a fair horse and, as I was in my thirty-eighth year now I wanted to ride at Liverpool before I was too old.

The next point-to-point was at home at Eyton-on-Severn where the river runs up the right hand side and, as I can't swim, I got a bit of leather and some tin tacks to make a home-made pricker on the side of the bit which ensured that this time I had no trouble steering. After very helpfully pulling Ted Dorrell by the seat of his breeches back into the saddle when he was about to come down, I went on and beat him twenty lengths.

The next outing was at Sir Watkin Wynn's but, on the day before, I had had to sack my groom and Rosemary and I managed to get hold of an old man out of the village who had been with horses some time before. He forgot to bring the rubber reins, put on a bridle with ordinary leather reins and the rain was pouring down. Everything was soaked. I had no chance of holding the reins properly on that very strong puller so I wound them round my wrists, duly won, landing a nice little £20 bet for myself but had the devil's own job unravelling myself from the reins before I could dismount. If I'd come down in the race I would have been killed for certain!

A week before Liverpool I was put to bed with bad 'flu and a high temperature. The doctor came twice a day, trying to get me right for Aintree. The Foxhunters' was on the Thursday and on Tuesday my doctor told me: "You can go, Tom, but you're not bloody fit!"

I got to Aintree on Wednesday and, feeling like the wrath of God, walked the course with Rosemary. This was a mistake. In my condition it frightened me to death. From the ground the fences seemed huge — remember they had still not been sloped or bushed out invitingly as they are today — and I was struck by the sharp angle at which some of them were sited. I was to find that, far from noticing this when you are riding, you met them all just right. There was a drop to each fence on the landing side, which was peculiar to Liverpool, and there were several awkward corners, especially after Becher's Brook and at the

Canal Turn. Certainly the height and spread of the famous open ditch, the 'Chair', in front of the stands seemed alarming from the ground. For the fence was taller than a man and three feet wide, the ditch in front was six feet wide and the guard rail on the take-off side was 18 in. high. Now, of course, Becher's has been modified so that the drop is nothing like as bad as it was and all the fences are considerably smaller. The Water is nothing like as wide today as it was then. Furthermore my horse had never seen any sort of water because, of course, they don't have water jumps in point-to-points. I was still feeling like death and my knees were all rubbery when I went in to change. There were only about a dozen starters and, as soon as I realised that nearly all the other riders were just as nervous as I was, I began to feel better. Then Gordon (later Sir Gordon) Richards, the greatest Flat-race jockey of all time, a Shropshire lad whom I knew well, came and sat beside me. He wished me luck and told me that, although of course he had never ridden over jumps, he still felt nervous before a big race. That from the man who rode many, many more winners than anyone else in the history of racing, was a great comfort!

Fortified by the good wishes of that great little man, I managed somehow to get Cable Home down to the start with great difficulty. As soon as the flag fell he ran away with me all that long gallop to the first fence which he hit hard and fell. I hung on to him, jumped back on and chased after them. Still fairly shaken from that heavy fall I don't remember Becher's first time round but I know that I took the lead at the Canal Turn only to come down again at Valentine's. Again I jumped back on and set off still quite unable to hold one side of him once he started galloping. Another fall in that long back straight and then a hell of a fall at the Water. I climbed on again and this time not only had I lost my stick but my left hand wasn't much good and my right hand was in a fairly bad state too. Past the stands back to the start I tried to pull him to the left but he wanted to go back to the paddock on the right. So, as a compromise, he went straight for the rails in front, hit them and precipitated me over his head. I still held on, remounted and, hearing somebody say there were only two standing, went off for the second time round the course with 2½ miles to go. He jumped all the way down the railway stretch, over Becher's, where I remember Sonny Hall shouting: "Take that bloody thing home, Jones — he'll kill you!", round the Canal Turn, over Valentine's until the last open ditch where he took off too soon and landed on the top. I slid down his neck pulling him after me only to find that he had one hind leg stuck fast in the foundations of the fence which were made with cord wood about 3 ft 6 ins high laced with wire and covered with birch. A mounted policeman and several people arrived to help. Eventually we cut him free and put the saddle back on. I started walking him back with a mounted policeman by my side but after a hundred yards I said that I was not going to walk back and somebody gave me a leg up again. I had just got onto the racecourse by the stands when Cable Home and I heard the horses in the 5-furlong Flat race after the Foxhunters', galloping up behind us. Away Cable Home went again, quite out of control, about a hundred yards in front of them and hurtled past the winning post turning at break-neck speed into the little gate on the right which led to the paddock. How he didn't break my legs I shall never know!

When I had taken the saddle off and went to change I was congratulated on all sides. Everyone wanted to shake my hand or pat me on the back. I was much more of a hero than that extra tall, superb horseman, Major Guy Cunard, who had won the Foxhunters' on San Michele. After weighing-in from his race Gordon Richards congratulated me. "Well done, Tom", he said. "It looks as though you won one race and beat me as well!".

Rosemary drove me home, gave me a bath and put me to bed where I slept until nine the next morning when the letters started to arrive — congratulations from all over the country as well as a number of offers to ride bad horses!

Barney Nugent, who owned the Dolphin Hotel in Dublin, wrote saying that he had never enjoyed anything so much in all his life and he offered me free hospitality at The Dolphin for ever. He was as good as his word. I went there many times afterwards and he never even let me buy a drink. I wish he had, or I would have stayed there more often.

It has always been recognised as very hard to adapt even the best horses in the same season from jumping those huge Liverpool fences to ordinary park or point-to-point fences. I rode Cable Home at Eyton two weeks later and he came down at the last fence when winning. I sold him in the autumn for £800 to a man called Dick Darlington. He won many point-to-points during the next four years and finally fell for the first time since he left me at the South Staffordshire point-to-point, breaking his leg at the very same fence where he was brought down the first time he ran.

CHAPTER XIII

Nuns . . .

Every time I visit Concord College at Acton Burnell I'm filled with pride. My grand-daughter Anna, Edward's little girl, is there now. My wife Rosie and my daughters Judy and Pat were all educated in this lovely place. Its outstanding 6th Form education attracts students from all over the world and I can truthfully say that I put it all together.

When, after ten years as tenants of the convent at Acton Burnell, the nuns decided to buy it, I was asked by the Mother Superior to help her put the place in order. My daughter Judy was there already and every Monday morning I used to take a gang of the girls who were weekly boarders.

Reverend Mother Edward took me all round the convent introducing me to the nuns who performed various tasks. I will always remember a marvellous sprightly woman called Sister Bridget, who was in charge of the heating. There were five different central heating blocks all over the convent and there seemed to be old-fashioned boilers everywhere. For some reason the children always called me the Professor. Sister Bridget would say: "Come on, Prof, come and find out what's wrong with this boiler."

By the time I'd investigated I'd be covered from head to toe in soot and I'd say: "Bridget, you're a perfect nuisance!" Of course it was great fun but I quickly got a firm in Shrewsbury to install one heating system with just one boiler for the whole convent.

Although I wasn't being paid a penny for my work — from the beginning I insisted on giving my services free — I began to enjoy every minute of it. Mind, I was teased endlessly at The Mytton in the evenings. All the old nun jokes, most of them unprintable cliches! And the milder ones like 'Why do nuns always go about in pairs?' 'So that there's one nun to see that the other nun gets none!'

Having fixed the heating with a good, modern system I turned next to the electrics which were chaotic and really dangerous. Put in haphazardly at different times over the years, much of the wiring was completely out of date. Something had to be done quickly or there could have been a major disaster. The thought of a fire with all those nuns and girls was quite horrifying. It was obviously going to be a big job and, although it wasn't costing me anything, I felt that I was protecting them from themselves because they were not particularly worldly to say the least. Inspiration came to me. I had a friend called Harold Dodd who kept the pub at Crosshouses which belonged to Wem Breweries. A qualified electrician who had been in the Air Force during the war, he had been given the pub on one condition, that he would see to all the electricity in the twenty Wem pubs. He had only one man working for him called Frank who helped with the electric work and the running of the pub.

After getting estimates from several big local firms, one lunchtime over a pint I asked: "Harold, would you like to rewire the convent?" His estimate was half the others and, helped by Frank, they made a perfect job. To this day in the Hall, there's a big cupboard which he made with a clear plan of all the wiring, switch boxes and so on. Fool-proof — and nun-proof!

It was the first big job which he had ever undertaken and now he is almost national with hundreds of employees. In very comfortable retirement he told me that he would never be out of my debt. I had given him the start that everyone needs.

Soon Mother Edward was replaced as Reverend Mother by Mother Lauris, a wonderful, attractive, vivacious woman, a Lady in her own right and a go-getter who wanted things done and done in a hurry. The first thing she wanted was a rest place for the nuns in the middle of a wood and, with her escorting nun running behind, she led the way herself. Dashing through the wood she got hung up in some briars with her veil and after

I'd untangled her we found a lovely little place in the middle where there were no trees, a little glade about thirty yards square. So we made a path in order that I could get a tractor through, cut bushes down, gravelled the path, cultivated the patch, seeded it with grass, put some seats in it and made a lovely retreat for the nuns.

Next week: "I want some playing fields, Tom". A friend of mine had just got one of the first bulldozers — really just a crawler tractor with a bucket in front. I asked him if he could level off a huge rabbit warren with a great big mound in the middle. He tackled the job for £800, which was more than the land was actually worth! But he gassed all the rabbits and levelled it off before I covered it with factory lime, spreading 20 tons to the acre, mixing it all up with soil and re-seeding it. The result was splendid level playing fields, which are there to this day.

Next week Mother Lauris wanted the old derelict buildings, great rows of cow houses with lofts on top, stables etc., made into dormitories and class rooms. Her habit blowing in the wind, she nipped up a stepladder into the loft. I followed and we couldn't see for cobwebs until we got a torch and went round the floor together. We eventually decided to turn the lofts into dormitories and all the bottoms into classrooms. I ordered all the timber, organised the builders and, before long, I was doing all Mother Lauris' business, going in to see her every Monday morning to do the accounts and see that the place was in order.

I thought they had unlimited money and, indeed, was spending the stuff like a Jew with no hands! Mother Lauris couldn't care less about the money as long as she got the work done. She was so right because, before long, her superiors in Rome put the brake on but by that time it was too late. The work was done and done really well. What fun we had. I asked her one day: "Why did you do this? You're so vital and enjoy life so much. I can't understand you being a nun."

"Tom," she said, "don't you realise that you get more happiness and satisfaction out of life by giving? I get on my knees every night to thank God that he has given me the strength to do all the work that I have got to do. Giving my life to these children and to the world is what life is all about.''

There was, of course, always somebody with her and she used to hold my hand while we talked. One of my happiest memories of her is laughing her head off when she came down from those lofts covered from head to foot in dust and cobwebs. Mother Lauris was never rattled, never angry. Anyone else would have been wild when we discovered that the nuns and the girls had disobeyed orders and blocked up all the drains to a depth of twenty feet with their sanitary towels. It cost £500 to clear them! By now I wasn't surprised at anything Mother Lauris did and so, when she asked me to teach her to drive, I bought her an old Bedford van for £15 and took her for regular lessons in the Park. Now apart from the playing fields, which were under construction, there wasn't a level field and I'll never forget the first time I took her. We drove up a bank, through a gate and up another steep bank. At the top of the field we turned round and, as soon as we started down, her foot touched the accelerator, causing the van to lurch and we came down the bank in a series of jumps. Every time her foot touched the accelerator, she would pull it off and the van would slow up — bump, bump, bump. In the end I had to switch the engine off and put the hand brake on and pull her up. By this time we had gone about a hundred yards down the bank, jumping all the way! However in no time at all she learnt to drive. I told her: "You're a natural, Mother Lauris!"

Sure enough she passed her driving test first time and I bought her a new Bedford Dormobile. One morning she told me that she wanted to buy furniture for the dormitories and classrooms from Birmingham. So I supplied her with the addresses of the wholesalers and one morning she set off, taking two of her nuns with her.

Birmingham is quite bad enough to drive in today, but in those days it was nothing short of purgatory. Mother Lauris and her nuns left home at about seven o'clock in the morning and arrived in the big city at a quarter past eight. They drove up New Street (before the one-way system was put in) and when Mother Lauris saw an opening on the left that looked like a street, she drove into it, parked the Dormobile, locked it up and away they went to do their shopping. They ordered new desks, new beds, bedding, cutlery, crockery and every imaginable sought of thing that they wanted, enjoyed a good lunch and arrived back to find a policeman standing by their van with his notebook out. He had come on duty at two o'clock and was obviously very shaken when three nuns walked up. He said: "Is this your vehicle, madam?"

"Yes, it is", said Mother Lauris.

"You know that you're committing an offence? It's been here since two o'clock."

"Oh indeed not," she said. "We were her at a quarter past eight this morning."

"That's as may be, madam", he said. "But this is not a street at all. It's a shopping precinct!"

When she arrived back home she was laughing her head off. The Reverend Mother had got away without a fine. That one could get away with anything!

I mentioned earlier that nuns always go about in pairs. One morning Reverend Mother said: "Tom, I have to go to London. Can you take me to the train?"

"Of course", I said. "What time is the train?" To catch the 11.15am meant leaving in the middle of the girls' morning break. When I arrived I found a crowd of girls waiting outside the door and I couldn't understand why they were all giggling, until Reverend Mother's travelling companion appeared and then I understood; a truly massive nun, 18 stone if she was an ounce with a backside like a Suffolk Punch. Luckily I had brought a new Austin pick-up with a bench front seat and gear change on the right of the steering wheel. God knows what I would have done with a gear change in the middle of the floor! I opened the nearside door and Reverend Mother got in followed by the companion. Slamming the passenger door on her I walked round to the driver's side and found that there was absolutely no room at all even for a little fellow like myself. The girls were going mad as Reverend Mother kept trying to budge up and finally I managed to get in, whereupon five of them slammed the door on me. We had a very rough ride into

Shrewsbury and when we arrived Mother Lauris said: "Tom, I've left my money behind!" I found a tenner to lend her and away they went!

By now we were employing a first-class maintenance man and an excellent gardener called Jim Tyldesley. We had mended all the old greenhouses and installed a new boiler to heat them. With the help of the glasshouse, a big walled garden and an orchard, Jim grew an amazing amount of fruit and vegetables. Feeding 180 people was quite an effort and not many gardeners would have managed it. Rhubarb, plums, damsons, pears, apples, all in bumper crops. The only trouble was that when each fruit was ripe, the girls had to eat it for every meal. Rhubarb for breakfast, rhubarb for lunch, rhubarb for tea and even rhubarb for supper!

One autumn when we were eating apples and the girls were having apples for every meal of the day, they would put all the peel and the cores into a great big earthenware stein, pour some water on it and leave it to ferment into what, in their innocence, they called apple wine. Of course there were so many apples and they put so much sugar into the stein that it made most extraordinarily potent cider, which they duly bottled.

Now every so often there was a Reverend Mother's Feast, a special occasion for which the cooks prepared lots of goodies and a splendid time was had by all. For Reverend Mother's Feast just before Christmas this particular year they decided to open about fifty bottles of apple wine. I tasted some on my Monday morning visit and it seemed alright to me, a bit sweet perhaps but very drinkable. Little did I realise ... !

But in the evening, in front of all the visitors from whom the convent was collecting contributions for charity, there was quite a scene. I never imagined that there could be so many drunken nuns, lying about giggling and obviously completely paralytic. This was one occasion when Mother Lauris was not best pleased!

Eventually when the whole place was really shipshape and running like clockwork as a model business, Mother Lauris prepared to leave, her work done. I had run the order into considerable debt but she was quite unconcerned about it.

In all our time together we had had only one bad experience and in that I was comforted by her magical presence. It was one of the worst jobs that I ever did in my life when we decided to have a look at the crypt underneath the floor of the chapel. As in some horror film, we lifted up an old trap door and, with two big torches, gingerly made our way down worn stone steps into this huge crypt. I don't believe that anybody had been down there for years because there were cobwebs everywhere and imagine our feelings when our torch beams picked out dozens of coffins all over the place, coffins which years had decayed and rotted away leaving only racks of bones and, in some cases, the tiny bones of babies. I got the funeral directors out and left them with the task of trying to identify the remains.

Mother Lauris is now, I understand, in charge of a convent in Rome to which I have often been invited. I shall never forget that remarkable woman whom I had grown to love and respect "...you get more happiness and pleasure out of giving than ever you will out of receiving. I've given my life to God and I go on my knees every night asking him for enough strength to do His will." She changed my outlook on life completely.

CHAPTER XIV

And Stallions . . .

I often turned up at the convent in boots and breeches because I was so heavily involved with my horses at this time.

As I said earlier, I have been very lucky in my employees and this applied to my grooms as well, with one notable exception. For the first nine years after the war I was lucky indeed. Den Thomas was an outstanding feeder and looked after the them so well. We had such fun, winning a lot of shows and races, especially during the five years when Rosemary Cox was with me to help exercise the horses. Den stayed until March 1954 when he was left some money by one of his relations and took a smallholding at Baschurch. As I had by now got another stallion I gave him Distinctive whom he loved. He remains a very good friend who I'm always glad to see.

When he was leaving I advertised for a groom and engaged a man who turned out to be quite useless. He looked the part and had good references but I wouldn't be surprised if they'd been forged. When I went on holiday in October I left him in charge. This was when I had just bought the brand new Austin pick-up. When I returned I found that this new vehicle had done 2,400 miles in my absence and the end of the month my petrol bill at the garage was £70 higher than the month before.

To make matters worse, when the visiting mares had left I had filled the boxes with small turkeys, getting them ready for Christmas. On my return I counted them and found I was short of forty. A few days later the landlord of the pub at Morville telephoned to see if I had any more turkeys as the last were delicious. I asked who had delivered them to him and he told me that it was my groom. I sacked him on the spot. I should have had the police but I'm too kind-hearted!

So I advertised again and this time my luck was in with a vengeance. An Irishman applied with a wife, a small baby girl and twin boys about six years old. His references were impeccable. I took him on immediately and put the family in a caravan by the vicarage building. They had the saddle room and two boxes as well and were very comfortable until I could get them a council house in the village. This was Gerry Murphy and his wife Eileen, a wonderful woman, who has died just recently. They were with me for twenty-six very happy years. He was an outstanding groom. In Ireland he had been with Dr. Vaughan, the breeder of all the Rakes including one of the greatest steeplechasers, Cottage Rake, winner of three Cheltenham Gold Cups. Gerry broke them all in, rode them away and nagged them to the complete satisfaction of the maestro Vincent O'Brien. Later, after I bought Pendragon, Gerry was wonderful with the mares and foals and also with my hunters. I was always superbly turned out and, as I usually had young horses coming along, he would break them and ride them out hunting to start with. We have been great friends from the very beginning. We have always seen eye to eye on everything.

When I gave up breeding after Pendragon broke his neck, I let Gerry have the boxes with free hay, straw and grazing, to use as a livery stable and he looked after my hunters free of charge while I was Master of the South Shropshire for seven seasons. It was an excellent arrangement and I was very sorry to see Gerry and Eileen go when I finally retired in 1981. He still comes over to see me; one of the finest men I have ever known in my entire life.

In addition to Cable Home and Morning Sun there were several other horses in those years immediately after the war. One Good Friday I bought a package of horses from a man called Sydney Everitt who lived near Ditton Priors. A mare called Sieglind who was heavy in foal, a three-year-old colt, a two-year-old and a yearling. All for £500. The mare foaled on Easter Monday and I did them well through the summer before selling four of them for £495, leaving me with the three-year-old for just £5. He had been broken and was a good ride. I turned him out in the paddocks with three mares, two of whom I had bought for £27(!) and he proved a fairly precocious little chap because he got two of them in foal. Two nice colt foals appeared the next year. I thwarted his chances of doing it again by castrating him and the following spring sold him for £300 for a girl to ride. After twelve months her father telephoned to say that his daughter was courting and had no more to do with the horse. Would I have him back? I agreed to take him back at the same price as long as he threw in the saddle, bridle and rug. We made a deal and this lovely little bay five-year-old, a pony standing only just over 15h. but a perfect model with depth and strength, called Siege Law, turned out to be a perfect hunter ridden by my lovely Rosemary Cox.

She and I both rode him in point-to-points and, despite his size, he did really well. He had only two troubles. Rosemary had taught him so much dressage that in the rough and tumble of a race you had to be careful how you applied your leg. Too much pressure with one on one side and he might well obey the aid and swerve out. Also he never really took hold of his bit until the closing stages of a race.

He was placed with Rosemary and with me and then I ran him at home at Eyton in the Adjacent Farmers' race. Alec Crow had a very good big horse but I still backed mine at 8/1. In the paddock he looked like a foal compared with his rivals. I kept him up on the pace and at half way caught hold of him and gave him one in the ribs. He really started to enjoy himself and three from home jumped into the lead. He flew past this great big horse of Alec's but I pulled him back two lengths behind him and jumped the second last in that position. At the last I gradually crept up to Alec's horse, kicked my little chap on and we won by eight lengths.

I rode him myself over hurdles, having wasted down to my absolute minimum weight and, for the first time, suffered the discomfort of a 1 lb saddle. He ran well and was placed but was really too small for the hurly burly of professional novice hurdles. I sent him to a trainer called Whiteley at Preese Heath who had a very good chaser belonging to Billy Brookes and, much to our surprise, once he had got Siege Law fit he found that he could beat this horse very easily. So we entered him at

Sedgefield where nobody knew us, but unfortunately the day before the race I broke my leg and couldn't go. I sent £50 to put on him and put up a jockey and away they went.

He was eight lengths in front at the last fence when he pecked and the jockey fell. We ran him a fortnight later at Ludlow and the same thing happened again. He was entered at Wolverhampton; I changed my jockey and told the new one that the little horse didn't pull much but to go to the front and stay there. He came over the last fence 22 yeards in front with 150 yards to go. Half way up the straight he came to the point where the course went round for the horses to go round again, where they had put some dolls. The jockey looked round to the right and in doing so he pressed the little horse with his right leg. He remembered what Rosemary had taught him about dressage and he turned sharply left and jumped over the dolls to go round again, with only 80 yards to go to the post! Sadly he developed navicular. Eventually I sold him to a bookmaker who won with him but the poor little chap, with that disease, had not long to live.

His dalliance with the two mares in the field as a three-year-old turned out to be a great success. One of his foals developed into a superb big chesnut colt with three white legs and the most extravagant mover. I showed him in hand at the West Midlands Show as a two-year-old and Harry Gittings, who was judging, put him first.

After that I showed him at the Royal, the Hunter Show and all round the top circuit. The only time that he was beaten was at the Three Counties at the end of may when, to my disappointment, we were put fourth. Mercy Rimell, with whom I had dinner afterwards, was second. The judge was Vivian Bishop.

Next year we won everything again. In all from nineteen shows we won seventeen.

In 1948 the Royal Show was at Shrewsbury and I particularly wanted to win the championship. I was beaten to it by a filly belonging to John Downs of Bourton and we were reserve. I couldn't understand this because the filly had never won before and, indeed, never won again in the ring but she did turn out to be a good point-to-pointer.

Now for the championship there were two judges of whom Vivian Bishop was the second judge and it was he who put me down to Reserve Champion. I did not see him again until the last show of the year at Welshpool at the end of September. After the show over lunch I told him that out of nineteen shows he was the only man who ever put my horse down and I wondered what he didn't like about him. He asked if I'd ever ridden him because, when I did, I would find out. He was quite right. The horse was wrong in his back. Indeed it was this fault in his back that gave him his extravagant action but it meant that he could not get off the ground to jump.

Next year I showed him ridden as a four-year-old at the West Midland Show but, since I was not happy about the way he was going, I sent him to one of the best showmen in the country, Johnny Moss at Gloucester, for a fortnight beforehand and he rode him at the show. Moss was a tremendous character, a cocky little individual with all the tricks of the trade, he would, for example, wait until the very last moment, when all the other horses were about to be judged before making a flamboyant entrance. We won that class alright and I sold him for £800 cash, to a corn merchant from the Wirrall. Two years later, when the son apparently was fed up with riding, I bought him back for £400 including rugs, bridle, etc. I sent him to Billy Brookes, our local national Hunt trainer, to school over hurdles but he knocked every obstacle down and I tried hunting but he never could jump. Eventually I got rid of him. Undoubtedly Vivian Bishop was a very good judge!

By now I was going to Newmarket regularly and I had renewed acquaintance with an old friend, Colonel 'Angie' Lloyd, one of the joint founders of the British Bloodstock Agency, now the most famous in the world. Our fathers and grandfathers had been friends and it was natural that Colonel Angie and I should always have had a lot in common over the years. He was a splendid, charming man and an outstanding judge of a horse.

The first stallion I had was a horse called Hullabaloo whom I bought at Newmarket for something like 100 guineas. I used to charge £20 for his services and he covered quite a lot of hunters and ponies as well as some Shire mares. A very good show-jumper who became well known, Lady Jane, was by Hullabaloo out of one of those big mares. One day when hounds met near by we were short of a horse to ride. Den Thomas rode Valate, a brilliant hunter but an impossibly slow point-to-pointer who 'stayed for ever in one place', and I rode Hullabaloo. We found a fox and away we went. The first fence we met, a split oak post and rails, real solid ones three good rails high, Den shouted: "Boss, are you going to come?" I said: "Yes, go on, Den. Give us a bloody lead!" I got the stick up and gave him a rap and although he'd never jumped a fence, he took off, just caught the top rail and how he got the other side I'll never know but after that he became a brilliant hunter and never hit a fence again. He covered thirty or forty mares a year. Quite a few of us used to go up to Newmarket for the famous December Sales, once described by the American auctioneer and bloodstock expert Tom Finney as "the lifeblood of the world's bloodstock industry". We used to stay at a private house and had a lot of fun. One evening when a horse came through the ring which I liked the look of, I looked at the catalogue and found that he had been sold earlier in the sale and was being put up for sale again. For some reason I nodded my head and he was knocked down to me for 110 guineas. He was an entire colt called Little Pipp who had been bought two days earlier by the BBA for 950 guineas to go as a stallion abroad. However, discovering that he was a rig, they sent him up again. About half a dozen of my friends, wanting to see what I'd bought, followed me down to the BBA boxes in that lane just past the saddlers and crowded round me as I opened the door. My new purchase, with his ears flat back on his neck, whipped round and lashed out with both heels. We all fell in a heap outside. "What the hell have you bought?", said someone. "All I know is that his name is Little Pipp — I don't know anything else about him but he certainly frightens me to death!", I said.

I gave an old man £1 to feed him and next morning I asked Colonel Lloyd: "What the hell was that thing I bought last night, Little Pipp?"

Angie said: "You bought a bloody good horse there, Tom — if you can manage him!" He added: "Yes, actually he is a decent animal who has won fair races and was good enough for us to buy him as a stallion. We had him vetted but he didn't pass the vet because he has a stone up."

So I gave Charlton a good tip and asked him to load the horse up and send him to Upton Magna station.

He was obviously tired from his exertions because we got him home with no trouble at all. About the third morning I went into feed him and he put his ears back only to shoot me straight out of the door. Then he turned round and kicked holes in the wall. He was a real savage devil. I couldn't expect anybody else to go into him so I went in with a big stick and eventually managed to get hold of him and place a piece of rope on his head collar. Then when I went in with a bucket, to feed him, I could catch hold of the rope. Otherwise you couldn't get near him. Luckily for me a proper horsemaster called Wall, Trevor Wall's father, from a real Flapping family in the area, had just come out of the Army and came to me looking for a job. Between us we tamed him and entered him up first at Worcester, where Bob Turnell rode him and came back to report: "Tom, this will win a race."

Next time out at Nottingham Bob couldn't ride him and so I put up an Irishman called Ned Hannigan. It was pouring with rain, he had to run in somebody else's colours and, after negotiating the floods, crossing a bridge over the river, we got to the course just in time to declare him. I splashed through the mud to the Tote and had £4 each way on him. Next thing I knew I saw this horse with yellow colours about fifty lengths in front, right under the stands. My little horse had won. I drew £494 off the Tote that day. We eventually got back to Atcham here at about midnight. the main road was flooded and two of my men came back with tractors. They had been making quite a bit of money towing people through the water!

Next morning the cowman said to me: "I was pleased you won with our old horse. You put that £1 each way on for me, didn't you?" I said: "Of course I did, Bert."

Over breakfast the doctor came in: "Glad you won

yesterday, Tom. You put my £2 each way on for me, didn't you?'' By the time I'd given Ned Hannagan a present of about £50 I finished up in debt! But it was good fun and a fortnight later we won with him again at Southwell. He won five races for me and I turned down an offer of £800 because I wanted all my friends to see him win at Ludlow.

The night before Ludlow races a crowd of us assembled in The Barley Mow at Newport after the local point-to-point when two men came into the bar and one said: ''You going to Ludlow tomorrow?'' His friend answered: ''Yes, I think so. I've got a tip. I've been talking to the owner and its bound to win.''

''What's that?''

''A horse called Little Pipp''. I cocked my head and never said a word. Then a friend of mine came into the pub. ''Hello, Tom'', he said. ''Got Little Pipp ready for tomorrow then?'' The other chap looked at me, turned round and ran out!

We took him to Ludlow the next day but he met a swinging hurdle, cut his stifle and lamed himself in front as well. He finished fourth and, as he was obviously going to be laid off for a bit, I let the Wall family, who loved him dearly by now, have him for £200. They really knew their horses and got him sound standing in a brook for most of the next summer. He repaid their loving care handsomely winning a great many valuable Flapping races for them. They kept him until he died and I can truly say I have never seen a horse so well looked after.

Now Little Pipp was savage for a good reason but he was a real good, brave horse. Captain Jinks, on the other hand, was a genuine pig. I had seen a lovely mare finish fourth at Chepstow, so thin and in such terrible condition that I was sure she could be made up with decent feeding and worming into a splendid animal. What a grand sort she was. But the owner would not sell her without also adding in a grey horse called Captain Jinks. So, wanting the mare so badly, I bought the two for £500. I got them home the next day and turned the mare out. She just got thinner and thinner until, in about a fortnight, we found her dead in the field. The post mortem showed that there was a hole in her guts. She had been doped and the drug had burnt a great hole in her. So I was left with Captain Jinks for £500.

We summered him and started trying to hunt him the next season but it was impossible to do anything with the brute. On New Year's Eve we had a big fancy dress ball at The Forest Glen to which Billy Minton, father of the highly successful bloodstock agent David Minton, and I went as a couple of St. Trinians' girls. My eldest daughter went as the Mad Hatter. Sadly it was one of those evenings when too much drink was taken by the wrong people who caused trouble and it all ended in a rather nasty row. Eventually having done my best fairly forcibly to restore order, I arrived back home a lot the worse for wear next morning when the men were just coming to work. The drink had worn off but I was still very angry. Angry with the people who had ruined the party. I said: "Den, put that saddle and bridle on the grey horse. I want to give him a jump this morning."

I changed out of my St. Trinian outfit into a sweater and breeches, had a cup of coffee and got outside just as daylight was breaking. I started off on a little course I used to school the horses. He jumped the first fence well and I turned him into the next left-handed, jumping into a field of sugar beet. The day before the wire netting had gone straight down the field and what I didn't know was that the shepherd had come and turned it across the field. When the grey horse refused at the fence I set about him and next time he went over it running away with me. My eyesight was not good the horse must have been blind he ran straight into this wire netting. We turned a complete somersault and when I tried to get up my left wrist was turned right back and my right wrist was bent right forward, both badly broken. Den Thomas, who had seen the accident, came running across the field, got me to the house and quickly to the Infirmary by nine o'clock. The house doctor looked at it and said he could do nothing until my friend Doctor Jack Beatty arrived. Now Jack had also been to a New Year party and was late for work so that by ten o'clock I was absolutely bursting to spend a penny. Somehow I managed to get to the lavatory but I couldn't undo my fly buttons. I shouted and a little dark-eyed Welsh girl came in. I said: "For goodness sake get me a male nurse. I must spend a penny. I'm bursting and my wrists are broken."

"I'm used to that sort of job", she said, unbuttoned my breeches and, eventually, found this poor apology of an appendage so that the relief was marvellous. I've always felt I'd like to meet that young lady again to prove to her that I was a real man!

Eventually we did get Captain Jinks jumping properly, hunted him quite a bit and then ran him at Ludlow in a two-mile chase. He was coming into the last fifteen lengths in front winning very easily when his jockey thought he had passed the post, dropped his hands and was beaten by a neck. Next time we ran him again on the same course a horse jumped into him, cutting his hock right through the joint so that he had to be put down. £500 down the drain and two broken wrists!

With my arms plastered across my chest I used to go on the bus into Shrewsbury. The conductress was a grand girl. "You'd better get some money out of my pocket", I said. So she put her hand into my trouser pocket, saying: "Which side do you dress on?"

"I dress on that side, but it won't hurt you!", I said. So one morning I put on a pair of trousers with a hole in the pocket. She soon found out which side I dressed on!

The next stallion I bought was Distinctive, a decent horse who had run successfully on the Flat in the Rank colours. I paid 840 guineas for him and Tommy Weston, that flamboyant jockey who used to make a habit of losing his cap in a tight finish when he was going to win by a short head, tried to persuade me to run him in the Champion Hurdle because he was sure that, if the horse was held up, he would win the race. Looking back I wish I had taken his advice. A beautiful quality horse who got quite a few winners from some very moderate mares.

I was lucky in my owners. Lady Mary Grosvenor always sent me mares as did Mrs. Campbell, whose family owned the Bibby shipping line. Distinctive established me as a breeder and before he left I was leased a good sprint stallion by Panorama called Pandemonium, who was getting a lot of two-year-old winners.

He came through Colonel 'Angie' Lloyd but sadly, while covering a mare in his second season, he had a heart attack and died. A glorious death!

As it was in the middle of the covering season and I had a number of mares booked, I immediately contacted Colonel Lloyd and asked if he could find me another horse. The only thing I insisted on was a good straight hind leg, the classic hind leg which helps a horse to get its hocks right under it before it jumps. A horse with its hocks away in the next parish may be alright for races up to a mile, in the same way as hares and greyhounds have their hocks away, but for a good jumper you need a straight hind leg. There's a wonderful picture of Pendil jumping at Kempton which shows you exactly what I mean.

Angie Lloyd was a good friend and a great operator. No wonder the BBA is the best agency in the world. He took just the same trouble as far as I was concerned whether he was dealing in hundreds or in hundreds of thousands. Two days later he telephoned at breakfast time to say that he thought he had got just the horse for me. He was one of the best bred horses in the world, by Lord Derby's great stallion Alycidon, winner of the St. Leger and the Ascot Gold cup, out of Bell of All, the Nasrullah filly who had won the 1,00 Guineas and just failed to stay the distance at Epsom finishing third in the Oaks. Although he was a very good-looking bay colt with superb classical hind legs, he was so straight in front that he was difficult to train and never ran as a two-year-old. As a three-year-old he lamed himself and was unable to fulfil his classic engagements. He was to pass on his virtues and his faults to his offspring.

At 800 guineas he was a snip and I was soon full up with mares, starting at £48 a service and finishing up at £248. When he broke his neck in 1965 I had him insured for £8,000 but, in the six weeks after he died during which he had eight really good winners, I had offers from all over the world for up to £50,000. The trouble with jumping stallions is that they take so long to show their true worth but, as Pendragon was to provide me with one of the greatest thrills of my life by enabling me to breed what was arguably the finest steeplechaser in the world at the time, I will make no excuses for running ahead of it and completing his story. Some time before Pendragon arrived, while I still had Distinctive, I went to the December Sales at Newmarket with my old friend Bob Bebb, David Minton's grandfather. We had been enjoying a really liquid Newmarket and, towards the end of one day decided that it was high time that we bought a couple of mares. It was one of those magical December Sales evenings with the animals walking round on straw, to prevent danger from frost, under the arc lights outside and the auctioneer's voice carrying from the brightly-lit ring into all the crowded bars. We were both pretty pickled but, when it comes to dealing, I never lose my instinct. First I bought a mare called Sabrina and then, looking through my catalogue in the bar I told Bob: "You better get bloody busy and buy this mare, Ziska. She's a half-sister to Bob Get's Busy". We went out to have a look at her and although she only stood about 15.1 hands, and had done nothing much, she came from a good female line and she was a beautiful little model. Bob bought her for 160 guineas.

I brought them both home together and covered them both with Distinctive. Two nice filly foals were the result. Bob called his foal Deliska and mine was Disabrina.

Disabrina won at Pontefract and I then sold her to Denmark where she won the Danish and Swedish Oaks.

Deliska failed to win as a two-year-old but, trained by Reg Hollinshead, finished second in a good race as a three-year-old. Then, with Billy Brookes and Hollinshead she turned out to be a really good consistant performer winning a number of races and being placed many times on the Flat and over hurdles. A really sound, game little mare she was covered twice by a local stallion and was then barren for a couple of seasons. By now Bob was a very sick man so I told him, because he was such a good old friend: "Bob, I'll fetch that mare, look after her and cover her with Pendragon free and we'll go half shares in any produce."

Sure enough I got her in foal first time. I raised the colt and, having done him really well and broken him as a three-year-old, entered him for Ascot Sales. The Tuesday before he was due to go to Ascot Bob, who was now very ill indeed, called here and asked Gerry Murphy my stud groom to see if I would give him £300 for his half share. When I got the message, I telephoned him that night and said: "I'm going to make at least 1,500 guineas from him and I am putting a 1,500-guineas reserve." Tim Moloney gave 1,600 guineas for him.

Tim had bought it for a man called Macdonald who telephoned me one night in October to tell me that he had just won £4,000 with my colt. I said: "If you take my advice, you won't race him again this year, send him back to me and I'll do him for you. You can have him back next spring."

He replied: "Not bloody likely!", but a week or ten days later he telephoned again to tell me that he had run Pendil against my advice. He had finished down the field. Would I have him back, please? The next day he came back here. I had sold him standing 15 hands 1½ in.; when he came back to me he had only grown half an inch. So I kept him until the first week in March and wintered him so well that he was now standing 15 hands 3½ in.

Then Macdonald sold his businesses and emigrated to Australia, sending his horses up to Doncaster Sales where Fred Winter bought Pendil for £3,400 guineas. Trained by Fred Winter and always ridden by stable jockey Richard Pitman, Pendil won six hurdles and twenty-one chases including the Arkle Challenge Trophy at the National Hunt Meeting, the Massey Ferguson Gold Cup at Cheltenham and the King George VI Chase at Kempton twice. Between the autumn of 1971 and the end of season 1973/73 he was only beten twice. The Dikler beat him a short head in the 1973 Gold Cup while in the 1974 running of that race he was brought down at the second last when lying third. He broke down in February 1975 when finishing third in the Yellow Pages Pattern chase at Kempton. That injury kept him off the course for twenty-two months but then, nursed back to soundness with the skill we came to expect from his trainer, he re-appeared at his favourite racecourse Kempton to win a 2½-mile chase with much of his old elan. He won two more races, but just when another chance at his bogey race the Cheltenham Gold cup became a distinct possibility, he slipped up on the road at Lambourn, damaged his neck and had to be retired.

A fast, fluent jumper with a real turn of foot, he stood head and shoulders above his contemporaries at distances of 2½ to 3 miles. Whether he also possessed the stamina to last out the extra two furlongs of the Cheltenham Gold Cup remains a matter of conjecture as recurring leg trouble, coupled with his neck injury, ended his career and he has enjoyed a wonderful retirement, spoilt and cosseted with our good friend, the eminent racing journalist Jonathan Powell, where we have visited him, now aged 28.

CHAPTER XV

They Don't Make Them Like That Any more

The word 'gentleman' is not considered 'politically correct' today. It is considered and anachronism not worthy of our new 'classless society' but there are still men worthy of that description and undoubtedly the finest man I ever met in a long life was Bernard van Cutsem.

At this time I was suffering badly from boils and carbuncles which my wife refused to have anything to do with. One day when I wanted to go hunting a huge boil burst on the back of my neck. I bathed it as best I could and asked my ploughman to put a plaster on it. His comment: "By God, Gaffer, have you pulled a calf out of that?!", which shows how bad they were. But I went hunting that day alright. When I left for the December Newmarket Sales, on that Sunday in 1947, I had a pimple just under my chin but by Thursday it had developed into a huge carbuncle. That afternoon I was standing by the rail watching the horses go round and feeling pretty miserable when suddenly the thing burst with a vengeance. It must have looked absolutely disgusting. A quiet voice said: "That is very bad luck." I turned and saw a tall, thin, immaculate man with the face of a Regency aristocrat who looked as if he should have been carrying a sword. "You had better come with me", he said. Leading me out to his Bentley he drove me to his doctor who attended to me and put a bandage right round my head. Then Bernard van Cutsem took me back to the sales and, as we got out of the car, he asked where I was staying. When I told him The Golden Lion, he said he would pick me up at 8.45 am to take me down for a further dressing. I simply couldn't believe that any stranger could behave in this way.

While we were waiting for the doctor we started talking and, back in the car park afterwards, he asked me when I was going home to Shropshire. When I told him that my friend had to see a sale at 7 pm. he said that he would pick me up at 4 pm to meet some farming friends of his.

Sure enough, at his lovely home in Exning, he introduced me to his 'farming friends', the Earl of Derby and the Duke of Devonshire. "John, Andrew", he said, "this is my yeoman farmer friend from Shropshire."

On the way back Bernard said he was very interested in what I'd being talking about and wanted to know when I was returning to Newmarket. When I told him that I would be coming back in April he said that he would like to take me to look round his estate.

On my return from Newmarket I found that my son Edward had developed pneumonia and by Christmas Day he was very ill indeed, in fact, if he'd been an animal, I wouldn't have given him much chance. So I sent for Dr. Miller of Cressage. Certainly he drank a bit — an occupational hazard of his profession! — but drunk or sober he was far and away the best doctor in Shropshire. He came and gave Edward an injection, got a steam kettle going and made a blanket tent. At about 7 pm the crisis came and Edward came through. To this day I think we owe his life to Dr. Miller. I also owe to him a cure for my boils and carbuncles. Just after that early in the New Year I had another carbuncle on my neck and Dusty Miller told me to go back in two days time when it was ready. He put a needle in the middle, drew out all the rubbish, dressed it and poulticed it and told me to come back for some injections. Every morning for twenty-four days he injected me with something from a black jar in a different part of my body every day. Since then I've never even had a pimple.

So in April I went back to Bernard van Cutsem at Newmarket, looked round the estate at Exning and also at his large stud at Side Hill on the other side of Newmarket where he was standing two good stallions. Money was no object, but both places were agriculturally in a mess. I advised him to get cattle and to graze them with the horses. Horses are selective eaters and dung in certain places, but cattle are like Hoovers.

Sure enough each day a man collected the dung but the grass was not grazed off. My advice was to have enough cattle on every paddock to keep the grass short. Even if the cattle did not pay the horses would do that much better. I reckoned he needed eighty cattle and I bought him that number of really good bullocks at Ludlow, practically pure-bred Herefords. I sent them down to him by train and we put them in matching lots, eight to a paddock. The second year he had a job to sell the cattle so I brought them back here and sold them for him. He left it all entirely to me.

Bernard was a big shooting man, one of the best shots in the world. Towards the end of his life I always thought he showed fantastic guts; he went on shooting at the very top level in those big shoots with two loaders and three guns while he was suffering from cancer of the jaw.

In one field they were growing mustard to provide cover for the pheasants and I told his son Hugh that it was quite ridiculous to grow mustard for no profit. With sugar beet you would have cover for your pheasants and a good cash crop as well. So I managed to get him 25 acres for sugar beet and Bernard was delighted.

I discussed feeding the horses with him — in the natural state horses are very selective but they eat a lot of herbs.

Now George Ridley of Bridgnorth, an old seed merchant and long-time friend of mine, mixed my own seed for my paddocks with grasses, weeds, herbs, etc. You had had to have the lime absolutely right balanced with phosphate and potash. When some weeds appeared the horses would eat them immediately but others would just get to the flowering stage and in two or three days they would have gone. Others would not be eaten until they had seeded but I found that at some stage of the life of a weed or a herb the horses would eat them and they would be getting all the minerals and natural herbs that nature had grown for them. So I got the seed from George Ridley and we seeded the paddocks at Newmarket. George had soil samples and so he knew exactly what to supply. It took us a few years to get all the paddocks done but the mares foaled a lot more readily after that. We started mowing them before the grass got very old. Horses want young fresh grass. What the bullocks would not eat we mowed off. By farming his land in the old-fashioned way we were very successful.

At Bernard's suggestion brother John and I went down to Devon and produced a report on the Castle Hill, South Moulten estates of his wife, Lady Margaret Fortescue.

There are so many stories about Bernard who was a fearless, highly successful gambler on the horses and at cards. When he brought off the last big coup of his life, the Royal Hunt cup at Ascot with Old Lucky, the Press crowded round in the unsaddling enclosure and one of them asked rather stupidly: "What's the plan?"

Bernard looked down somewhat pityingly, drew on his cigarette and said quietly: "That was the plan!"

Although resented and disliked by many as aristocratic, autocratic and snobbish, he was in fact the most gentle and courteous of men, loved by his staff and his animals, by women and, dare I say it, by all real men. A Guards officer in the war, he was essentially a leader and did a great deal for Newmarket and for racing in general. He was always the most generous of hosts, particularly at the sales. At one of his happy lunch parties, guests included the late Comte Roland de Chambure, a comparatively young leading French owner/breeder with a somewhat high opinion of himself who asked during the main course: "Bernard, what are these birds we are eating?"

Without thinking Bernard answered: "Partridges".

"Of course I know they are perdrix", said de Chambure. "But they are particularly good. They are very, very nice birds"

"We call them Frenchmen".

"Frenchmen? Why?"

Bernard, busy pouring champagne into another guest's glass, looked up and answered: "Because they have little red legs and run away when we shoot at them!"

He made me a member of Newmarket's exclusive club, the Jockey Club Rooms, and entertained Rosie and me in great style and luxury at Exning. He saw that we were treated as honoured guests with the Jockey Club on the racecourse and we sat down to lunch with the likes of Bunker Hunt and Marcos

Lemos. I was so proud of Rosie. Even at that early stage of our life together I realised how lucky I was to have a lady who always looked smart and whom everybody loved.

I looked after Bernard's estate until his death from cancer in 1976 and I can truthfully say that I have never missed any man more.

Every spring I would go to Ireland to buy ninety cattle for Bernard. When we turned them out we found they paid a lot better than those bought in England. Sometimes I stayed with Tom Dreaper, the famous trainer of Arkle, Flying Bolt, etc. who had tremendous success with one of my first crop of Pendragons, Crown Prince, a brilliant three-year-old winner of the Liverpool Hurdle and hailed by the sporting Press as possibly the best novice of all time, who sadly had to be put down after he broke his leg in the box.

As a friend of van Cutsem's many doors were opened to me in the racing world and I enjoyed spending a night or two with Tom. His horses drank more stout than he drank himself. I reckon the great Arkle, who was there at the time, was drinking a gallon of stout a day!

CHAPTER XVI

Ireland

The ferry from Holyhead or the flight to Collinstown; whichever way you do it, you end up in a different world. It was August Bank Holiday 1946 when I first went to Ireland with Frank Davis for the Dublin Horse Show.

It was a tremendous thrill for all of us Englishmen when the British team that swept the board, even in the Olympics, with Harry Llewllyn and Foxhunter, Wilf White and Dougie Stewart, won the Aga Khan Cup. It was of particular excitement for me because I had sold a horse to Wilf White a short time before. It was the first time that I had seen an Irish bank and that one at Ballsbridge looked quite frightening but it was amazing how the horses got over it.

At the show I met Charlie Ross, who was at one time one of the biggest cattle dealers in Ireland. He sent my father cattle for many years and every Friday when they had the Irish Stores sales in Shrewsbury he would send anything up to 200 cattle for the auction.

By now he was in his sixties, and was more or less retired but, although he seemed an old man to me, he was a wonderful contact. He was living at Black Rock and selling cattle in a small way.

The whole experience was a revelation to me; to go over in the boat with a couple of dozen Irish priests propping up the bar. Had they been to a Convention? No, they'd all been to Haydock races and were having a whale of a time on the way back.

After years of rationing in England the food in the Emerald isle was unbelievable. Huge pre-war style breakfasts at the Hibernian ... and my word how much hard liquor everyone drank as well as the Guinness!

193

The green, green grass of the fields and you only had to put a piece of it between your thumbs and blow and some of the most beautiful cattle in the world would come trotting up. Charlie bought in the west of Ireland at tiny crofts where maybe only one or two were bred. I would buy his best to take back to van Cutsem and it always paid off.

What parties we had, hunting, racing, eating and drinking. Nobody ever seemed to stop drinking in Ireland in those days.

Once old Mrs. Ross took me round the country buying cattle and one night in Listowel for the races, I managed to find accommodation for Mrs. Ross in the kitchen of one house and for myself in a bed-and-breakfast house next door. I walked down to the dance in the village that evening and found some very nice girls there, of whom two in particular looked a bit different. When I asked one of them to dance she turned out to be a German girl and for the rest of the evening I danced with both of them. When we came out of the place they were walking in my direction and I discovered that we were staying in the same digs.

When we arrived they went upstairs and I stayed below to have another drink but when I went up I found that our rooms were opposite and they had been waiting for me. No sooner had I got onto the landing when one of them caught hold of me and pulled me through the door. They were already stark naked. Between them they stripped me off — I had had a lot to drink and was certainly not refusing — pulled me into bed with them and had their wicked way all night. By early morning I was completely worn out, but what an experience! It transpired that they were hitch-hiking round Ireland and spoke very little English. If I went into detail of what they did to me that night, this book would not pass even the modern censor!

At 6 am I staggered to my own bed — there were four men in my room — and found the man I had been talking to in the bar the previous night lying in the bed by the window steadily drinking out of a bottle of whisky, obviously to save time pouring it out into a glass. After a number of glorious years like that going backwards and forwards to Ireland, really enjoying myself and doing good business with the cattle, when I started my new business in 1961 I had no further time but I was very friendly with a man called Michael O'Kayne and I got him to send me cattle. He arranged for me to go to Birkenhead on Sunday mornings and each week at least 1,000 cattle would come off the boats. All the Angus beasts would be picked out by a Scotsman, put on one side and no one else could buy them. They went up to Scotland and were sold as Scotch beef having had perhaps one night in Scotland!

Nevertheless I had second pick and chose as many as I required, arranged for a lorry to pick them up and sent them off to Shrewsbury where they were slaughtered. This method worked for many years but I then reluctantly had to call a halt to my dealings with Ireland.

In 1948 I went over for the Irish Derby and stayed at The International at Bray. There was a good bus service from there to Ballsbridge in Dublin where I went for the Sales during that week. When I got back on the bus after the sales on Friday I was accompanied by a couple who had obviously got married that day. They were staying at The International. We had a drink together before dinner and there was great excitement because the barman had just returned form a cocktail competition in London where he had the first prize and many diplomas. There were free drinks all round and we had quite a session before dinner. I made friends with four Scotsmen who took me to the races at The Curragh the next day where we all backed the Derby winner and, returning to our hotel, celebrated with brandy followed by champagne chasers.

We were joined by the married couple and at 1am the bridegroom Wally was asked by his bride to go to bed because he was very drunk. He told her that he was staying but she could go on up. So I said: "Come on, Wally, you ought to take her to bed". He replied: "If you want to take her to bed, you take her," and, hiccuping loudly, he staggered back to his drink.

So, gallant as ever, Jones took the bride upstairs. When we got into their bedroom she asked me to help her take her dress off. I did so only to discover that she had nothing on underneath except her knickers. The next thing I knew we were in bed. I won't go into details but we had a very exciting time. I did not stay too long in case Wally appeared. Eventually I went back and joined the rest. Before long a very drunken bridegroom was helped upstairs by another of the visitors. At 8am. the next morning Wally's wife walked into my bedroom, told me that Wally had been completely pickled when he got into bed and grumbled all night about the bed being too uncomfortable. She discovered that the cause had been my cigarette case on his side of the bed! I had enjoyed every moment of my Irish experiences and I will always love the country and its people.

CHAPTER XVII

FMC

February 1952 saw the death of King George VI, the good, shy man who had never wanted to be king, but who performed his onerous duties so splendidly, supported by his wonderful wife Queen Elizabeth.

Looking to the future, I discovered that Bates & Hunt, the Chemists, of which I was now a Director, owned a large building in Wellington that they wished to let. It stood behind a shop front belonging to a Shrewsbury man who was willing to sell it for £4,000. The two together would have been ideal for me to re-start my butchery business on the decontrol of meat by the Ministry, so I set all the wheels in motion to buy and rent the two premises respectively, all to be signed and sealed on the Thursday morning.

Wednesday evening brought a surprise telephone call from Bill (later Sir Gwyllum) Williams, vice chairman of the NFU, whose chairman was our mutual friend Jim Turner, now Lord Netherthorpe.

"Tom", he said, "Jim and I have been discussing your ideas for the meat trade which you put forward all those years ago. The three of us should meet in London right away. Can you come up tomorrow?"

I replied: "No, I'm meeting the solicitors with a view to buying the right premises so that I can start my own business as soon as possible". But I'm too gullible. Bill flattered and cajoled. After an hour on the telephone he persuaded me that, if the idea (which after all was my idea) came off, we would have a Meat Marketing Board as I had suggested. We would have full control of all meat and the support of all the farmers. A business like the one I planned for myself would be no good.

So, telling my wife to postpone the solicitor's appointment, I caught the early morning train from Shrewsbury and, after day-long discussions in Bedford Square with Jim, Bill and Knowells, the NFU secretary, they managed to convince me that we would soon be wholesaling most of the country's meat and supplying all the retailers. We decided to start a provisional marketing board to put our house in order ready for decontrol and, at the same time, we applied to the Ministry for permission to form a proper Meat Marketing Board as early as possible.

Afterwards we enjoyed a sensational night out in London, of which I remember little. The next day, somewhat hung over, before a delicious beef lunch at Simpsons in The Strand, I telephoned my solicitors and cancelled my bid for the premises. It was the greatest mistake of my life.

To recap, my idea in 1943 was to have a Meat Marketing Board to run in conjunction with the Milk Marketing Board. The trouble with farmers was that they always jumped on the bandwagon and, if anything appeared to be selling well, they started to produce it irrespective of whether it was suitable for their land or environment, thereby causing gluts and shortages. This was why I wanted a Meat Marketing Board to control production as well as sales.

From 1938 to 1954 all fatstock had been graded by the Ministry as suitable for human consumption irrespective of weight — only a slight variation in price according to weight. Farmers had got their animals as heavy as possible and never remotely thought of quality or customer demand. Indeed in 1948 I was actually booed at an NFU meeting when I got up and said that farmers should breed and feed for consumer demand, not for weight, since in the end the customer would want quality not what was then being forced on him, forced on him by the short-sighted farmers and by the Ministry. Now, sadly, 80% of the beef and of our sheep are the produce of continental bulls and rams and the Danish pig, as I discovered on a wonderful visit to Denmark, is the best in the world.

Although Jim, Bill and I started what we called the Provisional Meat Marketing Board in 1952, it was March 1954 before the Government finally told us, after the most scandalous delay, that we would not be allowed to have a Meat Marketing Board because of their promise to all wholesalers and auctioneers at the start of the war that they could have their businesses back on the decontrol of meat. So, in July 1954, far too late, we started the Fatstock Marketing Corporation, in full competition with auctioneers and wholesalers.

Initially most of the farmers were faithful. The first week our turnover was over £2 million — but what rubbish! The best had all gone to auction and had been snapped up by our competitors. Inevitably there were several rackets. For example, through the war years, they never got round to punching holes in the sheep's ears but just put dye on their ears to show that they had been graded. Some rather dubious characters discovered how to get rid of the dye and one man was making himself about £500 a week by buying sheep in Shrewsbury on the Tuesday, cleaning the ears and taking them up to Stoke 8 days later. By co-operating with Detective Inspector Harris we succeeded in arresting the man, who was sent down for 6 years. Another man, who was never caught, used to bribe the grader in the abattoir. We found a wastebin full of sheep's ears!

At one of our first meetings I insisted that we must have refrigerators. This idea was immediately knocked down by Bill Williams who said that once meat had been put in a fridge or freezer, it reduced in value. Imagine an expert at the very top of his profession talking like that! There was worse to come.

On the first Saturday we had thousands of pounds worth of meat left on our hands, unsuitable for our clients, which we had to give away or sell at a loss to the knackermen.

I had maintained at a meeting in London in April that, as we were not going to have a monopoly, we should approach our customers, find out their requirements and supply them with exactly what they wanted at a price which would enable them to show a profit. Once again I was laughed at.

To take an extreme example, whereas in prosperous areas like Shrewsbury or Cheltenham, butchers wanted the best cuts for their customers, up in the poor districts of Lancashire they wanted the lesser cuts for their hotpots and stews. It was no good sending a complete beast to either because there was bound to be a great deal of wastage. But once again my idea was laughed out of court.

For our first meeting in London ten days after we started I managed to put a proposition through that at every abattoir that we controlled we should engage a big retail butcher to be what I called a Relieving Officer to take off our hands any meat that hadn't been disposed of, by Saturday morning, at the best price he could get. As I was in charge of Shropshire, Cheshire, Staffordshire, North Wales, Birmingham and Liverpool, I had a big job finding the right man, as indeed did all the other thirty-one directors. But I did find the right man in Shrewsbury, a super chap whom I advised to put in refrigeration and to get all the school and canteen orders in the area. This he did and he is now, I am happy to say, a millionaire living in the Isle of Man. I did nothing else for a month but get every abattoir properly fixed up and in doing so, I created a number of millionaires.

Another big trouble was that for sixteen years farmers had not had to worry about quality but only weight. Although they had entry forms to describe their stock to be sent in a week before delivery, they hadn't got a clue. The descriptions were completely false in most cases. It looked alright on paper but, as different areas wanted different quality of stock, when the beasts arrived they were very often not as they had been described and so we were back to square one, to the need for good Relieving Officers.

In September 1954 things got so bad that I managed to push through another resolution. Although we had promised the farmers that we would move all the fatstock, in my opinion because of ignorance and greed, those same farmers were letting us down, sending us the rubbish and selling the best in the auctions where our competitors were buying and they were taking our customers.

I proposed that we should only take 60% of our requirements direct from the farmers and buy 40% in the auctions. My word what an uproar there was! The vote was absolutely even but luckily Jim Turner, in the Chair, voted for me.

So I was put in charge and I had to find buyers all over the country to buy at the auctions. It was the worst job I ever had but eventually it was successful and made the whole operation a bit better. The FMC was never a real success because the Board were all farmers and not businessmen. Our abattoir managers were the second best because the wholesalers had beaten us to it because of the Government's delay in not letting us know whether we could or could not have a board. They had also got the best buyers for the auctions.

So, I'm afraid I lost some of the most valuable years of my life which could have worked well and consolidated my future instead of wasting it on an ideal which was ruined by the short-sightedness and greed of farmers and of many of the board members — who were, of course, also farmers.

But at least now, looking back to the days when I was buying up great businesses like Marsh & Baxter for the FMC, and when people call me a trail-blazer, I can comfort myself with the thought that I did indeed think up and found the biggest operation that has ever taken place in this country's meat trade.

I had so many ideas for a business of my own as even in those days I wanted to sell cuts of meat to butchers instead of carcasses and also to make all my offal and trimmings into pet food. Nowadays you can see how right I was. 90% of beef is sold boneless and in primal cuts. I remember talking to my father and saying I would find a market in bulk for a lot of the waste offal that the butchers threw away.

In 1958 I could see that the supermarket business was growing in this country and got up at a meeting in London and said that we should put our house in order getting ready to supply supermarkets with meat. They laughed me to scorn. The supermarkets would never sell meat, they said. They could never compete with the retail butchers like Dewhursts and Baxters. I suppose I could tell you a lot about the everyday running of the FMC, the ''farmers' meat corporation'' as many people thought it was, but it was never really very successful. Farmers who were supposed to be the chief beneficiaries, were very disillusioned and quite honestly, they did not supply the

FMC with the meat that the retail butchers wanted. If the farmers had really had the FMC at heart and had looked after those retail butchers, producing the right article at the right time for the right people, all would have been well.

Talking about being in the right place at the right time, it will by now have been obvious that, thanks to the good Lord, this factor has played a major part in my life. In 1957, when we were in the bacon trade — as I mentioned earlier, one of our first deals for the FMC was to pay several million for Britain's biggest pork firm Marsh & Baxter — we could not compete with the Danish farmers and one morning I found myself on the train from Shrewsbury going to an afternoon meeting in London. Throughout the journey I was working on my FMC papers and preparing for the afternoon meeting and about twenty-five minutes out of Paddington I put them in my brief case. A well turned-out man sitting opposite me who spoke very good English with a slight accent asked: "Are you something to do with FMC?" I said: "Yes, I'm one of the directors."

"Well, I am a Danish member of parliament and I am very interested in your FMC. Are you going to a meeting?" I told him that I was, at half past two. "That will just give you time to come to our Danish Club and have lunch with me", he said. "Then you can get in a taxi to go to your meeting."

When we arrived in London he took me to the Danish Club and it was the first time I had ever had Danish food — all laid out with everything you could think of on a big table. We had a very interesting conversation and when I left at about two o'clock to go to the meeting he said: "If ever you can come to Denmark, get in touch with me".

I had been so impressed with the Danish bacon that I decided I would take him up on his offer and go to look at their trade. I thought that Jim Turner would definitely pay my expenses. He didn't but I wrote to my Danish MP friend, told him that I was coming over for a week and asked him to arrange accommodation for me. I had a letter back by return saying that he would put me up in one of their top hotels in Copenhagen and that he would meet me at 9 o'clock on the Saturday morning.

By luck not long before that I had sold a three-year-old filly to go to Mr. Johansen in Denmark. He was the man who made those little three-wheeler bubble cars. He was very well disposed towards me because my filly had turned out to be the top classic filly in Scandinavia.

This particularly nice man also wrote back by return to say that he would come to my hotel and asked me to telephone him. He would then come and pick me up on the Sunday morning.

The MP took me to the immaculate estate of a Danish count who farmed it himself in the most superbly efficient way. It was one of the tidiest places I have ever been on in my life. He was milking about 150 Danish Red cows, a very, very good cow, lightish red with good conformation and excellent milk yielders with high butterfat. He was using a Friesian bull on them to produce beef. The cows themselves were smaller than Friesians, bigger than Ayrshires but with far better conformation. They were all in superb condition. He must have had about 200 Landrace sows on whom he used all Landrace boars but he told me that the owners were not allowed to have boars of their own. All the boars belonged to the co-op; all farmers had to be members of co-ops; and there were about three or four co-op societies with so many farmers in each and they would have one excellent research station. When I say excellent I mean it was out of this world. No boar was allowed to be used unless it was proven. I found the proving of the young boars left absolutely nothing to chance. I was told that all the research stations in Denmark were the same outstandingly high standard.

Their methods of breeding which I can go into perhaps in another book resulted in them producing 2.5 litters of pigs every year which made a huge difference to the profitability of the animals.

They taught me that once the sows were weaned they were put onto a very low plain type of food to keep them going, if anything slightly to lower their condition and certainly not to put any meat on. They said that in this way they make bigger litters. They argued that in feeding rich food at that early stage after the sow had gone to the boar, the placenta would grow and if the body was growing and the animal putting fat on at the same time, the placenta would then be at a standstill and some of the pigs that were attached to it would die. By their methods of underfeeding in the early stages of pregnancy they said they got far bigger litters. Better ones, too. When the sows were about two months in pig they would start feeding them really well and getting them into good condition for pigging down. Their methods were so good that they were averaging 9.5 pigs a litter whereas at home I, who thought that I was one of the most experienced pig farmers in England, was averaging 8 pigs to a litter.

The research stations were not only designed to produce the right boars but also to produce meat as near perfect as possible. Every type of pig meat, pork and bacon after it had been cured would be sent to the local research station where it would be tested and all the cooked meats were then tested by taste, selecting tasters at random for tasting sessions. Unless all the people approved of the batch of ham which was being tested, they wouldn't give it a licence for export to England. Most of it was consumed at home but some could be sent to Germany!

Back to the Count's fabulous estate. I was absolutely amazed at the farming efficiency. On the arable side all the grass was chopped and blown into silos and they also made silage from sugar beet tops and sugar beet pulp, wet pulp that again would go into these big silos. There were no hedges anywhere on the farm but electric fences.

In the cowhouse with these 150 cows all in one building, they were tied up by their necks in stalls just as we do at home but with a big difference. I was made to realise that our methods are far too slipshod. A cow's back rises about 9 in. or 10 in. when she is dunging with the result that in England some of the dung inevitably lands on her bed so that when the cow lies down she is always dirty. They had to be washed every morning or they would be in a mess, but not in the Count's cowsheds. At the back of the cows he had an electric wire, just ordinary electric fencing wire about 3 in. or 4 in. above the cows' backs so that when they arched their backs to dung they would get a shock which meant that they always stood back in the gutter to dung for themselves and their beds were kept absolutely clean

I was mad to have some of Landrace pigs at home but the Danish government would not allow them to be exported to this country. I pulled all the strings I could but there was no way they would let them go. Soon after that we did start importing Swedish Landrace but they weren't as good as the Danish. The Danes had had the original Landrace pigs, the best, and they were sticking to them.

Having spent three days going round small farms, big farms, research stations, factories and abattoirs and getting a good insight into everything I was amazed by the efficiency of the farmers and the fact that the land was worth a lot more than ours. Whereas our land in those days was worth about £250-£300 an acre, theirs was worth £1,000 an acre but it was well worthwhile.

When I returned to my hotel, had a bath and got changed, I went down to dinner and found that my generous Copenhagen hosts, thinking obviously that I would be lonely, had arranged for a charming girl from Taiwan to sit at my table. We got talking and I found that she spoke excellent English as she had been to college in America for four years and was on her way home where she was going to be a teacher.

They had called at Heathrow to refuel but something went wrong with the plane and they had landed at Copenhagen. So she had to stay the night. We got on so well that I suggested that we might go to the pictures. Nearly all the films in Denmark were English or American with Danish subtitles, which is probably why the Danes speak English so well.

After a while sitting in the cinema my companion quietly held my hand and then put it up to her mouth, kissing my knuckles and putting one of my fingers in her mouth. This was a really surprising turn-on and of course I put my arm round her and we soon went back to the hotel where I ordered a bottle of champagne to be sent up to her bedroom which, funnily enough, was next to mine. When I opened the bottle of champagne and we started drinking it, I undressed her and she undressed me. She was absolutely beautiful with the most perfect figure and I had one of the most wonderful nights of my life. The next morning we had breakfast together and she accompanied me to the airport. I have seldom been so sorry to leave anyone in my life as I was to leave that marvellous Taiwanese girl.

CHAPTER XVIII

Tender Weekend Joints

In 1960 I resigned from the FMC and also from the NFU of which, of course, I had been chairman in Shrewsbury. I had given eight precious years of my life to the FMC and nearly all my adult years to the NFU. In both cases I had become disillusioned for one simple reason. Much as I love my fellow farmers as a breed, the majority appear to be far too self-centred and always to have an eye on 'the quick buck'. In every branch of farming they go on producing whatever they think will make them money at the time without ever taking the trouble to find out what the customer wants. Think of those Danish farmers with their superlative research stations and you'll see what I mean. Their first concern is for the customers who will be eating their products.

I wanted to start on my own, to put my ideas into practice but, as always, you really need a great deal of capital. Thinking about the sort of animal that the customer wanted, I invented barley beef and started producing 10 a week by feeding them on rolled barley and protein with hoppers which I patented to take the dust and killer husk out of the broken hulls so that they grew to 8½ cwt. in ten months — carcasses of about 500 lbs. which, because of their youth, would be very tender. I asked Perkins of Liverpool whether he was interested and he gave me an order for ten carcasses a week as well as 20 pork pigs to make up a load to go to Gloucester to supply stores in South Wales. The meat sold so well that in two weeks he wanted 20 cattle and 40 pigs and 100 lambs a week. After eight weeks he doubled again. Luckily by now I had friends also producing barley beef and so had no trouble in getting the necessary cattle, sheep and pigs.

One Sunday in 1961 at The Mytton I had a long talk with Joe Scott who had sold out his Sunblest business to the Finefare Supermarket group of which he remained a director. It was he who put me on to Perkins, their man in charge of meat at Liverpool. But when the following day I telephoned a man called Bowater who was in charge of meat for Vesteys, British Beef (wholesalers) and Dewhurst (retailers), met him at Smithfield Market and told him that I wanted to put meat into supermarkets but didn't think that I had the capital to do it, he laughed at me and said that supermarkets would never sell meat in any quantity as they could never compete with people like Dewhurst, Baxters and the other retailers.

My business was so successful that by 1965 I was supplying Finefare, Safeway all over England, Spar and Tesco locally — in fact 300 cattle, 3,000 sheep and 1,300 pigs a week. I called my business with my own initials, T.W.J., Tender Weekend Joints Limited. At the same time I gave that name, TWJ, to one of the best horses that I owned. One day at the Newmarket October Yearling Sales I saw a huge handsome bay yearling standing all of 16.2h even at that age, walking round the ring and noticed that he turned in his off fore foot very badly. He was beautifully bred by Lord Derby's top-class horse Mossborough, who was standing as a stallion at Bernard van Cutsem's Side Hill Stud at the time. I examined the offending foot and discovered that, on the country stud where this yearling had been reared, the foot had been neglected. The inside had grown while the outside had worn down and so badly that he twisted his toe. When he was knocked down to me for 115 guineas Bernard said: "Tom, why on earth did you buy that cripple?"

"I think it's only his foot and I am sure that I can get it right."

"Well, if you can, send him to me and I'll train him for nothing."

I took him home and for seven months the blacksmith came once a fortnight. He made a shoe, cut it an inch from the toe and heel and welded some spring steel on to it, and filled it up with lead, accomplishing a near miracle. The horse, now standing over 17 hands, was moving almost straight. So much so that I sent him up to Bernard who got him fit and gave him a run on the Flat at Brighton. He was delighted with the way that the big youngster performed but he told me to have him home again.

"He's so heavy topped that if I go on with him I will break him down. Turn him away, let him develop, school him and hunt him. That horse will make a top-class chaser".

First, after we had castrated him, he was ridden shepherding all summer by a great friend of mine in Wales,then, after I had broken my leg hunting, he was hunted through the winter by another friend in Wales called Derek Gethin to whom I gave a quarter share.

Derek reported he was going so well that we should run him in a point-to-point. In a field of fourteen in the North Hereford Open race he finished close up fourth behind one of the top Open race horses in the country, Mr. Joe. Next morning Hugh Sumner of Typhoo Tea, at the time one of the country's leading National Hunt owners, telephoned and after a little haggling I sold TWJ to him for £3,500 with a contingency of another £500 when he won his first £500 race. I added a further contingency of £1,000 if he won the Gold Cup or the Grand National.

First time out at a Worcester evening meeting when I was buying cattle I backed him at 20/1 with a fiver each way and he won by eight lengths. He won eight races on the trot and I could see my other £1,000 coming but in a race at one of the Cheltenham minor meetings he was brought down at the water jump and broke his leg. I had backed him every time and won £840. This money was going to come in very handy.

Tender Weekend Joints was flourishing — almost too well perhaps, as it was to turn out. Not only did I buy my first refrigerated vans about this time but also I introduced into England 'Vacupac' or Cryvac which had been proving a great success already in the Argentine. You cut the meat up into prime cuts, took out all the bone — leaving a whole sirloin, rump, topside, silverside and so on. Then you put your joint into the vacuum, draw out the air, seal it and put it into a chiller at about 38^0. For nine weeks it will tenderise and improve. I took my manager down to Bedford. When we opened up the Cryvac the meat was as black as the ace of spades but within ten minutes it was beautiful and pink. We cut some steaks off it, cut it up and put it onto the counter next to some of the meat that I had supplied. It has two advantages. When the trade is going up you can buy a lot of meat, Cryvac it, put it into a chiller and keep it for nine weeks. So you can get your profit there because you always have something in reserve. With Cryvac you don't lose anything. It retains its colour and it tenderises. So I bought a small plant. The system is now operated all over the world.

In 1963 my father, who had not been too well, was nearly ninety, I arrived back from a three-week holiday in Las Palmas to find that the old man was very poorly indeed. He had been blind for about two years and now had great trouble with diabetes. That first Saturday night I slept the night in his bed with him or rather I spent the night in bed with him. We didn't sleep much because he had a catheter in and was in terrible pain. The next morning I went to see his excellent sympathetic old doctor who gave me some morphia pills for him. At about half past nine I went home and an hour later was telephoned to say that my father had died. The night before, knowing that he had not got long to live, he asked me if I would look after his sister, my Aunt Margaret who lived in Wellington and, indeed, I looked after her until she died in 1973.

In July of the following year Aunt Margaret asked me to take her sister, my Aunt Mary who was staying with her on a visit from South Africa, back to Cape Town. Aunt Mary offered to pay my fare if I would take her and I could not refuse an 87-year-old lady, even though perhaps I would be neglecting the business at a very crucial stage.

We travelled out to South Africa on the Windsor Castle which took nearly a month. Aunt Mary was a delightful companion and my journey was enlivened by a most attractive red-headed freckled physiotherapist called Jenny, who put my slipped disc back in the Bay of Biscay and then massaged me in the most wonderful intimate way for the rest of the trip. I didn't need to do any more running round the deck. They say that making love does you as much good as a four-mile run. From early dawn every morning of that voyage I must have run about twelve miles!

We had two extremely prestigious travelling companions who soon became good influential friends. Jim Woolley, who was travelling with his wife Edith, was managing director of ICI in Johannesburg and Sam Cohen, owner of the South African supermarket chain, OK Bazaars. It was a great help knowing both of these men.

I made the most of my time in Africa, travelling all over South Africa, Rhodesia and Kenya where, not only did I inspect farms but also lunched with the President Jomo Kenyatta and with his Minister of State. At the end of this book, in an appendix, I have inserted a letter which I wrote on my return as a result of this visit. It was at a show at Eldorette where I had lunch with Kenyatta and sat between him and Kanaji. Kanaji told me that he knew all abut strikes from his time in England and I was not surprised to read next week that Kenyatta had told six trades union officials to sign a no-strike document on penalty of immediate gaol. As his Minister of State said to me over lunch: "Strikes are the ruination of any country".

It was lovely to renew acquaintance with my first fiancee Betty, on my second visit in 1968. Through Sam Cohen, who was particularly interested in my views on the meat business, also I made many good friends. Moreover Lord and Lady Delamere, farmer friends of my father and now very prominent in farming, racing and breeding out there and Lady Mary Grosvenor, of the vast Westminster estates, who had always sent mares to my stallions, were wonderfully hospitable. It was great to go to the races out there because, for example, there was a good two-year-old by the Stewards' Cup winner Palpitate, a son of my former stallion Pandemonium. Palpitate had been at Lord Delamere's stud in Kenya but he had sold him the next year and he was now standing in Rhodesia. Then I saw on my racecard a two-year-old by Ship's Bell who was a half-sister to my Pendragon by Doutelle. By a happy coincidence the two-year-olds by Ship's Bell and Palpitate finished first and second. Betty introduced me to the owner of the winner and I received an immediate invitation to look round his stud.

211

Thanks to my old friend Mike Killer, who was waiting for me in Cape Town, during a fortnight there I went racing three times at Kenilworth, Milnerton and Durbanville. I was very happy to take with me my darling daughter Pat (Wooty) who had been enjoying herself out there and whose mother insisted that she came home with me. Sam Cohen arranged for us to look round the top abattoirs and the biggest retailers and wholesalers in all the Cape Town area. When I stayed with Lord Delamere I realised that my stock was even higher out there because an animal which I had bred called Yuhuru and sold to Jack Ellis had won the Kenya Oaks. Racing is a wonderful bond worldwide.

At the end of 1968 after staying in the Orange Free State with Florence, she took me to see all her friends, including some nice people at Standerton near Johannesburg, who bred thoroughbred horses and stood a couple of stallions. We drove 300 miles on magnificent roads, stopping for lunch at a place called Bethlehem and two days later we went to a race meeting at Lasuto in Basutoland, a somewhat Godforsaken place right up in the mountains. Lady Mary Grosvenor who lived not far away had telephoned to ask us to meet her there. She had her own tent and entertained us royally with much champagne and good food. She had three runners at this little meeting where the excited natives made the most incredible racket. Lady Mary won two races and their own King Johnny won another. This reminded me of a bumper race in Ireland when there were no other triers because everybody wanted Prince Aly Khan to win. Here they made sure a victory for King Johnny's horse and the excitement was intense.

It is surprising how many problems face the farmers in the various countries of Africa. After my lunch with Jomo Kenyatta at Eldorette Show he arranged to meet me for an official lunch at the new Stanley Hotel. I arrived at the hotel at about midday and after a few drinks at the bar the President came in and we sat down to lunch. I found him to be a very intelligent man. We talked mostly about the meat trade and he arranged for me to go next morning to the abattoir and the factory at Atti River, where I was to meet a man called Morgan who was manager of meat for all Kenya.

I left him at about 3 o'clock, went back home and had a quiet, peaceful evening. The next morning I borrowed a car from John Dorrell and went to Atti river as arranged. Morgan was a very clued-up man and he outlined their problems, the biggest of which was to find customers for their meat because of the disease factor. They had no regulations for foot-and-mouth or anything like that and so very few people in the world, except those in the Middle East, would touch their meat. In fact they had so much meat and such a job to sell it that their prices were about half those in England. However, as in South Africa, they would bone the animals out on a line system and process all the bones and fat. To see all the fat being boiled coming out and put into packets was amazing and Fray Bentos made a lot of their beef into corned beef. We saw the whole process right the way through and I was so impressed with the quality of the meat that I told Morgan that when I got home I would try to sell some for him. He took me back to his office and we stayed there until about 6 o'clock in the evening when he took me out to dinner at a Chinese restaurant and gave me an excellent meal.

When I was in the meat factory I saw them packing meat into boxes and I particularly remember the fillets being packed into cases which were stamped "Frozen fillets from KMC" with a date on them. Funnily enough I was in Smithfield market a few weeks later and I saw these packets of meat being unloaded onto one of the stalls.

In our green and pleasant land we have no idea about dust bowls and a desperate shortage of salt. Frequently in Africa the only salt that the natives can get is from the urine of a male animal. I have seen the natives going up to a beast with a stick and a bucket, encouraging the bulls to urinate in the bucket. They would then mix the urine into their food.

On another occasion I was staying with a cousin who had about 1,000 cattle and they had no salt for weeks. He used to buy it in five and ten ton loads. On the morning when a load arrived he put about five bags in his pick-up. In each of these huge paddocks there would be around 120 cattle. He told me to

213

keep driving while he emptied some salt into a trough in the middle of the field. The cattle must have smelled the salt because they came towards us at full gallop bellowing and he only had time to put about three bags of salt in before they were on top of us and we had to get going. The cattle then piled up on top of each other trying to get at the salt and were so desperate that three of them were killed. Whereupon the natives slit their throats, dressed them and had a huge feast. What they couldn't eat they cut into strips and dried in the sun for 'biltong'.

It was on a pig farm that I saw another hazard. Bill kept about 80 or 90 sows and grew a lot of barley and maize to feed them. One morning I was walking around and heard a lot of squealing. I went into the pig pen and in the farrowing house was a sow who had had ten piglets the day before and now she was covered with safari ants. These are as big as your little finger. I ran outside and shouted to some of the men to get the sow out and ordered the old Indian mechanic to pour a tin of waste oil all over the sow to kill them. When we went back into the pen there were ten rucks of little bones. The ants had eaten every tiny bit of the piglets. I learnt that the ants were the ultimate scavengers of Africa. You start with the lions, hyenas and all the other predators and if there was anything left the ants would clear it up. This was quite a lesson to me.

Away from the farming and the commercial side one of my best memories of Africa was the game reserve at Killagooni about eighty miles from Nairobi on the road to Mombasa. We arrived at Killagooni just before dark and I went into the lodge. It had a thatched roof, a great big verandah all the way along the front with chairs and comfortable settees where sixty or seventy people could sit all night and watch the animals in the game park. About a hundred and fifty yards below the verandah there was a drinking place. Water and salt were laid in about half an acre and the animals would come at night. The place was all floodlit so that you could see them come to drink. In the distance you could see the elephants. The moonlight was almost as light as day and as they came, these elephants would look red because the mud all around was red and the elephants rolled about in it. As you watched they didn't appear to be moving fast but they would come and drink and roll about. Then I saw the amazing sight of a rhino arriving. There was a big bull elephant up to his belly in the drink and the rhino wanted to get in but he wouldn't come while the elephant was spraying water all over himself from his trunk. The elephant finally got out and went straight towards the rhino who ran away. It proved to me that the elephant is still king of the jungle. All sorts of animals, including a leopard, came to drink at this place. It was magic. We eventually went to bed. We were comfortably accommodated in little two-bedroomed chalets with a verandah overlooking the park and water holes. We woke in the morning when a little black man came in to give us a cup of tea early,because to see the animals properly we had to be up at dawn.

With about six carloads of people and a guide in a Land Rover, we drove round the park and saw many elephants, including fifteen cows with their babies, one of whom was only a day or two old. It was a lovely sight. You had to be careful and ready to get out of the way quickly because they were apt to attack you.

Down at the Savo River the water comes out of the ground and goes all the way to Mombasa. Where the water comes out there is quite a big lake, at least an acre in size. We got out of the car and walked down a pathway to the lake. You could see across to the other side where crocodiles and about twenty hippos played about. I took some beautiful photographs of the hippos ducking their heads, blowing water into the air and snorting. We turned right further down the river to find a large place made out of glass with some steps down which you went to seats where you could sit and take photographs. Six of us went down and the guide threw fish food. The fish came, all different colours of the rainbow. It was a lovely sight. When we eventually left we drove miles through the reserve and came across a wooded area suddenly revealing two big bull elephants. I'll never forget it.

During the time I was in Africa I never saw real green country and I longed for it. I longed for the green fields of Shropshire. As I was now approaching sixty, I, who had been regarded as an expert, lunching with the President and who had turned down a fabulous job with Brahms in Cape Town, to buy 600 cattle a week for his business in South West Africa for £3,000 a year, plus a beautiful house by the sea, a car and all expenses paid, felt the need to return to my roots in the Shropshire countryside.

My business was thriving. We had worked up to a turnover of at least £40,000 a week which would be about £300,000 today. All the farmers in Shropshire respected us and knew that we were giving them a really good service. In fact I would say we were strengthening the trade right throughout the area, including North Wales and Anglesey.

Our old friends Finefare and Safeway had always remained loyal but there were other supermarkets and by 1969 our chief rivals Leanstock had been taken over by Heinz with, of course, unlimited resources. Clearly we, too, were now ripe for takeover.

All one night I stayed awake and thought it over. I had never been one to shirk a fight but there was more to life than boardroom battles and as dawn broke, I realised that this was a fight which I really did not want to win even if I could. I was a farmer of the old school, a horsemaster and, above all, a countryman. I had been a trail blazer and I had had the joy of seeing my ideas implemented but in any case knew that I was under-capitalised to take on the giants and, besides, at this crucial moment of my life I was offered the honour of becoming Master of the South Shropshire Foxhounds, the realisation of one of my greatest ambitions. Changing my black coat for a red one in the world's greatest sport must be better than all those boring boardroom battles.

I sold my business and accepted the Mastership. I never regretted it for one moment, I sometimes think of good turns which misfired in one way or another.

One such was the case of Miss Whylie whom I mentioned earlier in connection with the activities of the War Agricultural Committee, of which, you will remember, I was a member.

At the beginning of the war she had been threatened with eviction because her farm was a Grade C farm but I had argued for her and she was allowed to remain in her home as long as the committee farmed the land.

In 1950 the War Ag was still in operation and one day I was asked by her doctor, an old friend of mine, to go and see this old lady who was now seventy years old. Apparently she had been up all night with her five dozen assorted dogs and had been unable to keep an earlier appointment because she stayed in bed until 2 o'clock.

I found her farm in appalling condition. The land was covered in weeds and riddled with rabbits who, of course, ate everything in sight; two bullocks who had lost their hind quarters completely or got rheumatics; twenty horses so old that they had no teeth in their heads. There were also two donkeys. Some years afterwards, when a film was being made in London of the donkeys working in the cemetery, we had a request for them to be sent back to be filmed. However, on the way to the railway station was the local cemetery and they would not pass it! We had to take them back home, load them in a trailer and take them to the station in the trailer. They were away about a month being filmed and eventually came back 'home'. The paint was peeling off all the buildings including a large indoor riding school, and so on. I had never seen cows so thin and this ancient starved bullock who had lost all his hind quarters looked like a bison with huge fore quarters and six-foot horns. The whole thing was a chaotic mess.

Apart from anything else it was an obvious case for the RSPCA but it transpired that Miss Whylie was a long-time member of that organisation.

However at the tribunal I stood up for her arguing that it would have been perfectly in order for them to turn Miss Wiley out back in 1940 but that this was her only home and for the last ten years it had been farmed by the Committee. It was not a disgrace to Miss Whylie but it was a disgrace to the Committee. To turn her out after ten years would be diabolically cruel.

So the Committee agreed, asked me if I would be prepared to put the place to rights if Miss Whylie gave me £7,000 to do so. I took on the job and within five years it was showing a profit. By 1960 when I finished all the horses had died in those ten years as well as the donkeys. Miss Whylie insisted on all of them being buried on the place. This meant digging enormous holes and I soon found that the only way to bury a stiff dead horse was to cut off its legs first!

I'm afraid that Miss Whylie was typical of a lot of cranks in the modern world of animal rights, sanctuaries and 'antis'. She posed as a great animal lover but in fact the kindest thing would have been for all these animals I found on the farm to have been put down years before. And my mind went back to a West Midland Show before the war when I saw the same Miss Whylie, who did a lot of show-jumping at the time, thrashing her refusing horse so viciously and for so long that she was booed by the crowd.

By 1971 when it looked inevitable that the United Kingdom had to join the Common Market, having been to France many times over the previous few years with the co-operation of the chairman of the Farmers' Union, his opposite number in France and the man in charge of agricultural tourism, I arranged a series of fact-finding tours of French farms and markets for our farmers. Apart from all the other aspects which opened their eyes, perhaps the most important was the tremendously high standard of French meat production and presentation. For example, by comparison with their beautifully white products on show in French markets, many of our carcasses of lovely Welsh lamb at the time looked as though they had been savaged by Alsatians!

On that occasion we had the Welsh BBC with us and they recorded the whole trip, showing it the following Monday and arousing a great deal of interest all over the country.

I'm afraid that British farming today is in a mess for many reasons — subsidies, the EC, ignorance of animal husbandry, a lack of feeling for the land and, above all, the selfish insistence right across the board of continuing to produce without studying the wishes of the customer. Take one single example, apples, of which we have always had in this country the finest in the entire world — Worcester, Cox, James Grieve, Lord Lambourn ... the list of wonderful English apples is endless. What happens? Believing that we must find an answer to a very moderate apple produced by the French called Golden Delicious, our fruit growers produce a revolting variety called Discovery which is then flooded into all the shops. Woolly, with a thick, bitter skin and little flavour, everything which the customer does not want. Growers wonder why they are forced out of business when they insist on continuing to grow the old-fashioned thin asparagus grass despite the fact that the customers prefer the thicker hybrid varieties.

People listen to town-bred college-educated agronomists who have little real genuine knowledge of the land. There's an awful lot of ignorance about. A recent President of the NFU said that 'burning off' is the sign of a bad farmer. Now a proper burn where the short straw is spread is a good thing. You cover the whole ground, burn it and it kills off a lot of diseases. You just clean the ground up.

The reason why we were so productive in this country is that we still used our old method of mixed farming. Old four or five-course rotation where we built up fertility and got more nitrogen out of the air than by using any other method. Plants through their leaves draw the nitrogen out of the air, store it in the roots and increase the fertility of the land. And again all the root systems of the grasses, clovers, etc. go into the ground and feed the worms who eat all the bacteria and there is so much cover and sustenance for wildlife and birdlife. The way we seem to be farming today — its corn after corn for years and years. Some people in this area have grown wheat on the same land for sixteen or seventeen years. Admittedly they are getting good crops but fifteen years is a very short time in a lifetime. We are changing the whole structure of the soil. There's little natural left for the worms in the ground to feed on — the humus. There will be none left in time. So we have had to breed fresh strains of corn that will live in this almost sterile soil and will try to fight the bugs. Then there is nothing left to fight with and to get a good crop we have to spend a fortune in sprays. God knows what else we are not taking that Nature has given us, which is the benefit of the air and the rain and all the that the Lord put into the soil and which we are now killing. By spraying we are killing off an intricate natural system and people's insides today

219

must be so full of antibiotics and things as so-called cures for diseases, which in the old days a good dose of salts would have fixed. We don't know what good, healthy food is. We are breeding a race of people who have no antibodies. In the old days you could drink slurry out of the pool and it would do you no harm because you had antibodies in your body which would kill the germs. Today everybody is very vulnerable to disease. We have no antibodies because all the drugs we take prevent our bodies from making them. You know what happens if a foal doesn't get its colostrum. The colostrum contains the antibodies and if the foal doesn't have it, it dies. No young animal can live without the antibodies to fight off disease. Let's be fair, we are feeding our animals God knows what, especially the pigs and the poultry. Goodness only knows what it is doing long-term for human bodies.

The French, being sex conscious, prohibit caponising animals and poultry, presupposing that the hormones get into the blood stream. They must do. It means that we have got to find something to counteract it in our bloodstream which, no doubt, the chemists and scientists will do or we're going to become a race of sterile people! The future generation will not be able to enjoy themselves as we have!

Perhaps I am old-fashioned in many ways but I would like to go back. I was so proud of being a farmer and so proud that we could grow crops better than anywhere else in the world. I remember my grandfather telling me that land is a heritage. There is only one object in farming. We farmers are sent into the world to make the land better for the next generation. All my life I have tried to improve land. I have loved the land.

Farm workers wages are still far too low. The English farmer, ever since the war, has had grants and subsidies. The farmer receives these grants and subsidies which have kept the inefficient farmer in business. With no grants and subsidies the good, efficient farmer would have produced a lot more food at less cost and he could then have afforded to pay his men a decent wage. Fat subsidies have ruined agriculture in this country.

I am all for helping the hill and marshland farmers to make

their land grow more grass and more feed for store cattle to send to this part of the country for us to feed. Yes, I'm all for helping the hill man. But the farmer farming the good land should not be subsidised.

All that said, I still love our farmers and have always done everything I can to help them. God bless farming and hunting!

CHAPTER XIX

The Beginning Of The End And A New Beginning

I had hunted with the South Shropshire all my life and enjoyed them much more than the North in whose country I lived, although only just on the other side of the River Severn which was the boundary between the two hunts. I had been on the committee since 1945 and, indeed, my farm at Acton Burnell was in the South country. During the war I had helped Major Clapham run the kennels, keep the pack going and hunt hounds when he was not available.

So I was absolutely thrilled that the chairman Captain Bill Corbett asked me to be Master when John Barrow finished in May. I started as joint Master with Brian Roberts but this was a difficult partnership because Brian had had a nasty accident in October, badly damaging his eyes, and could not ride much again until the following March. So he was out for the season. Michael Rowson, the kennel-huntsman and I had a wonderful time. We really hit it off together and everyone, especially the farmers, made us very welcome.

I knew all the farmers in the country well and had dealt with them in one way or another over the years. As soon as I became Master I used to make a point of going to market every Tuesday — I was, of course, still farming at the time — and if any of the farmers in my country were offering stock, then if I did not buy it myself, I made sure that it fetched a good price and afterwards, in the bar, it would cost me a fortune buying drinks. Nevertheless it was good PR and well worth it. When Brian left he was followed by Marek Kwiatkowski, a fine huntsman. We had two very happy, eventful seasons. He was followed by David Herring, who stayed for three seasons during which I acted as Field Master because I could no longer

223

afford to carry on as full Master. After all I was supplying Michael with two and sometimes three horses as well as all the feed and bedding for six horses. Our guarantee then was only £4,500 a year and it was costing me at least £2,000 a year out of my own pocket, but although it was a very expensive job, it was well worth it and I gained a great many friends.

Apart from studying the farmers, the most enjoyable part of the job was provided by the children. I remember one day when we had a nice two-mile point right on top of the Long Mynd. I had a lot of children out who were going really well when we came to a place where there were some nice post and rails — good ones about four feet high and solid. I shall never forget it and as far as the children were concerned it probably made their hunting day for them. I said: "Anybody give me a lead over the post and rails?"

"Oh yes, sir," said a little girl called Mandy Beedles, who was about twelve or thirteen at the time and had a splendid pony.

I said; "Anybody else? Go on, go on." I let them all jump these rails and I said: "Will somebody come and open the gate for the old man?"

These kids loved it. They all went home and said: "We jumped the rails and the Master couldn't jump!" It made their day and it made mine. The whole time I hunted the hounds I loved it. I loved the children and took a great interest in them, and I was particularly keen to teach them manners. Whenever it was possible I would send one child out with the Huntsman and one with the Whip. Not to get in their way but so that they could be somewhere near in order to open gates, hold their horses if they had to get off, that sort of thing, learning the job. At the end of a season I would give a Hunt button to the child who had done the best job and helped most during the season. They loved it but I must admit I was so fond of the children because they were the future of hunting and although some people say I spoilt them, they were so good to me. When I finally finished, about six of them came to me, said how sorry they were and I burst into tears.

In the autumn of 1971 I had a nice surprise when a lot of my

224

old suppliers of fatstock asked me to provide them with store animals, especially with sheep.

We started cub hunting in August on Mondays, Wednesdays and Saturdays and it made my life very hectic particularly because Monday, Tuesday and Wednesday were market days, while on Thursdays and Fridays I was buying on the farms. So, for two days a week I hunted until 10.30 and then left someone else to drive my horses home. From mid September however I had of course to remain full days.

It was at this time that Rosie came back into my life. Throughout those cub-hunting days when I was having to get up at 4.30 am for the six o'clock meet I was always very hungry until, like a ministering angel, Rosie started to turn up with coffee and sandwiches. She arrived one Monday morning just when we had run a fox to ground in a big dingle. I was riding a topping little horse called Simon Scot, who stood 15.3 hands but would jump anything. He was 11 years old and at one time had been travelling companion of the great Arkle. I had bought him from Tom Dreaper. So I asked Rosie to hold him while i went to see Michael and when I returned found she was riding him. I was thrilled. She told me that she had not been on a horse since she was ten years old. Shortly afterwards Mrs. Pat Lincoln Lewis lent her a horse called Magic which she rode until the end of the season and he taught her a lot about self preservation that was to stand her in good stead for the years to come.

Thereafter she quickly joined the committee of the South Shropshire Hunt Supporters and took on the running of the bars and the catering at dances and other activities, making quite a lot of money. Our most successful barbecue was held in my barn at Atcham when we had booked that well-known group The Wurzels who were No.1 in the hit parade that week with 'Combine Harvester'. No fewer than two and a half thousand people turned up. What a night! The money was divided between a local charity and the South Shropshire Hunt, who built a new slaughterhouse with the money. In December 1972 just after Christmas I had a really nasty fall when my little horse put his foot through some hidden pig netting in the grass. He reared up and came over, wrapping himself in the wire and, like a fool, I didn't come off so that he rolled over with me right under him. I smashed in my ribs one of which punctured my lung. Rosie looked after me, put me down in the cowhouse with some rugs while we waited for the ambulance. When the ambulance arrived I was unconscious. I became conscious half way to Shrewsbury and woke up to find Rosie holding my hands. As a result I was out of action for the remainder of that season, during which Rosie rode all my horses and became a permanent fixture with them and, thank God, with me.

In 1974 she started to live in Bayston Hill and we rode and hunted together. Like most horses from the same stable where one went the other followed. Poor Rosie had some dreadful experiences. On one occasion she was riding a grey horse called Cecil, whom I had bought for her and stood only 15.3 hands, while I was riding a great big grey called Chin (she was always wagging her bottom lip!) Hounds crossed a road into a beet field. I was standing on the road with the rest of the field and told them to stay put. The week before we had had several thunderstorms. The sheep had been grazing the beet tops and the ground sloped down to a hollow where the rain had washed the sheep muck and the mud down to a depth of about three feet. Hounds suddenly spoke and went off at full cry. I turned my mare and jumped into the field.

To stop her horse from following me up the road Rosie had turned his back to me but he must have seen me out of the corner of his eye, turned left and jumped the hedge down an 8ft drop into the slurry. He turned a complete somersault into that muck, burying poor Rosie. The next thing I knew was a greenish-black horse galloping alongside me. I caught him and someone led him back to Rosie. She remounted and, when hounds checked, climbed up again covered in slurry from her hat to her boots.

We had a good run and turned down a long, grassy lane at Arthur Jones' farm at Bayston where there was a five-barred gate about half way down I was watching hounds on the right, glanced around and saw that someone had nailed a rail over the top of the gatepost, making it nearly 6 ft. high. I kicked my mare and too late remembered that Rosie was right behind. All

I heard was: "Oh no!" and, as I pulled up, Rosie and Cecil landed in one piece while the rest of the field had pulled up.

By 1973 we were showing such good sport that we were getting visitors from neighbouring packs; from the Wheatland we had a few regulars including Dena Marsh, daughter of a former Wheatland Master, the late Colonel Peter Marsh, who took some following and often gave us a lead. From the Cheshire came Jane McAlpine, who used to bring friends with her. Quite a few came from the David Davies and on one Boxing Day when hounds met at Bayston Hill there were no fewer than fourteen from that hunt, including Pat Fletcher, one of the best men across country I have ever met, and also Derek Gethin who used to bring his family, all of who were real goers.

On this occasion we found a fox on the Hill and had a very fast 35 minutes with a point of some 3½ miles so that, out of a starting field of 94, there were only fifteen left when we ran the fox to ground and eight of those were form the David Davies. We all returned home for big bowls of hot stew with Rosie.

On November 13 1977 (my birthday) Rosie came to live with me at The Grange. We were so happy and did everything together. That year we lambed 200 ewes. Rosie took over the lambing and proved first-class at the job. We had 324 lambs and had just about finished when my son Edward came in one night saying that he had a problem. He had 197 feeding ewes and had taken them to market and had them sent back because they were all in lamb.

Rosie said she would lamb them and so, very foolishly, we bought them. A week later they started lambing — 18 lambs in the first day and only half the ewes had any milk. How she managed I don't know. We only lost two ewes and produced 244 lambs but, of those, 47 were on the bottle. Rosie lost a stone in weight because, even with the help of her two daughters Caroline and Sue, it was a full-time job. But they all learned a lot and are still expert in that field.

For some time Rosie had been driving me to markets and sales all over the country and I had taught her to buy. We were moving a lot of store lambs and feeding ewes. Rosie bought the feeding ewes, including some for export, as we were selling

227

about a hundred ewes to go abroad and it was important to buy the right sheep for the abattoir, to get the right weight and quality in order to obtain the top price. She soon became expert at both. In fact we made a very good team and to the amusement of a lot people we used to foot-rot,drench and inject all the store sheep while they were still in the pens before they left the market so that when they reached their destination they were ready to go straight out into the fields.

In 1977 we had 100 fat cattle in and a little over 100 acres of corn, most of which went under water in an unseasonal flood which resulted in a fearful amount of dust during harvest, at the end of which we decided to take a break, intending to spend a night in Blackpool on the way to the Isle of Man to see my brother John. That evening we went for a walk on the seafront and suddenly I collapsed. Rosie was unable to get any help because people thought I was drunk. She got a taxi, took me back to the hotel and called a doctor who was wonderful and told me to keep very quiet. I spent a week in bed in the hotel and on my return home went to see a specialist, who confirmed that I had asthma. I had 32 attacks in a week and had to have a spell in hospital to get it sorted out. The specialist Mr. Wilson told me that I must give up the Mastership and so, reluctantly, I sold all the hunters except for two four-year-olds, two yearlings and the children's ponies. We rode the four-year-olds round the farm every day to see the stock.

Even though I had had to give up hunting, the greatest sport in the entire world, these were some of the happiest days I ever spent, riding round the farm checking on the young stock with Rosie and we became closer than ever.

We had had some wonderful times hunting but I'm afraid Rosie, riding second horses, had some rather rough rides. My motto had always been shorten your reins, ram on your hat and go. Rosie's was look and think first — but to no avail! So when by 1980 I was so poorly that the doctors told me that if I did not get out of the corn and hay dust I would be dead in three years we decided to sell up and build our bungalow. Unfortunately soon after the decision was taken Rosie was knocked down by a van in Shrewsbury and was unable to walk for several weeks. She was still on crutches on the day of the sale. When all the stock, implements and most of the miscellaneous lots had been sold I was just in time to see my ice skates and racing saddle going up for sale. That was just a bit too much for me to bear. I grabbed both and bolted for the house, locked myself in the lavatory and shed a few tears. I had my leg pulled for it afterwards when the girls and Rosie said that if they had done that with the horse, pony and lamb that they wanted respectively it would have been very crowded in the loo!

After the sale and subsequent move to Grangelands, we continued to buy and sell sheep of all sorts, press-ganging Caroline, Sue and friends Jackie, Jean and Tom Habberly for crack-of-dawn searches for sheep with torches for loading and moving to market at least three days a week. By 1990 however, my knees had got so bad that I could barely walk across the garden and finally had to retire. The following year I was given two new knee replacements. Both operations were successful and we will always be very grateful to Mr. McGeoch for his skill in giving me the ability to live a pain-free life again.

Although I have dedicated this book to Rosie, who has given me more love and help than anyone else in this world, I would like to finish by saying something about my children and grandchildren. I must thank them for all the love they have given me over the years. I am so proud of their achievements, and of my 12 grandchildren, four great-grandchildren, and of Rosie's two daughters.

I would raise my glass to each and every one of them, but nowadays my doctor does not allow me that pleasure! But perhaps you, the reader, would raise *your* glass to them, for me.

APPENDIX

Sir John Holt M.P.
8 College Hill,
Shrewsbury

11- 6 - 71

Dear Sir John,

I refer to our conversation on Wednesday 9 May 1971 regarding my reasons for commencing tours to France, and the reaction of farmers/butchers who went on the first trip.

Briefly, my experience of farming and the met trade in general has been learned the hard way:

i)   I started butchering and retailing meat in 1930

ii)   I sold my business just before the 1939/45 war and concentrated on farming at Atcham, near Shrewsbury

iii)   During the period of meat control 1940 to 1954, I graded sheep for the Ministry in Shrewsbury market. I was nominated on to the Board of the Provisional Market Board (which later became the F.M.C.) in 1952, by the farmers of Shropshire, Staffordshire and Cheshire. I served on the main board until 1960. In 1957 I proposed that the F.M.C. should prepare to sell meat to Supermarkets, but the proposal was rejected.

iv)   In 1963, I started my own business again by retailing to Supermarkets and by 1970 had attained a turnover of £40,000 per week. I then sold my shares to a large concern, but have been retained as a consultant.

     During this period we exported sheep, cattle and pigs to the continent, over and above the home trade.

It was during the time of these export contracts with France that my attention was drawn to the standards of the French meat trade. Their sheep were extremely good; full of lean meat and attractively dressed. The same applied to their beef.

In 1968 I visited the Rand Show, South Africa and found to my surprise that a large percentage of the beef animals came from Europe. I then realised that the problem was breeding the correct stock for **consumer demand.**

The subsidy system and grading standards of these Isles were laid down in 1954 and had not been changed since. The farmers of the UK were breeding and feeding to a standard of grading which was completely out of date, and did not take into consideration the most important factor, which was consumer demand.

The Supermarket meat specialists require lean boneless meat. Argentine meat now comes in boneless and in cryovac packaging, again, this meets a demand.

The Meat and Livestock Commission set up under a Labour Government costing millions, has done very little to tackle this problem, or even come up with suggestions.

When we enter the Common Market, we have a huge selling potential. But, *the Continent requires lean meat*, and due to our subsidy and grading system our farmers are producing carcasses with too much fat, *even for our own housewives!*

The first tour to France was an outstanding success. The French Farmers' Union were most cooperative, and arranged visits to the Paris Smithfield, farms and a coach tour of the arable farming area outside Paris. I hope the N.F.U. will reciprocate as fully, should the French farmers desire to visit Britain. The members of the tour party will confirm the following points:

i)   The French lamb carcasses are better in meat, dressing and presentation.

ii)   The French cattle had better confirmation and were leaner than most cattle in this country.

iii) The French have done to our Leicester sheep (imported 100 years ago and now called Ile de France) what the Danes did with our Yorkshire pig which they now call Landrace. They changed it by selective breeding into a totally different animal – lean, with big hind quarters and loins, and a fine shoulder more suitable for consumer demand.

iv)   The large arable farms (probably not typical of the country as a whole) were well maintained and cropped.

v)   The price the French farmer received for this fat stock is 30 per cent higher than his English counterpart in spite of the fact that English farmers receive subsidy.

The next tour is on July 4th and will consist of interested farmers from Northern Ireland, Scotland and England.

I hope these comments will be of help to you.

Yours sincerely,

Tom Jones
Tom Jones